PATTERNS OF POLICING

PATTERNS OF POLICING

A Comparative International Analysis

DAVID H. BAYLEY

Rutgers University Press
New Brunswick, N.J.

Library of Congress Cataloging in Publication Data

Bayley, David H.
   Patterns of policing.

   (Crime, law, and deviance series)
   Bibliography: p.
   Includes index.
   1. Police—Cross-cultural studies.   I. Title.
II. Series.
HV7921.B38   1985   363.2   84–24908
ISBN 0–8135–1094–5

Dedicated to
My Colleagues in Police Studies
Worldwide

Contents

Figures

Tables

Preface

This study represents the culmination of almost twenty years of personal research on national police institutions. The most concentrated effort was devoted to India, Japan, and the United States, the results of which are available in other publications. Over the years, it became increasingly apparent to me that no scholars or practitioners were making systematic attempts to analyze police development internationally. Indeed, there were hardly any comprehensive descriptions of policing around the world. Wondering, then, whether the insights I had developed into policing through intensive case studies would hold up when applied more widely, I applied to the National Science Foundation in 1976 for a grant to study contemporary police functioning in an accessible cross-section of countries. The National Science Foundation generously acceded to my request, the award being given grant number SOC 76-15474. Additional support from the Earhart Foundation and from the Graduate School of International Studies, University of Denver, provided the time and assistance necessary for me to analyze the material collected and, ultimately, to write this book.

It is impossible to recount the obligations incurred over nearly twenty years of scholarly effort. Advice, hospitality, friendship, and unstinting assistance have been given me by a large number of people throughout the world. I cannot recount names without unwittingly slighting some and certainly trying the patience of the reader. I shall, therefore, mention only those who personally undertook to provide me with information used in this book. The sweat of their brows is mingled with mine. They are Lewis J. Alverson, John A. Bishop, Prem Chand, Gale Davey, Art Dill, Pierre Gabrielli, N. Krishnaswamy, René Kuhn, Grant Lappin, Jackson Loy, Howard Mann, Isamu Nitta, A. R. Nizamuddin, Eric E. Nordholt, Leif Petter Olaussen, R. N. Pande, Leonard Post, K. F. Rustumji, Jon S. T. Quah, Gilbert Raguideau, K. G. Ramanna, Rudra Rajasingam, T. Rajasingam, Roy Rushmore, Mahesan Selvaratnam, Harbans Singh, Takashi Suetsuna, Harold Thonoff, Richard Wilson, Paul A. Zolbe, and Jane Zoll.

That this book could be written at all is testimony to the fact that open societies and open police forces exist in the world. I can personally attest that this is true in France, Great Britain, India, Japan, Norway, Singapore, Sri Lanka, and the United States. Rather than finding excuses for denying access, government and police in these countries welcomed me, provided informed assistance, opened records, and allowed me to inspect facilities and observe operations. In so doing they not only acted according to the ideals of democratic societies; they also showed that it is possible to forge professional links across the barriers of custom and politics even in an area of enormous sensitivity. There are other countries in the world besides these where similar research might be done, but altogether the number is not large. The existence of this group should be a matter of deep satisfaction to all people who value intellectual and political freedom.

Closer to home, I was fortunate in being able to work with six patient, conscientious, hardworking, and exceedingly competent graduate research assistants. Now embarking on their own careers, they were Jennifer Bailey, Beth Byerly, Carla Foote, John Graham, Steven Lamy, and Reuben Miller. To them fell the painstaking labor of organizing the statistical data I carried back from abroad, rendering it into machine-readable form, and performing the statistical analysis. I thank a kind providence that we have survived our labors with the computer with deepened mutual respect and affection. The manuscript was prepared by uncomplaining, efficient, and reliable Liz Isaacson.

I am particularly grateful for the very insightful comments made on all or parts of the manuscript by Peter K. Manning and Clifford W. Shearing. Although I incorporated many of their suggestions, I have chosen to ignore others, recognizing that we disagree on important conceptual and empirical points. Let the debate now begin.

Comparative scholarship conducted abroad, especially when it is done in short bursts in many places, requires separation from one's family. Loneliness is an unavoidable part of this kind of work. The only redeeming feature is the recognition rekindled again and again of the value beyond words of having a family with Chris, Jenny, and Tracy in it.

PATTERNS OF POLICING

PART I
INTRODUCTION

CHAPTER 1

Toward a Theory of Policing

This book examines the police in the modern world, describing and trying to explain variations in patterns of police operation and development. The analysis takes the form of examining relations between
police and society—the ways in which each affects the other. The distinctive purpose of the book is to construct general propositions about
police functioning on the basis of comparative contemporary and historical information. Specifically, the book addresses three questions:
How did modern police systems develop? What tasks do police perform? And how independent are police as social actors? These topics—
evolution, function, and politics—constitute the major divisions of the
book.

POLICE AND SCHOLARSHIP

Before grappling with the fundamental conceptualizations that inform
both the organization and analysis of this book, a word is in order about
the place of this book in the accumulating scholarship on the police.

By and large, the police have not been subjected to comparative
analysis. Until very recently neither historians nor social scientists appeared to recognize that police existed, let alone that they played an
important role in social life. Writing about the police almost everywhere was left to policemen themselves, who either told stories or addressed nuts-and-bolts issues. The indexes of standard histories of most
countries show no entries at all related to the police. The thirteen-
volume *Cambridge Modern History* (1911), for example, has no head-
ing for *police*. Notable historians writing about their own times persistently fail to mention police, and not because police did not exist.
The great Roman chroniclers make no more than passing mention of
them, though the Vigiles were a substantial force from 6 A.D. (Reynolds
1926: 26–28). A marked exception to this pattern of chronic oversight
are the histories of Russia, which devote a great deal of space to the

development of the Tsar's police (Florinsky 1953). There is a lesson here. Police are noticed only during dramatic events of political repression, as in Hitler's Third Reich, during the Paris Commune in 1872, in the counterrevolutions in Europe 1848/49, and during confirmation of Meiji rule in Japan in the 1870s. For the same reason, spies and political police claim attention far more often historically than patrol and watch personnel. Routine order-maintenance and crime-prevention are persistently ignored, even though they are a much more important part of the daily life of ordinary citizens than political repression.

Fortunately, neglect of the police role has changed dramatically during the last decade, certainly in the English-speaking world. Until then the best of a meager lot were British studies (Critchley 1967; Hart 1951; Reith 1938, 1948, 1952, 1956). None of these antedated the Second World War. Now historical study of the police has become fashionable, producing several excellent country studies, a spate of articles, several edited readers, and even commentary on the accumulating literature. As heartening as the recent activity is among historians, it remains to be seen whether it will be more than a short-lived fad.

Social scientists have been even more delinquent than historians in studying police. In the United States, from the eve of World War II until the mid-1960s only six articles on the police appeared in the *American Sociological Review* and the *American Journal of Sociology*; two in the *Public Administration Review*; and none in the *American Political Science Review* (Earle 1973, p. 15). These articles were rarely analytical, being characterized by one commentator as "pragmatic and experimental, and also, on occasion, hortatory, particularly as regards public morality and law observance" (Pfiffner 1962). Political scientists, even comparativists working internationally, ignored police altogether. In the words of David Easton and Jack Dennis, the police "have fallen into a position so peripheral to the core of political science that it is virtually impossible to find a sustained theoretical discussion of the varied functions they fulfill in political systems" (1969, p. 210). Since the mid-1960s this situation has changed, with sociologists especially and a smattering of political scientists and economists looking at police functions in society. Comparative international work is still rare, however, as indicated by the fact that Raymond Fosdick's *European Police Systems* (1915) is still properly regarded as a fundamental text. Of the 175 dissertations written on the police between 1974 and 1979 in the

United States, only 6 dealt with foreign forces, and 1 of those was on the United States occupation of Germany (University Microfilms 1979).

The neglect of the police in scholarship is curious indeed. It is especially perplexing in the case of political scientists. The maintenance of order is the quintessential function of government. Not only is the legitimacy of government in large part determined by whether it maintains order, but order is a criterion for determining whether government can be said to exist at all. Conceptually as well as functionally, government and order are related.[1] Although political scientists have recognized the importance of studying the contributions of government—its "output"—they have consistently neglected its central responsibility. This is reflected in the fact that there are numerous studies of legislatures, courts, armies, cabinets, political parties, and bureaucracy in general, but hardly any of the police. Police activities also determine the limits of freedom in organized society, an essential feature in determining the character of government. Though governments exercise constraint in other ways, surely the manner in which they maintain order directly affects the reality of freedom.

Popular writers of fiction have shown a much more acute sense of the importance and salience of the police in life. Police appear repeatedly in Chaucer, Shakespeare, Hugo, Dostoyevsky, London, Conrad, and Greene, not always centrally but as stock characters in the drama of life.

The discrepancy between the importance of the police in social life and the amount of attention given them by scholars is so striking as to require explanation.[2] What factors might account for the persistent failure of scholars to deal with the police? I would suggest four. First, police are rarely important actors in great historical events. They are not involved in epic battles, heroic marches, or splendid retreats. Their activities are too routine, their presence too pervasive, and their clientele too ordinary to be the stuff of high drama. They do not make general social policy but address human problems in a particularistic way. The fate of nations does not obviously hang on the results of their encounters. Significantly, when police play large roles in politics, scholars do pay attention to them, as in Russia in the nineteenth century and Germany in the twentieth. Surely, too, the upsurge of scholarly interest recently in police in the United States is due to their propulsion into the foreground of social confrontation. If the Vietnam War had not provoked violent protests and racial discrimination not sparked frightening riots in large cities, would scholarly interest have risen so sharply? The attention of scholars may follow the dramatic currents of politics more closely than they would happily admit.

Second, policing is not a glamorous, high-status undertaking. Its tasks, even those connected with criminal investigation, are dull and repetitious, conducted on behalf of very ordinary persons in surroundings that are often tawdry or decrepit. Policemen everywhere comment ruefully that joining the police is not a way to meet improving people. Moreover, unlike the professional military, senior officers in the police have not often been drawn from among the educated upper-class. In studying the police, one does not associate with persons recognized generally as socially important or distinguished. Though the situation is changing, policing is still regarded in most countries as dubiously professional. Thus, both in terms of political importance and social standing, police hardly qualify as members of the elites that scholars so disarmingly put at the center of their attention.

Third, policing may also have been neglected because it is morally repugnant. Constraint, control, and suppression are undoubtedly necessary in society, but they are not pleasant. Though war is not pleasant, either, it can at least be made to seem heroic. Warriors can dramatically do battle for the sake of great causes, such as democracy or national liberation. This pretense is harder to maintain for policemen, though it may nonetheless be true.[3] Policing represents a people's use of force against itself, and this is somehow more shameful and embarrassing than using force against outsiders. The failure of scholars to study policing may represent a denial of the necessity for coercion in domestic affairs. It reflects a reluctance to be associated with forces of control, of conservatism, of the status quo.

Fourth, formidable practical problems confront those who conduct research on the police. Not only is access to the police problematic in most countries, but documentary materials are not routinely collected, catalogued, and deposited in libraries. There is a vicious cycle at work here. Because there is little interest, there is only slight demand for the kind of bibliographic aids that facilitate analytic scholarly work. As a result, an unusual amount of legwork is required to study the police, which in turn reduces the attractiveness of the police as an object of scholarly attention.

In summary, a scholar who studies the police must be willing to do extensive fieldwork in unprepossessing surroundings, to brave bureaucratic intransigence, and to become politically suspect and socially déclassé. Only a handful of scholars have been willing to do this.

FORMS OF POLICE

In order to study the police one must be able to recognize them in their historical diversity throughout the world. This is not easy to do. Police come in a bewildering variety of forms, from the New York City Police Department to the "People's Police" (Druzinikii) of the Soviet Union, from the French Gendarmerie to the Provincial Armed Constabulary in India, from the American county sheriff to the Norwegian rural *Lensman*. Moreover, many agencies that are not thought of as police nonetheless possess "police" powers. The Coast Guard in the United States, for example, along with the Customs Service and the Immigration and Naturalization Service, are authorized to arrest and detain. Even more confusing, private persons do policing as well—detectives and security guards, militia, *posses comitatus*, and neighborhood crime prevention associations. Historically public order has been maintained by knights in medieval Europe, samurai in Japan, vigilantes in the United States, "trained bands" among the Cheyenne Indians, *potwaris* in India, *hans* in China, and Hundreds in England. Are all such agencies "police," therefore appropriate objects for study? Unless there is agreement on the meaning of "police," as well as on the presumptive signs by which they may be distinguished, any generalizations about police will be challengeable.

Whenever the word *police* is used in this book, it will refer to people authorized by a group to regulate interpersonal relations within the group through the application of physical force. This definition has three essential parts: physical force, internal usage, and collective authorization. Recognizing that definitions are never right or wrong, except in relation to usage, but are matters of convenience, why do I insist on these elements in defining *police*?

The unique competence of police is the use of physical force, real or threatened, to affect behavior. Police are distinguished not by the actual use of force but by the fact that they are authorized to use it. As Egon

Bittner (1974) has said, "the policeman, and the policeman alone, is equipped, entitled, and required to deal with every exigency in which force may have to be used to meet it." Even when they do not use force, it shapes every interaction they have (Shearing and Leon 1975). Other agencies may prescribe coercive measures and even direct their use, as legislatures and courts do respectively, but police are executive agents of force. They actually apply it. Though police are not the only agents in society that are allowed to lay hands on people in order to mold behavior, they would be unrecognizable as police without this authority.

The stipulation of internal usage is essential in order to exclude armies. At the same time, when military formations are used for order maintenance within a society, they should be regarded as acting as police. Indeed, the separation of police from military institutions is an important matter to examine.

Authorization by a group is the third defining element. It is necessary in order to exclude from the term *police* persons who use force within a society for noncollective purposes. This would include robbers, rebels, and terrorists, as well as, on some occasions, parents, employers, landowners, schoolteachers, and priests. Another way of saying this is that police are not self-created; they are tied to the social units from which they derive authority. Today we are accustomed to thinking of police as being created by states, but a moment's reflection will show that this is much too restrictive. All sorts of groups authorize internal use of force that is accepted as legitimate. People are subject to different sorts of police, each predicated on a different kind of social unit. Police may be authorized in the United States by the central government, states, counties, cities, and private interest groups; in Africa by tribes, countries, cities, and revolutionary movements; in South Asia by villages, states, castes, and tribes. Groups capable of authorizing policing should be seen as nesting inside one another like Chinese puzzle boxes. This is true not only for modern complex societies, but also wherever people have loyalties to multiple interrelated social groups. Social units that authorize police vary in kind and scale. Among the most important are families, clans, tribes, interest groups, and territorial communities. States, then, are not the only kind of community that may create police.

The social basis of police authority does not, however, determine how that authority may be organized. For example, police authority is often implemented in terms of territorial boundaries by groups that are not constituted in terms of territory, such as tribes and interest associations. Universities, mining companies, and armies wield police authority within geographical areas even though membership is not decided by inhabitation. The converse is also true. Countries may exert police authority over members even when outside their boundaries. Similarly, to say that a social group authorizes policing does not mean that it is carried out in a unified way. Police power may be delegated to other kinds of social agencies—such as churches, businesses, guilds, and families—or be decentralized to subordinate groups of the same sort—as in the case of states to cities, counties, provinces, and districts. Authorization by a social unit implies nothing about either the nature or the organization of community direction.

In practice, of course, it is often difficult to know whether persons using force within a community have been authorized to do so. The difference between police and brigands is a matter of judgment. Confusion occurs when authority is disputed. Civil war is a clear example, as is competition among bureaucracies in a state with respect to the use of force. It also occurs when loyalties of people shift among groups, so that the authority of one is eclipsed by the other. Tribes become submerged in states, guilds in municipalities, extended families in economic interest groups, churches in states, and clans in tribes. A key feature of political change throughout history, therefore, is competition among groups over the authorization as well as the exercise of police power.

Confusion in recognizing police is especially likely to result when government is customary and authority implicit. Yet custom can authorize policing as much as statutes. Knights of the manor were a kind of police, because they enforced order and brought criminals before the lord's court. The same is true for warriors in American Indian tribes who expelled people from the community on the order of tribal councils. So, too, are kinsmen who are allowed by custom to punish persons who have harmed a relative. Police exist whenever the application of physical constraint can be shown to be regarded as legitimate by the community. Since the existence of legitimacy is problematic, disagreements will inevitably arise about whether police exist. We must accept this possibility unless we eliminate the requirement that policing involves authorization by a group.

Particular problems occur, therefore, when a police force loses legit-imacy and is no longer accepted by members of the community. Does it cease to be a police force? Certainly not, at least not immediately. Its status as acting for the community is necessary conceptually for police to be said to exist, just as four legs are necessary in the definition of a horse. But exceptions do occur. Some police lose their legitimacy, as horses lose legs. In such cases it is not a contradiction to say that a particular community has an unacceptable, illegitimate, unauthorized, even illegal police. However, a group of enforcers who have never been or have not for a long time had standing as acting for the community cannot be regarded as police.[4]

But legitimacy, which implies approval, is not the only indicator of authorization by communities. Surely police should be said to exist when one nation occupies another or a minority dominates a majority by forceful means. Even the subjugated would not contend that the po-lice were not acting in the community's name, simply that control of the community had been wrongly appropriated. Authorization, then, can mean recognition of status as the community's monitor. Status as pre-eminent agent for the community may itself be imposed by force. Le-gitimacy is lacking, but standing is not.

To reiterate, police are authorized by a social group to apply physi-cal force within itself. Without these elements, police do not exist. Are there any societies, then, that do not have police in this minimal sense? Not many. One can imagine social groups, even entire societies, that run on a consensual basis so that membership entails subservience to group norms and violations bring voluntary resignation. By and large, however, such voluntary associations are usually embedded in larger involuntary social groups, such as family, tribe, livelihood association, village, nation, or state. The most fundamental of life's affiliations have always and in every place provided for physical constraint against members, if only in the limited form of exclusion from the community. To the extent, therefore, that man is an involuntary social animal, po-licing is nearly universal. Though societies without policing are pos-sible to conceive, they are exceedingly rare. One such may be the Nuer of the Sudan. As described by E. E. Evans-Pritchard, these people had a common language and customs and were recognized by themselves and others as being distinct. At the same time, they had no persons au-thorized to resolve disputes within the group, to apply force, or command fighting to cease (1940). Although the Nuer tribe was an involuntary association, it had the barest minimum of authority (Nair 1962, chap. 1).

The definition of police used here deliberately errs on the side of inclusiveness. The advantage is that it allows comparative study of a wide variety of institutions of forceful constraint in society. This is particularly important if the development of police institutions through time is to be undertaken. If, for example, uniquely contemporary characteristics of police become part of the definition of police, then historical analysis is precluded. On the other hand, inclusiveness in a definition generates problems of manageability. We might find it difficult to trace the evolution of all forms of policing. What is one to do?

The solution is to select features of policing that are particularly important or interesting in the contemporary world and examine their development, searching especially for factors that account for their emergence historically. In effect, this strategy amounts to working backward in time from contemporary forms, rather than examining historical mutations in all kinds of police institutions. For most of the world's people today, the police that are most authoritative and salient in their lives are those that are public, specialized, and professional. These three characteristics are almost synonymous with modern policing—almost, because private policing has expanded so rapidly that in some countries its members are as numerous as public police. Because the attributes of publicness, specialization, and professionalization characterize the police that have the greatest perceived clout contemporarily, they will be the features of policing that I have selected for analysis initially. Though it is useful to think of these characteristics as dichotomous—public/private, specialized/nonspecialized, professional/nonprofessional—they comprise many gradations between extremes. The development of each of these features will be examined in detail in Chapter 2. For the moment, let us look at their relation conceptually to the definition of police.

Publicness or *privateness* refers to the nature of the police agency. This can easily be confused with community authorization, which is one of the elements of the definition of police. Authorization to act in a community's name does not entail public agency. Authorization and agency are conceptually distinct. Sovereign social units, like city-states or modern countries, do not always have police forces raised, paid, and directed by government, even though they may have elaborate legal codes. Rome in the early Republic, approximately the third century B.C., left law enforcement to individuals (Kunkel 1973, p. 29; Lintott 1968, chap. 2). Victims and their relatives were allowed to capture persons who had harmed them and to administer condign punishment. Policing in Rome was in private hands, but it would certainly be mistaken to say that Rome did not have police in the sense of persons authorized by the community to use physical constraint legitimately in human affairs. Similarly, in the United States today there are as many private policemen as public; important territorial areas, like business premises and hotels, are almost exclusively policed by private agents. Yet one would not argue that those regions were not policed legitimately. The point is that the frequency with which the application of physical force is entrusted to private as opposed to public agencies by communities and the circumstances under which it occurs are matters to be determined empirically.

Specialization, too, should not be confused with elements of the definition of *police*. A specialized police force concentrates on the application of force; an unspecialized force is authorized to use force but does many other things as well. French and Prussian police in the eighteenth and nineteenth centuries were general-purpose instruments of government regulation, making health inspections, checking weights and measures, issuing building permits, and ensuring adequate food supplies. In smaller and less complex societies, policing is often done by customary leaders, sometimes assisted by warriors, who are responsible for government generally. Even in modern nation-states, as we shall see in Chapter 6, police do many things other than constrain behavior in physical ways. Moreover, other government agencies may be authorized to enforce law through forceful means but do not specialize in it. In the United States, for example, agencies like the Postal Service, Coast Guard, and National Park Service enforce laws forcefully as part of achieving more ramified objectives. They do specialized work, but they do not do specialized *police* work. Policing becomes specialized when agencies are directed to concentrate primarily on the application of physical force.

The characteristics of public/private and specialized/nonspecialized may be variously combined in practice. The Colorado State Patrol is a public specialized police; the American Internal Revenue Service is a public nonspecialized police; Pinkerton Agency detectives are private specialized police; and family members who undertake forceful dispute settlement under community sanction are private nonspecialized police.

Professionalization refers to explicit preparation to perform the unique police function. The term is awkward, especially since it has become a term of art in police circles, referring to status desired rather than behavioral attributes achieved. *Rationalization*, in the sense of self-conscious management, might be a better term, but it too has connotations that obscure meaning. Professionalization involves merit recruitment, formal training, structured career advancement, systematic discipline, and full-time service. The dimension of professionalization versus nonprofessionalization cuts across the other two categories. Although most public specialized police today are professional in some measure, private police can be professional too, just as unspecialized police can be.

The three sets of attributes pertaining to agency, focus, and rationalization are logically distinct; they can occur in any combination. Since a particular combination characterizes modern policing, an important part of the analysis to follow will be to determine whether they emerge historically in a particular sequence. Does public agency replace private agency before or after specialization? Does specialization occur before professionalization? Does publicness emerge before professionalization?

Figure 1.1 summarizes schematically the concepts employed. The attributes of physical force, internal ambit, and social authorization (numbers 1, 2, and 3) define the police. All three must be present to have police. Because an important kind of police, namely modern ones, tend overwhelmingly to be public, specialized, and professional, these attributes (numbers 4, 5, and 6) are critical to the analysis of police evolution. These attributes are not necessary to the existence of the police. Agencies that are private, nonspecialized, and nonprofessional are as much police as those that are public, specialized, and professional as long as they use force within their communities legitimately.

At the same time, police forces vary in many other respects as well, such as structure, training, forcefulness, reputation, strength, and social composition. Any attempt to describe and explain policing that is less than encyclopedic requires limiting analysis to a few salient topics.

Figure 1.1

BASIC CONCEPTS

A. Definitional elements
    1. Applied physical force
    2. Ambit
    3. Authorization

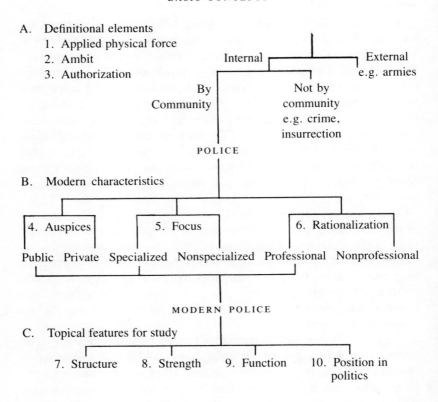

B. Modern characteristics

C. Topical features for study

In this book these will be police structure, strength, function, and political position (numbers 7, 8, 9, and 10). Their inclusion is justified
solely by their topicality. They are matters that people generally consider important when police systems are compared. Although all police
organizations could be compared in these respects, only those that are
modern—public, specialized, and professional—will be. Otherwise
the book would be unmanageable.

ORGANIZATION OF THE BOOK

The analysis of police presented here is shaped by considerations of what is essential theoretically, contemporary historically, and persistent in informed interest. Part I treats historical evolution. Specifically, Chapter 2 analyzes the emergence of public, specialized, and professional police organizations. Chapter 3 describes the structure that modern police forces have and examines reasons for variation. Chapter 4 discusses patterns in the growth of police forces, focusing on personnel. Part II looks at the work performed by modern police forces. Chapter 5 begins with an analysis of what police work is, how it should be conceptualized, and what the sources of information about it are. It charts some of the major patterns of variation in police work among national police forces. Chapter 6 develops a theory explaining variations in police work. It might be more accurate to say that I assess whether a parsimonious theory is possible given what is currently known about police work. Part III, Politics, looks at the reciprocal relations between the police and its encapsulating political system. Chapter 7 explores how countries have sought to make police accountable. Chapter 8 reverses the perspective, examining the role that the police play in political life.

The analysis of police evolution in Part I draws on a rich but not exhaustive collection of historical materials. By and large, the research uses materials available in English, though some information has been privately translated from foreign-language sources. It reflects fairly accurately the state of knowledge of police development in the following countries: in Europe, France, Germany, Great Britain, Italy, the Netherlands, Norway, and Russia; in North America, Canada and the United States; in Asia, India, Japan, and China; and in a miscellany of ancient empires, simple societies, and contemporary Third World countries. As one would expect, the quality of material varies enormously from place to place. Except for a handful of countries, writing on the police is meager apart from official documents. Documentary and analytical material is most extensive at the present time for the United States. Great Britain is not far behind, and Canada is gaining rapidly. France, the Netherlands, and the Scandinavian countries are just beginning to study the police. There is considerable material on Japan, almost all in Japanese, but it is rarely analytic and almost always official. India, too, has excellent official reports, largely descriptive, as well as a wealth of insightful and diverting anecdotal accounts of policing.

Because the information available about the historical evolution of police is patchy and varied in quality and my own understanding of changes in social circumstances historically in all these countries is necessarily uneven, the propositions developed cannot be considered conclusive. Rather, they represent an informed attempt to find general patterns of development, as well as general explanations for the patterns. I earnestly hope that people with more extensive knowledge of these countries or familiar with experience elsewhere will amend or even refute these findings. These propositions mark the beginning rather than the conclusion of a dialogue about the historical evolution of police. If this initial attempt at comparative historical analysis is conceptually sound and does not misuse the information available to it, subsequent research by others, whether moved by respect, pity, or outrage, should prove easier.

I have also deliberately eschewed a deductive approach to research based on a particular theoretical paradigm or ideological perspective. Our historical knowledge of the police is at best so incomplete that operating out of specific theoretical perspectives obscures rather than illuminates experience. At this stage of our knowledge, it is wiser, I believe, to fashion theoretical statements out of a lively appreciation of disparate facts, even at the risk of operating at fairly low levels of generality, than to be preoccupied with fitting empirical pieces into major paradigms. Since some of the propositions that are advanced later are surprising—counterintuitive, if you will—I believe the approach has been justified by results.

The information used in Part II to describe and explain police work contemporaneously comes in large part from my own intensive research in several Asian, European, and North American countries in the late 1970s, specifically India, Japan, Singapore, Sri Lanka, France, Great Britain, Norway, the Netherlands, Canada, and the United States. Although the countries chosen for study cover several continents, cultures, and degrees of economic development, they do not constitute a representative global sample. While the data collected demonstrates the extreme variability in police work in the modern world, it cannot be used to prove, as opposed to suggesting, reasons for the variation.

Access to any country's police is problematic because their work is often both politically sensitive and protected by consideration of citizens' right to confidentiality. This factor more than any other accounts for the bias in the sample. Some countries can be pried open by diligent effort, but many are not even worth trying. Few countries fail to raise barriers of some sort. I would suggest that a country's willingness to allow access to police records, personnel, and operations is an excellent indicator of the openness of political life and the character of regimes. Being an indigenous scholar, by the way, does not simplify the problem. Indeed, the converse may be true. Local scholars represent a standing threat to police institutions. The foreign scholar at least can be counted on to go away and to publish far away. Even when access is granted, cooperation by serving personnel may not be forthcoming. Like other bureaucracies, police forces are suspicious; they have their own interests to protect. Before access becomes meaningful interaction, police officials must learn to trust the researcher as well as to accept the importance of the research venture.

Part III reverts to the approaches taken in Part I of searching for patterns of reciprocal relations between police and society and then framing theoretical statements about the factors that give distinctive character to this interaction from country to country. Once again, although the information used is more extensive than in any other treatment of the police, the analysis constitutes an informed beginning to theory construction rather than conclusive testing.

The book concludes with a chapter about the future of policing in the modern world. In it I review the insights into police functioning and development pinpointed in earlier chapters. Then I present an analytical schema that delineates the strategic choices that countries face in crime control and suggest the policies that are most likely in different social circumstances.

One topic that many people regard as very important in the study of the police is their relative effectiveness in meeting responsibilities. While this is undoubtedly a critical matter, constituting the dominant preoccupation of serving policemen, variations in police effectiveness over time or space simply cannot be determined. The reasons are familiar to knowledgeable experts, even though they are generally ignored in practice.

First, although the prevention of crime and improvement of public safety is considered the responsibility of police the world over, other criteria are also considered important, such as adherence to law, absence of immoral behavior, generation of public trust, display of sympathy and concern, openness to informed scrutiny, capacity for generalized problem-solving, protection of the integrity of political processes, and equitable treatment of persons. Judging police performance is a controversial multivariate process, elements of which change from place to place and time to time.

Second, assuming that crime-fighting is the key feature of police performance, information about it cannot be trusted. The usual measure is the amount of crime reported to the police. The fact is that reported crime rates are unpredictably unstable, even when the recording process is not subject to deliberate manipulation. Even more troubling, active and attentive police work can have the paradoxical effect of raising rather than lowering reported crime. Reported crime rates are, therefore, too unreliable to use as a measure of police effectiveness. So familiar are the problems with reported rates that the burden of proof should no longer be on the skeptics but rather on the users of them. Victimization surveys get around some of the problems with reported crime statistics, but they have difficulties of their own, notably the faulty recall of respondents. They are also very costly, which explains why only a handful of countries have undertaken them, all of them wealthy by world standards.[5] At the present time, they are not a practical alternative in comparing variations in objective criminality.

Third, crime, which comes in an enormous variety of forms, has been attributed to many factors having nothing to do with police activity—age, sex, race, income, employment, industrialization, urbanization, community cohesiveness, values, psychological disorganization, and opportunity (Radzinowicz and King 1977, chaps. 3 and 4). Therefore, any test of police usefulness must assure that factors such as these exist to the same degree among places and times compared. Internationally, the range of variation among these factors is so great that a test of police efficacy, even if a reliable measure of criminality could be constructed, is quite impossible. Even within countries, comparability among police jurisdictions with respect to these variables is usually too much to assume.

Fourth, efficacy measures such as clearance rates, usually meaning the ratio of arrests to the number of reported crimes, are wholly spurious. Not only are they based on unreliable reported crime figures, but they measure what police do—making arrests—rather than what police achieve—preventing crime. Clearance rates can be considered measures of police effectiveness only if the primary purpose of the police is considered to be retributive. If their raison d'être is the protection of the public, then clearance rates do not provide relevant information.

Given the serious methodological problems that face a test of police efficacy, it is not surprising that attempts to relate variations in policing to criminality have generally failed (Clarke and Heal 1979; Wycoff 1982; Wycoff and Manning 1983). Current police practices, structures, and levels of strength are literally unjustified in terms of meeting the responsibility universally entrusted to them of controlling crime—not because the police may not in fact be useful, but because we cannot determine whether they are. The plain fact is that relying on what the police are currently doing to protect society is a matter of faith, not science. Continued use of reported crime figures and clearance rates as indicators of police utility is a fraud on a gullible public. Such statistics are the fig leaves of the police. Unfortunately, judgments about police effectiveness will continue to be based more on police salesmanship than on demonstrated connections between police activity and public safety.

PART II
EVOLUTION

CHAPTER 2

The Development of Modern Police

Policing in the world today is dominated by agencies that are public, specialized, and professional. Indeed, as far as most people are concerned, these characteristics partially define police and certainly facilitate recognizing them. Police are thought of as being employees of government selected and trained for a career service, whose responsibility is the forceful enforcement of law. This is a restrictive view, as the discussion in Chapter 1 has shown. Policing may also be done privately and without particular attention to the rationality of its management.

This chapter will examine the emergence of the combination of public agency, relative specialization, and rational management in world policing. In each case, the chronology of development will be described, and factors that seem to have impelled development will be specified. On the basis of the evidence available, theoretical propositions will be constructed about the evolution of modern police. The propositions are offered to prompt further study and especially testing.

THE NATURE OF PUBLIC POLICE

Communities authorize the use of force in regulating internal affairs and even create formal institutions of government and law without developing public police. Police become "public," as I shall use the term, when they are paid and directed by communities acting collectively. Both payment and direction are necessary to distinguish publicness from privateness. Police have been directed by government but paid privately. Before the nineteenth century, constables in England were directed by magistrates appointed by the crown but were paid privately, usually by persons avoiding the duty of obligatory service (Spitzer and Scull 1977). Members of sheriffs' posses, famous in American cowboy movies, were unpaid volunteers organized by official action. They were privately maintained but directed by a government official. (The posse, by the way, is an ancient invention, the word itself an abbreviation of the Latin phrase *posse comitatus*.) On the other hand, governments sometimes use public funds to maintain services that are privately directed. This is rare in policing, though private security guards for public buildings are an example; it is more common in medical care, street maintenance, and sanitation. Insisting that the public status of policing depends upon the nature of both payment and direction limits the number of instances of it that can be found historically, but it avoids the problem of comparing systems that are public in one respect but not in another. Partially public systems can now be clearly designated.[1]

Remembering that an essential element of the definition of police is authorization in the name of a community, how likely is it that a substantial police system will not be public? Wouldn't it be logical to expect that community authorization would bring with it public direction and support? If this were so, then private policing would turn out to be very rare. This is not in fact the case. Many communities, even many states, have relied exclusively on private policing. Up to the sixth century B.C. in Athens, only wronged persons could institute criminal suits; noninvolved persons, including the state, could not do so. The state prosecuted people by its own agency only for a few subversive and sacrilegious offenses (Bonner and Smith 1928, vol. 2, chap. 11). Though historical evidence is not entirely clear, the executive administration of justice until Solon appears to have been in private hands. Rome maintained public order in a similar fashion under the *Ius Civile* and the Law of the Twelve Tables until the middle of the third century B.C. (Kunkel 1973). Private individuals brought malefactors to magistrates, usually assisted by friends or relatives. Magistrates decided the guilt of an accused and turned the prisoner back to his captors for administration of whatever punishment was allowed by law—including death, slavery, and monetary payment. Until recently, the *jir* of the Tiv tribe in Africa was the community's only public agency for the administration of justice. Like Roman magistrates, they only adjudicated, leaving executive police action to private persons (Bohannan 1957, chap. 10). In all these cases, policing was performed in the sense of physical constraint legitimately applied in a community's name, but not under public auspices.

Generally in feudalism the lawmaking community and the law-enforcing community were distinct. The development of political sovereignty predicated on territory as well as the sentiment of nationality did not automatically lead to the creation of police capacity by the central government. Indeed, the persistence of decentralized authority to maintain public order was sometimes an explicit condition for the creation of a larger political community. Nor did the development of state adjudicative capacity lead to the development of state police forces. European kingdoms in the Middle Ages became "law states" before they became police states (Strayer 1970, p. 61). The conclusion, then, is that communities can authorize the executive enforcement of law without directing or maintaining a police force.

Enforcement of law in England during the early Middle Ages, for example, was carried out by lords with title to land—"thames" in the reigns of Alfred (871–900) and Edgar (959–975)—or nonlandowning people organized into Tythings (ten households) and Hundreds (ten Tythings) in what was known as the Frankpledge system. Although order was maintained in the king's name, offenses being against the "King's Peace," he did not have officials to enforce his own writ (Bloch 1961, chap. 30; Bopp and Schultz 1972, pp. 9–10; Keeton 1975, chap. 1; Lee 1901 [1971], chap. 1). A similar arrangement existed in France. For instance, according to the charter granted the people of St. Omer by William Count of Normandy in 1127, the lord of the castle, his wife, or his steward had authority to issue warrants for arrest when a crime had been committed. If the suspects were taken within three days, they were turned over to the lord; after that they could be punished by citizens at large. The citizens were not liable for property damage, bodily injury, or death that resulted (Herlihy 1968, pp. 181–184). Executive as well as judicial authority attaching to title to land granted by sovereigns persisted historically until quite recent times. The right of Prussian landowners (*Junkers*) to administer justice was not abolished until 1872, while that of the Russian squirearchy, though attenuated after the emancipation of serfs in 1864, lasted until the 1918 revolution (Florinsky 1953, p. 572; Holborn 1969, p. 401). In India and China the police power of landowners fluctuated with the strength of empires from time immemorial until well into the nineteenth and twentieth centuries, respectively.

The conclusion, then, is that communities can authorize the executive enforcement of law without directing or maintaining a police force.

But this raises a crucial conceptual point. Is it appropriate to call feudal landowners who maintain order *private* as opposed to *public* functionaries? Since membership groups fit within one another, how does one know which auspices are public? If manors are considered the primary effective unit of government during the medieval period in Europe, then retainers like *senchal*s, *prevot*s, knights, and bailiffs should be considered public police officials, although they certainly did not act in a police capacity all the time.

Publicness is easily determined after the establishment of states. But associating publicness only with state political communities is too restrictive. States are not the only important human communities where a distinction can intelligently be made between collective and noncollective instrumentalities. All sorts of communities, including many that are not defined in terms of territory—like tribes, churches, and castes—can have government in the sense of authority to act for a community. Recognition of the separate roles of rulers and ruled exists in small and large communities, both territorial and nonterritorial. A difference between public and private roles is recognized commonly in human communities; to associate publicness only with states obscures an almost universal distinction.[2] Public agency exists prior to the development of nation-states. And public police agencies may precede the formation of states, just as they may absent from them.

An alternative tack often taken is to broaden the definition of *state*, identifying it with the capacity to govern regardless of the nature of the community. Public auspices remain tied to states, but *statehood* refers to the collective capacity to govern. Since this capacity is almost universal, publicness becomes a common feature of organized social experience. The problem with this formulation is that *state* ceases to delineate a political community organized in a unique way. In my view, it is simpler and closer to usage to associate *state* with sovereign communities that are predicated on control of territory. This is surely the connotation of phrases like *city-state* and *nation-state*. Public and private should be distinguished wherever noncommunity auspices can be distinguished from community ones, regardless of the social basis of the community. In practice, of course, the smaller the community the more difficult it will be to do this: private and public domains become coextensive, community action and individual action are inseparable.

Police are public, then, if they are paid and directed by the community that also authorizes policing. Police are private if the authorizing community neither pays nor directs them. This formulation is compatible with an important reality in governing, namely, delegation of authority to act for the community. The police of Maryland in the United States, Uttar Pradesh in India, and Azerbaijan in the Soviet Union are not private. Why not? Because they are directed by government, by agents of the maximal community. Some subunits of communities are public and others private, depending on whether they are agents of the sovereign power. It follows that medieval manors are public entities, not only because the authority of the king was often minimal but also because they were explicitly derivative units of the kingdom. Vassalage meant sharing with the king the prerogative to rule. Similarly, geographical subunits of modern nation-states derive their authority from that of the encompassing political community. They are constituent in authority, though unequal in power.

Because communities nest within one another, contending for political preeminence, determination of whether police are public or private depends on judgments about sovereignty. If the Cheyenne Indian nation is considered sovereign during the nineteenth century, then their bands of soldier-police were public; if the United States is considered sovereign, then the Cheyenne soldier-police were private. The police of the East India Trading Company in the eighteenth century were private from the point of view of Englishmen living in England, but public from the point of view of Indians and Englishmen living in India. Application of the dichotomy between public and private agency can only be made intelligently when the relation between the respective communities, especially whether one is superordinate, is specified. Encapsulation of one community by another frequently means competition with respect to autonomy. Unless the units of police predication are specified so that judgments about sovereignty can be made explicitly, changes in the character of policing can be confused with changes in the primacy of political communities. The replacement of the police of a small sovereign unit by a larger sovereign unit is not a change in the character of policing. Both are public. On the other hand, when a political community substitutes police agents paid and directed by it for police agents of constituent groups that are not its creation, like tribes or industrial enterprises, then a change in the character of policing has taken place.

THE DEVELOPMENT OF PUBLIC POLICE

Public policing is an old, not a new, development. It is as old as the existence of sovereign communities that authorize physical constraint and create agents that they direct and maintain. This is borne out by the work of Richard Schwartz and James Miller (1964), which is the only systematic research on police institutions in primitive societies. They found that twenty out of fifty-one primitive societies surveyed had public police, including the Maori, Lapps, Riffians, Thonga, Syrians, Ashanti, Cheyenne, Creek, Cuna, Crow, and Hopi.[3] One of the earliest well-documented cases of the development of public police was in Rome, beginning in 27 B.C., when C. Octavius became *princeps*, taking the name Augustus. One of his first acts was to relieve the Senate of responsibility for civil administration in Rome and assume it himself. Since the fifth century B.C., civil administration had been in the hands of several grades of magistrates appointed by the Senate, some of whom, like the *questor*, had general regulative power for maintaining order in markets and public thoroughfares. These magistrates were not paid, their personal servants being used as professional staff. Augustus realized that a growing, teeming city of almost one million people, divided sharply by class and imbued with habits of violence, needed more efficient policing.[4] He created the post of *preafectus urbi*, filled by appointment from the highest ranks of the Senate, with responsibility for maintaining public order executively and judicially. The staff of the *preafectus urbi*, including the *preafectus vigilium*—chief of police—were paid by Augustus (Kunkel 1973, chaps. 1, 3, and 4). For the first time Rome had a truly public police—executive agents of physical constraint paid and directed by supreme political authority.

For the conceptual reasons already discussed, it is a mistake to regard public police as having died in Europe during the interregnum between the fall of Rome and the rise of modern nation-states. Policing became exceedingly decentralized, but so too did political sovereignty and the authority to make law. Gradually, new superordinate kingdoms were formed, delegating the power to create police but holding on to the power to make law. Later, public police officials were created who were directly responsible to sovereign power. In England this was the *sheriff*, a term derived from *shire-reeve*, who was made a royal official by the Norman kings in the twelfth century and was granted power to levy fines against criminals as well as the Hundreds for failing to capture criminals (Bopp and Schultz 1972, pp. 9–10; Lee 1901 [1971], chap. 1). He was responsible for organizing the Tythings and Hundreds, inspecting their arms, and calling out the *posse comitatus*, which consisted of all able-bodied men over fifteen years old. Complaints about the greed and highhandedness of sheriffs, such as making false charges against Hundreds, were common, as the tale of Robin Hood correctly portrays. As late as the sixteenth century, Hundreds were petitioning the crown for release from these fines (Lee 1901 [1971], chap. 1).

English sheriffs were public police officials, but they were not paid in the modern way—a salary for services rendered. Rather, they were allowed to appropriate a portion of money collected in the king's name—thus the temptation to overenforce the law. The money supporting them was nevertheless public, since the sheriff was acting as official collecting agent for the king. The same is true for the celebrated "trading justices" of London during the seventeenth and eighteenth centuries. They, too, should be regarded as public officials. Placing them on a stipendiary footing in 1792 contributed to a higher level of judicial conduct but did not change their status (Keeton 1975, chap. 3).

The constable is another important medieval English invention in law enforcement but cannot be regarded as a public police official. According to the Statute of Winchester, 1285, two constables were to be appointed by every Hundred; their duties were to inspect the arms of the Hundred as prescribed in the Assize of Arms and to act as the sheriff's agents (Lee 1901 [1971], chaps. 2 and 3). As the Frankpledge system decayed, Hundreds could no longer appoint constables, so authority to do so was successively transferred to parish, borough, county, and eventually "police authority." Until the nineteenth century the constable remained an executive agent of law, acting in the king's name but not paid out of public funds. Beginning in London in 1829, constables began to be paid, thus fundamentally transforming their character, although nearly a century passed before the change was implemented throughout the country. The modern English police constable is the medieval Tythingman, still acting under royal authority but now serving at public expense in a chosen career.

Setting aside the conceptual confusion about who were police during feudal times, the only law enforcement agents in England before the eighteenth century who could be regarded as public were the sheriffs and London's "trading justices." Starting in 1735, the first of a series of experiments began that were to nationalize policing. Two London parishes were given authority by statute to pay their watch out of local taxes (Tobias 1972). Later, in the middle of the century, John and Henry Fielding, Bow Street magistrates, began to pay men to serve as constables and to patrol at night (Armitage n.d., p. 123). Though ostensibly paid privately by the Fieldings, the expenses incurred were partially offset by grants from government. In 1792 the new stipendiary magistrates in Middlesex were empowered to pay constables from public funds (Reith 1948, chap. 5). In 1800 the Thames River Police, funded in 1798 by West Indian merchants, became the Thames River Establishment, supported by public revenues (Spitzer and Scull 1977). By 1829 London had become a patchwork of public and private police forces. The City of London had a municipal police force, while police elsewhere were supported by vestries, church wardens, boards of trustees, commissioners, parishes, magistrates, and courts-leet (Hart 1951, pp. 26–27). Because experimentation was so rife and the concept of public police still so unsettled, historians seldom agree about which police agents deserve to be called the first public police. The point I would underscore, however, is that the English developed a specialized police official in the constable seven hundred years before he became a public functionary in the sense of being both directed and maintained out of public funds.

The first public police of the French state may have been the provost of Paris, a post created by St. Louis in the thirteenth century. Headquartered in the Chatelet, which was also the city prison, the provost was assisted by a staff of investigating commissioners and "sergeants" (Stead 1957, chap. 1). In addition, the provost commanded a small detachment of mounted military troops and a nightwatch, participation in which was obligatory on all male citizens (Tuchman 1979, p. 158). John II (1350–1364) created a larger military force to patrol the highways and suppress the marauding bands of unemployed knights, foreign mercenaries, and army deserters who pillaged the land (Tuchman 1979, chap. 10). Their responsibilities grew to encompass suppression of crime generally on the king's highway.[5] Three centuries later Cardinal Richelieu (1585–1642) enormously expanded the administrative capacity of the state by creating the *intendant*, an appointed official paid by the king to maintain order, administer justice, and collect taxes in France's thirty-two provinces (*generalité*). In 1667 a specialized deputy for law and order, the lieutenant general of police, was created in Paris (Arnold 1969, pp. 12–13; Stead 1957, chap. 1). He commanded the Garde, initially composed of a mounted troop. By 1699 there were lieutenants general in all major cities.

Prussia, the keystone of German unification in 1871, developed a paid bureaucracy very soon after Frederick I, the Great Elector, became *primus inter pares* among the other *Junkers* in the middle of the seventeenth century. Higher civil servants, like the *Landrat* and *Steuerat*, had police powers, though they were simply part of general administrative authority. The first specialized public police official was the police director for Berlin, appointed in 1742 (Emerson 1968, pp. 4–5). As in other continental European countries, a numerous body of public police did not grow until the nineteenth century. At the same time, the *Junkers* were allowed to retain police powers on their estates. Thus, modern state police institutions, largely in towns, coexisted with feudal ones. Since both systems were constituent parts of the sovereign's authority, Prussia should be described as having a dual system of public policing.

Ivan the Terrible created Russia's first state public police, the dreaded Oprichniki, in 1564 (Florinsky 1953, pp. 200–202). Dressed in hooded black cloaks with brooms attached to their horses' heads, its members constituted a mounted military corps that scourged the countryside suppressing Boyar resistance to Ivan's rule. The Oprichniki became the secret police of the Tsar in addition to controlling markets, roads, and other public places. Peter the Great created a specialized public police official in St. Petersberg in 1718. The system was extended to the rest of the country by edicts of Catherine I in 1775 and 1792 (Abbott 1972, sec. 1; Monas 1961, pp. 24–29). In cities police rank and file were paid; in rural areas they were not, being lower-class persons who were hired and paid by people who wanted to avoid service, like Englishmen during the same period. As in Prussia, the landed gentry were allowed to maintain their own police system side by side with that of the central state. The landowners remained a law unto themselves even after the emancipation of the serfs in 1864 (Florinsky 1953, p. 101; Monas 1961, p. 274; Seton-Watson 1967, p. 26).

The ebb and flow of public policing in China and India extended over millennia. When powerful dynasties created large empires, paid police officials were invariably established—in towns as the Mauryas and Moguls did, in districts (*hsien*) as the Tangs and Mings did (Basham 1954, pp. 118–121; Starkarum 1963, pp. 91ff; Cox n.d., chaps. 2 and 3). When imperial power declined, nonstate police institutions based on small voluntary communities or the obligations of land settlement reasserted themselves.[6] Flux in the scale of government again confuses judgments about public policing. As in feudal Europe, two systems exist side by side, both with claims to being public, depending on the sovereignty they possessed. Unambiguously public police were not dominant in India until passage of the Indian Police Act in 1862, and abolition of the princely states in 1948/49, and in China until the Communist Party created a new and effective imperial center in 1949.

Public policing came to the United States with the first settlers. New Amsterdam, later New York, created a burgher watch in 1643, one year after it was founded, but did not pay them until 1712 (Bopp and Schultz 1972, chap. 2). Constables, marshals, and watches were appointed or elected in every settlement, with early recognition that payment was required to ensure effective performance. Compared with the other countries examined, public police became important in the United States about the same time as in England, later than in France, much later than in India or China, and about the same time as in Prussia and Russia. In the American West the unpaid posse remained a mainstay of law enforcement into the twentieth century.

These examples demonstrate how one determines whether public policing exists at a particular time or place. Publicness, a characteristic of forces that dominate policing today, is not a modern invention. Its antiquity is not usually recognized, primarily because of confusion with respect to the concept itself. There is another reason as well. History tends to discount the vigor of failed political systems, systems that gave way to other centers of power, especially if those new centers still exist today. Historical success makes it seem as if Rome had public police but the Duke of Brittany did not, that Emperor Asoka had but zamindars did not, that the state of Colorado had but the Cheyenne nation did not. Because England and France emerged from a welter of estates and manors, the sheriff and the *marechausée* appear to be the first public police. However, if amalgamation had not occurred, then Tythingmen and shire-appointed reeves might be seen as the first public police. In Japan the sovereignty of the emperor was restored in 1868, yet it would certainly be wrong to say that samurai who enforced law and order for the daimyo before that were private police. The samurai were agents of the only effective and legitimate units of government that people acknowledged. They were as public for the Japanese as were King John's sheriffs or Louis XIV's lieutenants general of police. Public policing only looks like a modern development when the vitality of noncontemporary sovereign powers is discounted.

Furthermore, although it is true that police in the world today are for the most part paid and directed by governments of states, it would be a mistake to conclude that privateness in policing is inevitably withering. There is no historical necessity in the movement from private to public police auspices. For example, the collapse of the Roman Empire destroyed state policing and forced people into desperate reliance on private mechanisms for ensuring security. Neighbors banded together into Tythings and Hundreds in England; clergy proclaimed days of peace and tried to exempt certain places and people from violence; lords formed transitory alliances to subdue rivals who broke the peace; and Peace Leagues took the field against robber barons (Bloch 1961, chap. 30). Today, as well, private policing is growing enormously, especially in advanced industrial countries. Public forms of policing do not permanently supplant private ones; the process is reversible.

CAUSES OF PUBLIC POLICE DEVELOPMENT

Considering the ubiquity of the public form of policing in history, one must strain to argue that particular sets of social or political conditions are required in order to have it. Public policing has existed in societies as different as ancient Syria, classical Rome, absolutist France, industrial Britain, feudal Russia, and contemporary America. Certainly none of the characteristics usually associated with modernity—industrialization, urbanization, technology, literacy, affluence—appear necessary to create public policing. Theoretically it is less interesting that all advanced industrial societies have substantial, indeed dominating, systems of public police than that many societies developed public police long before they became modern.

On the basis of their study of fifty-one primitive societies, Schwartz and Miller (1964) argue that some social complexity is required before public police emerge—specifically, monetization, functional specialization in some nonpolice sectors, such as religion and education, and creation of government officials not related to the chief. The authors weaken the importance of their discovery when they note that these features often exist without public police being established. Social complexity, then, is only a minimally necessary condition for the creation of public police. The same is true of restitutive sanctions, like mediation and assessment for damages, which, they find, precede establishment of public police. Social complexity and restitutive sanctions are so common in human history that they do not help to explain whether particular societies will or will not rely on the police.

Public police replace private police when the capacity of groups within society to undertake effective enforcement action is no longer sufficient to cope with insecurity. Such a change can occur in societies of very different character. Conversely, urbanization, increased affluence, and industrialization do not inevitably produce public police. They do so only when accompanied by unacceptable insecurity as a perceived result of decay in the vitality of traditional bases of community enforcement. In England, industrialization destroyed the effectiveness of the parish as a unit of community regulation (Silver 1967). In part this may have been the result of changing perceptions of public order needs, reflected especially in a growing concern with immoral pastimes, like drunkenness and animal baiting, as well as decorum, such as vagrancy and brawling (Philips 1977). In any case, by the middle of the nineteenth century the parish no longer commanded the wealth or loyalty necessary to support a reliable constabulary. The same thing happened in Prussia, Russia, and the American South when landowners on large estates discovered they could no longer protect themselves against the disorder generated by their suppressed laborers. In Rome, it was commercial aggrandizement, urban scale, and population heterogeneity that weakened policing based on kin and neighborhood. In short, when traditional private auspices for maintaining order are undermined, either new private groups must become effective centers for regulatory mobilization or the community as a whole will assume responsibility.

The transition from private police auspices to development of police institutions maintained and directed by government at the most inclusive level of political identification does not occur overnight. Norman kings, Tudor queens, and Whig governments in England tried to breathe new life into local police institutions for centuries. Sheriffs were created initially to supervise the Frankpledge system, fining Hundreds for failing in their duties. Countless directives issued from London for centuries urging justices of the peace to improve the quality of personnel chosen as constables. Private and public police auspices thus sometimes coexist, both in substantial scale. Changes in relative proportions take place slowly and are subject to reverses.

The factor impelling movement from private to public policing is not simply a growth in insecurity but a growth in insecurity traceable to a decline in the efficiency of customary enforcement auspices. A high incidence of crime by itself is not sufficient. To be sure, movement to a public system will be justified in terms of security needs, but this is true as well for the regeneration of private policing. Though crime figures are hopelessly inadequate for the periods discussed here, impressionistic evidence suggests that public police did not supplant private in times of unusual criminality (Lodhi and Tilly 1970). Private policing persisted in England in the eighteenth century despite rampant criminality, while public police were created in Russia and France in the seventeenth and eighteenth centuries without the prompting of ordinary crime. Violence was common in Roman life from at least 131 B.C., most of it inspired by politics. Courts and assemblies were frequently disrupted by mobs, their judgments coerced. Wealthy people hired bands of retainers—slaves and gladiators—to defend themselves and their property. Cicero, for example, is reported to have had three hundred thugs under hire in 61 B.C., mostly to intimidate his political opponents (Lintott 1968, chaps. 5 and 6). Yet Rome did not develop public police, apart from periodic intrusions by the legions, until Augustus. Conversely, rising crime may actually contribute to the strengthening of private policing if public police are perceived to be ineffective. Vigilantism in the United States in the nineteenth century is a case in point, as is the remarkable increase in private policing throughout the industrial countries since the middle of the 1960s.

A change from private to public police auspices represents an aug-
mentation of the regulative capacity of the maximal community. This
being so, it would be logical to expect that the dynamics of political
encapsulation—the growth of new political centers—would effect policing in turn. A priori it would seem that the extension of effective
political hegemony would be associated with the creation of public police. Surprisingly, this is not the case, for two reasons. First, the units
whose capacity for policing is extinguished may have had public policing themselves. British conquest of India did not create public policing;
it merely shifted control of it from one place to another. Second, the
assertive larger political community has no need to establish public police institutions unless its own interests are threatened. England's Tudor
monarchs and Prussia's Frederick the Great created powerful state bureaucracies, but both left traditional police arrangements almost wholly
untouched (Rosenberg 1958, pp. 35–38). The preservation of substate
enforcement auspices was part of the political settlement underlying the
initial growth of both the English and Prussian states. New political
centers may assert themselves through taxation, military prowess, and
the adjudication of disputes without developing marked police capacity
(L. Tilly 1971). Public policing is not the taproot of today's nation-
states. This point is often not recognized because states have been defined in terms of the capacity to maintain a monopoly of force within
the community. The fact is, however, that political communities may
have effective and authoritative government without maintaining and
directing enforcement agents.

The only time the formation of a new political community brings
about a shift from private to public police auspices is when constituent
units resist the process by violence. A section of the French nobility—
the Fronde—resisted centralized monarchical rule in 1649, at the cost
of their feudal prerogatives and monopolization of policing by the king
through the *intendants* and the lieutenants general of police. The English state, on the other hand, developed administratively without resistance from the landed nobility and gentry. The squirearchy shared responsibility with the king for administering the Common Law. They
acted as royal agents and justices of the peace, and in exchange the king
allowed them to direct the parishes executively. Legislative and judicial
centralization was combined with police decentralization under private
auspices. Within this political formula, English government steadily

grew in power until well into the nineteenth century (Bloch 1961, pp. 425–426). The exception proving the rule is Oliver Cromwell's experiment with a national Military Police from 1655 to 1657. The Military Police was the only attempt by the central government to create public police, apart from the sheriffs, during the nine hundred years from the Norman conquest to Peel's reform. It came about because the country was polarized on the issue of religion. Protestants and Catholics violently disputed the existing political dispensation, neither side being able to accept a central government ruled by the other. The Military Police, composed of about sixty-four hundred mounted militia, enforced Puritan Rule after the Civil War, their attention extending to lifestyles as well as political reliability. Although religious animosity strained English politics for a long time after Cromwell, the accession of William and Mary in 1688 confirmed Protestant domination and reunited crown and squirearchy, providing again a basis for private, decentralized policing. The system remained unchallenged for another century and a half.

In summary, public policing never permanently replaces private policing. Furthermore, public policing is difficult to explain, because it occurs in all sorts of social circumstances. If public policing were rarer in history or exclusively modern, the search for an explanation would be easier. Two factors appear to be most influential in producing a change from private to public police auspices: social changes that undermine the capacity of private groups to maintain acceptable levels of security, and the formation of superordinate political communities that is met with violent resistance by constituent groups.

SPECIALIZED POLICE

Specialization is a relative term referring to exclusiveness in performing a task. In policing, the defining task is the application of physical force within a community. A specialized police devote all their attention to the application of physical constraint; a nonspecialized police do many other things besides. The seventeenth century *intendant* in France was a nonspecialized police agent; the constable in England was a specialized one. The district magistrate today in Pakistan is nonspecialized, responsible for performing administrative, judicial, and enforcement tasks; the district superintendent of police is sp ecialized. Because police are rarely totally specialized, evaluations of specialization must be made comparatively. That is, they must be made in relation to a standard. Furthermore, having specialized police in a society is not the same as having a single police force. Specialization of function and monopolization of that function are different. Countries can have more than one agency whose primary function is the maintenance of public order. Italy, for example, has three police forces, Spain two, and the United States innumerable. Conversely, a force that monopolizes the application of physical force within the community may not be specialized; it may do other things in addition. The organizational structure of policing in a society, of which monopolization is one form, will be discussed in Chapter 3.

THE DEVELOPMENT OF SPECIALIZED POLICE

The earliest specialized police were watchmen, found almost universally among societies, from village *chowkidar*s in South Asia to the nightwatch in medieval Europe. However, although their function was certainly specialized, it is not always clear that it was policing. Very often they acted only as sentinels, responsible for summoning others to apprehend criminals, repel attack, or put out fires. To the extent that watchmen did apply force, they represent specialized police.

Specialized police have usually developed as part of the administrative apparatus of most of the world's great empires. Detectives, spies, and enforcers of public order are found in imperial records of the Mauryas (c. 321–c. 184 B.C.), the Guptas (320–c. 535), and the Moguls (1526–1858) in India, the Mings (1368–1644) in China, and the Heians (794–1185) in Japan.[7] The Romans developed specialized police known as Vigiles in 6 A.D., who by the third century A.D. were deployed in police stations and patrolled the streets both night and day (Reynolds 1926). As far as records are concerned, specialized police personnel seep into the sands of history when imperial vigor declines, going underground to emerge at a later date.

Among the states of Europe that we recognize today, the British were probably the first to develop specialized law and order agents. There were the *posse comitatus* and the constable of the Middle Ages.

The French *sergeant*, on the other hand, who appeared about the same time as the constable, was a more multipurpose official who did everything from serving judicial warrants to undertaking military operations (Strayer 1970, p. 78). At the same time Denmark, Norway, and Sweden created the *Lensman*, who enforced laws at local levels and collected taxes for the king. In Norway he was elected by the peasants but served under the direction of the king's territorial representative, known as the *syssler*. *Lensmen* still exist in rural Norway. In Denmark the *Lensman* evolved into a kind of county sheriff, and his privileges became hereditary. From the late twelfth century Scandinavian cities were administered for the king by *gjaldkere*, who collected taxes, enforced law, prosecuted offenders, jailed criminals, and assigned people to the nightwatch (Hjellemo 1979).

Since the Middle Ages, policing on the continent has been less specialized than in England. Certainly this was true for middle level police officials. Continental *intendants*, *prevots*, *Landrat*, *Steuerat*, and *Lensmen* did much more than enforce law and maintain public order. They were omnicompetent, serving as the king's representatives in all official matters. The nearest English equivalent is the justice of the peace, developed in the thirteenth century; but he, as the name implies, was more narrowly concerned with matters of public order and justice (Keeton 1975, chap. 3). Continental administrative officials whose responsibilities included policing may have had more specialized subordinates much like English constables. If this is true, the degree of specialization in Europe was stratified by rank. Policing within the framework of the emerging state was viewed on the continent as an inseparable part of crown administration. The word *police* originally denoted all administrative functions that were not ecclesiastical. In England, contrastingly, the maintenance of the king's peace was a distinct responsibility, antedating the rise of administrative capacity in other areas. Curiously, England appears originally to have been more of a police state in the specialized sense than continental kingdoms. The primacy and early specialization of law enforcement in England within state administration may have acted in fact as a bulwark in tradition against the rise of the continental European *Polizeistaat*.

Another difference between English and continental development was the sequencing of publicness with specialization. Referring to state institutions only, as opposed to feudal ones, English police became specialized before they became public; continental police became public before they became specialized. By roughly the middle of the eighteenth century, specialized royal police officers had been established in larger European cities. Copying the French lieutenant general of police, Tsar Peter I created a police chief in St. Petersburg in 1718, Emperor Frederick II in Berlin in 1742, and Empress Maria Theresa in Vienna in 1751 (Emerson 1968, p. 4–5). Though these officials had wider regulatory responsibilities than the English justice of the peace, they directed personnel who specialized in patrolling, arresting, and spying. In 1760 Paris had a variety of specialized personnel—detectives in each quarter; a patrolling watchguard, both foot and horse; squads of soldiers serving as sentinels; and archers deployed to rid streets of beggars and idlers (Radzinowicz 1957, pp. 540–541). The system had become so elaborate that an English traveler commented wryly that in France, lieutenants general order, inspectors inform, *exemts* apprehend, archers conduct, *commissaires* commit, *chatelets* condemn, and priests grant absolution (Mildmay 1763, p. 6). The other absolutist regimes undoubtedly developed specialized personnel too, but little has been written about them.

American police, like the English, specialized relatively early in national development. Constables and marshals were fixtures of colonial American society from the time of the first settlements. Throughout American history when enforcement was required, government created additional specialized officials. This has been true nationally as well as locally. Specialized federal marshals were created in 1789, one of the first acts of the new national government. The Federal Bureau of Investigation, established in 1924, continued this tradition, concentrating more exclusively on law enforcement than any other force in the country with the possible exception of some state patrols. Comparing American and British experience with that of continental Europe, it is fair to say that Anglo-Saxon police have tended to be more specialized when the territorial extent of their jurisdiction was larger; European police have tended to be less specialized when the extent of their jurisdiction was larger.

An important part of police specialization has been the removal of the military from the work of maintaining domestic order. Since military units also defend communities externally, their use domestically, which has occurred almost everywhere historically, represents imperfect specialization in policing. This kind of imperfect specialization has been a persistent feature of continental Europe, represented in the *gendarmerie* system. Developed initially in France, *gendarmes* were military personnel assigned responsibility for maintaining law and order in rural areas and along major thoroughfares. *Gendarmerie* was the name given during the French Revolution to the old *marechausée*, which in turn had grown out of the *compagnies d'ordonnance*. *Gendarmerie* became standard in European countries during the first half of the nineteenth century: Prussia in 1812, Piedmont in 1816, the Netherlands in 1814, Spain in 1844, and Austria in 1849 (Bramshill Police College 1974; Carr 1966, pp. 233–234; Cramer 1964, pp. 327–329; Fried 1963, chap. 2; Keppler 1974; Jacob 1963, pp. 11–12). Some contemporary descendants of these *gendarmerie* are the Italian Carabinieri, the Spanish Guardia Civil, the French Gendarmerie, the Netherlands Rijkspolitie, and the West German Landespolizei. Gradually, operational direction was turned over to civilian ministries, but the military often retained control over budget, recruitment, and even training. Links to the military are still strong in Italy and Spain, weak in France and Germany, negligible in the Netherlands. Where they continue to exist, police specialization remains incomplete.

In England and her colonies, military participation in policing was never institutionalized. The army was frequently used to suppress outbreaks of domestic violence, but its intrusion was regarded as abnormal, a breakdown in the proper administration of law and order. The most dramatic exception to this was Cromwell's Military Police, 1655–1657, and in the United States the army's deployment to preserve law and order west of the Mississippi River during the nineteenth century. Regarding the United States Army as a "police" force is an interesting example of a post hoc judgment about sovereignty. From the point of view of American Indians, it was not a police force at all but an army of occupation waging aggressive war. As with Cromwell's Military Police, the American army was quickly supplanted by civilian law enforcement agents such as marshals and sheriffs. Even on the reservations into which the Indians were driven, a specialized nonmilitary force was created. This was the Indian Police, formed by Congress in 1878 and directed by Indian agents acting for the Department of the Interior (Hagan 1966, pp. 2–5).

A major reason everywhere for continued military participation in policing was the need to deal with widespread, prolonged, or severe outbursts of violence by large numbers of people. But specialization eventually prevailed here too, so that by the twentieth century military intervention in aid of civil police had become rare. This final act of exclusion of the military from policing has followed different patterns from place to place. It involved an interplay among three forces: armies, police, and militia.

During the two hundred years bounded by 1650 and 1850, riots, rebellions, and insurrections plagued European countries and were met by military force. The military expedient worked successfully as long as violence was localized and of fairly small scale, involving parochial matters of food supply, prices, and sectorial employment. But vast social changes were afoot that were to change the character of unrest. As a result of the commercialization of agriculture and the destruction of cottage industries, people were forced into cities. The control of landed elites, based on ascriptive deference, was weakened, and in some countries hereditary classes were overthrown. Protest increasingly involved vast numbers of people, often spearheaded by the urban mob, and was directed against general political authority rather than local wrongs (Tilly, Tilly, and Tilly 1975). In these circumstances, introduction of an army became a political act, not simply a technical solution to a law and order problem. Furthermore, military units, often mounted and wielding sabres, were too forceful, killing and wounding indiscriminately. They created martyrs and earned the understandable hatred of the populace. As a result, military leaders became reluctant to act in a police capacity. Their distaste was reinforced by concern for the reliability of the army itself. The loyalties of the rank and file were often with the agitators, as were those of nonaristocratic members of the officer corps. These strains became especially acute in Europe with the rise of large conscripted armies in the early nineteenth century, representing a cross-section of social classes that replaced the mercenary armies raised by kings and landed gentry. Thus demands for increased political participation and greater economic equality threatened armies that were barely coming to grips with their own problems of mass mobilization. Soon neither professional military officers nor civilian politicians were keen to use the army as police—in part out of concern for the integrity of the military machine, in part out of concern for the legitimacy of government.

Another force was commonly used throughout Europe to deal with outbreaks of collective violence. That was the militia—irregular volunteer forces recruited locally that were armed and usually mounted. They were a defensive reaction by elites to violent attacks on the status quo. In England, militia were first created in 1660 following the Civil War; in France, after the Revolution in 1789, although the Garde Bourgeoise of the seventeenth century was a precedent (Bayley 1975). Where feudal institutions were strong, as in Prussia and France, militias were an extension of seignorial power. Militias became more prominent in Europe as demands for increased political participation in the nineteenth century moved like a wave across Europe from the Atlantic coast to the Urals. The problem with militias was that they reflected partisan political interests. They lacked general legitimacy, which explains why revolutionary regimes always reorganized them along more inclusive, democratic lines, while restoration governments reconstructed them from rural landowners and the *haute bourgeois* (Carr 1966, pp. 233–234, 283; Langer 1969, pp. 332, 391–392). Militias were not an effective substitute for armies in maintaining domestic order. Indeed, their intrusion tended to exacerbate problems, making law enforcement transparently political.

Faced with reluctant but too forceful armies and enthusiastic but unreliable militias, European governments in the nineteenth century withdrew armies from domestic riot duty, abolished militias, and developed a specialized, public police capacity. England was in the vanguard. In 1829 government created a publicly supported civil constabulary in London that was large enough to contain and disperse urban mobs. Instructively, the Duke of Wellington, England's foremost military authority, gave crucial support to Sir Robert Peel in creating the "new police."[8] Substitution of trained civil police for militias and the military spread throughout Europe during the rest of the century, though the military continued to play a more prominent role on the continent than in England due to the existence of substantial forces of *gendarmes*.

By the early twentieth century, however, urban unrest throughout Europe was met for the most part by armed units of civil police specially trained for that purpose. The English and Norwegian police alone disdained the use of arms altogether. The same historical scenario was followed by Japan during the 1870s. The conscript army created in 1872 as an instrument of national revitalization was unsettled by having to suppress violent regional uprisings that were a reaction to the destruction of the decentralized feudal system of the Tokugawas. In 1878 the responsibility for maintaining internal order was formally transferred from the army to the newly created police built along French and Prussian lines (Tsurumi 1970, p. 85).

The United States developed a unique solution to the problem of containing large-scale domestic turmoil. From colonial times, militias—sometimes voluntary, sometimes conscript—had been used to put down rebellion. Indeed, until early in the twentieth century, they were the only substantial armed forces available, apart from the police. The American Civil War was fought essentially by state militias and not by national armies either of the Union or the Confederacy. Militia units were used throughout the nineteenth century to put down popular agitation, much of it associated toward the end of the century with increasingly organized and violent labor disputes (Smith 1925, pp. 29–32). Like other countries, the United States learned the unwieldiness of using military units in such situations. It came to rely more and more on specialized police forces, keeping the militia in reserve. In 1903 the militias were nationalized, becoming a volunteer military reserve, and were renamed the National Guard (Hill 1969).

Modern policing is dominated by organizations that have become increasingly specialized during the past two centuries. In Anglo-Saxon countries, specialization involved primarily the substitution of civil for military units in dealing with domestic violence; in continental countries, as well as in Latin America, specialization occurred primarily within the civil administration of the state, involving to a lesser extent formal removal of the military from policing. By and large in modern states, the application of physical forces for the maintenance of domestic order has been entrusted to specialized nonmilitary organizations. This is not to argue that modern police do nothing other than forcefully constrain behavior; but the diversity of tasks performed by police today is, as we shall see in Chapter 5, more the result of their own adaptation to the requirements of maintaining order and less the result of the directed mixture of police and nonpolice tasks.

Among contemporary countries, the movement from nonspecialized to more specialized policing has so far not been reversed, unlike the situation with respect to private and public agency in policing. On a wider historical stage, there have been returns to unspecialized police, almost always as part of the collapse of political systems and the creation of new police auspices. This was true during imperial interregnums in China and India and after the fall of the Roman Empire.

THE CAUSES OF SPECIALIZATION

A compelling explanation for an increase in police specialization is difficult to construct. It is tempting to argue that increased social complexity in the form of stratification and differentiation brings it about, especially since both are characteristics of contemporary countries that have specialized forces. The problem is that specialization also occurs in the remote past, both in feudal institutions, as in the Frankpledge system, and early in state-building, as with the sheriff and constable. And the English experience is not exceptional. The United States, admittedly following English tradition, had specialized police well before the industrial age. Specialized police officials—the exact degree of specialization being debatable—are also found in empires such as the Mauryian, Heian, and Ming. Day- and nightwatches occur universally in human society and, to the extent that they have enforcement powers, should be regarded as specialized police. The conclusion is, then, that modern social circumstances may facilitate specialization but are not required for it.

It is equally difficult to find an explanation in politics. Certainly regime character is not obviously associated with specialization. In modern times both democratic and autocratic regimes have simplified the focus of their primary police agents. Although state assertiveness and centralization, which are associated with European absolutism, produced "police states," they did not produce specialized police officials as early as in the more decentralized, consensual England. In England, in fact, specialization antedated the rise of the modern bureaucratic state, with the degree of specialization remaining virtually unchanged from the thirteenth to the twentieth centuries. The growth of centralized bureaucratic power, a feature of modern states, may in fact retard police specialization. This seems to have happened at middle levels of administrative responsibility in the absolute monarchies of Europe. Furthermore, when the need for omnicompetent and unified control by government did confront the English in their far-flung colonies, police command became less specialized, not more, and was concentrated in the hands of multipurpose district magistrates and collectors (Bayley 1969, chap. 2). The *Polizeistaat* is not, therefore, a police-specialized state (Raeff 1975). Not only is the growth of centralized state power not required for police specialization, but it does not particularly facilitate it.

Differences in specialization in Europe, clearest at middle levels of state management, are associated with the contrasting traditions of Roman law and common law. A heritage of Roman law retards development of specialized police agents. Even today, as we shall see later, continental European countries tend to assign a wider range of responsibilities to their police than do Anglo-Saxon countries.

The removal of the military from policing is the one aspect of specialization where the historical record does not confound the search for explanation. A military role in policing persists, representing imperfect specialization, when a large standing army is created early in the state experience and when the development of state capacities is met with prolonged or severe civil strife.[9] *Gendarme* police systems developed in France, Prussia, Italy, Spain, and the Netherlands, where these conditions obtained. They did not develop in Britain, the United States, Japan, or Scandinavia, all of which were spared the need to develop substantial standing armies until late in their national experience. Moreover, in each of these countries national identity was not forged by conquest on the part of one region over the others, nor was the authority of national government contested by force. Though each has known civil strife, such episodes were either brief or occurred after traditions governing the relations between police and military had been set.

The military withdraws from policing in response to two factors: development of mass armies based on conscription, and changes in military technology that make the indiscriminate use of force difficult to avoid. It is important to note that civil strife plays a role both in bringing the military into policing and removing it. What is crucial is not strife itself, but its timing in relation to other events, notably the existence and nature of a standing army. Domestic violence early in state-building creates traditions of military penetration into policing; domestic violence weakens military penetration late in state-building when one of the two conditions exists. Violent domestic agitation tends always to bring the military into law enforcement, but the intrusion becomes more episodic as warfare requires mass mobilization and the technologies of massive destruction.

Police specialization cannot be accounted for in terms of social and political change, except in the case of military participation, because specialization, although a characteristic of modern policing, is not peculiar to it. Nor do increased insecurity and a heightened demand for order provide the essential impetus for increased specialization. In part, police specialization appears to have grown because management philosophy in modern nation-states requires it; specialization is assumed to be useful both in terms of ensuring adequate accountability and in enhancing efficiency. The same is true, as we have seen, of the attribute of publicness. The analysis of specialization is hampered particularly by lack of information about the work of police personnel, especially at the lower ranks, in all but the modern period. Often they appear not to exist. My guess is that their absence is more apparent than real. Where detailed historical studies have been done, as in England, specialized police have been found. If future research confirms the supposition that specialized police are often too common to be mentioned by local authorities, then comparisons between England (and its dependencies) and other countries will no longer be anomalous. Instead, the hypothesis will be reinforced that specialization is not uniquely modern.

THE DEVELOPMENT OF PROFESSIONALIZATION

Professionalization is a modern attribute of police more clearly than either publicness or specialization. It is also a more complex attribute. Professionalization connotes explicit attention given to the achievement of quality in performance. Minimal indicators of a professional police are recruitment according to specified standards, remuneration sufficiently high to create a career service, formal training, and systematic supervision by superior officers. To some extent the word *professionalization* has become a term of art in police circles today, covering features such as functional specialization of personnel, use of modern technology, neutrality in law enforcement, responsible use of discretion, and a measure of autonomous self-regulation. These elements are controversial, part of the term's honorific baggage, and will be ignored.

Timing the confirmation of professionalization in a police force is problematic for several reasons. First, even in its simpler sense, professionalization has diverse parts. In England, the Bow Street Runners, created by John and Henry Fielding in the middle of the eighteenth century, were selected from among constables with one year's experience, were trained and supervised by the Fieldings, and were paid from public funds, though in the form of rewards out of fines rather than salaries. They could be regarded as primitive professional police (Reith 1948, p. 31; Pringle n.d.). Other partial experiments in professionalization were the Thames River Police, 1798, and the curiously named Unmounted Horse Patrol, 1821 (Critchley 1967, pp. 42–45). The great breakthrough came, of course, with establishment of the London Metropolitan Police in 1829. Recruitment was made on the basis of sex, height, weight, character, and ability to read and write. Training was mandatory, though it consisted almost exclusively of close-order drill (Gorer 1955).

Second, attempts to establish professionalism may be both fitful and uneven. In Russia during the 1860s great care was given to raising the level of bureaucratic performance, especially the elimination of corruption, sloth, and incompetence. Appraisals made in the mid-1870s, however, indicated that the reforms had largely failed (Abbott 1972, pp. 257–258; Abbott 1973). In the United States, control of police departments by political parties was not eliminated until well into the twentieth century, though some cities successfully professionalized administration in the late nineteenth century. The notorious "spoils system" assured that appointment as a police officer depended on party loyalty. Extreme fragmentation of police authority in the United States compelled the issues of professionalization to be discovered and fought over repeatedly throughout the country. Even today, chief law-enforcement officers, like sheriffs, are chosen by ballot in many rural areas rather than by vetted appointment (Lane 1979).

A notable exception to the stuttering pattern of professionalization occurred in Japan. Copying boldly from Europe, the Meiji government created a professional national police system in about a decade, beginning with the establishment of the Tokyo Metropolitan Police Department (Keishicho) in 1878. By 1887 personnel throughout the country were rigorously selected, largely from among former samurai, and trained in prefectural police schools (Hackett 1971, pp. 103ff.; Oura

1909). India, too, experienced systematic though penny-pinching professionalization under the British after the shock of the Mutiny (1857) caused responsibility for governing to be transferred from the chartered, private East India Company to the Parliament in London. The Police Act of 1862 created a national police system within which regulations governing recruitment, training, supervision, and discipline for all ranks were gradually introduced. The lesson to be drawn from Japan and India, confirmed in the experience of countries that have become independent after World War II, is that the more recently police reform has been undertaken, the more likely it is to involve professionalization that is national in scope.

Third, professionalization proceeds at varying speeds at different rank levels. France and Prussia began to create a nonamateur bureaucracy at senior administrative levels in the seventeenth century. England allowed public offices, including army commissions, to be bought and sold well into the 1870s (Rosenberg 1958, pp. 51–52; Webb and Webb 1963, pp. 1–67). On the continent, professionalization percolated downward over almost two hundred years. In England it occurred in a much shorter period and encompassed all rank levels.

Fourth, qualitative judgments must be made to determine whether any facet of professionalization can be said to exist. For example, do standards with respect to height and weight of applicants constitute merit recruitment? India has had these for over a century, but literacy was rare enough that "writer constable" was a meaningful designation through independence. Similarly, there is an enormous difference between a wage that attracts capable personnel and a wage that assures employment of incompetents and misfits. Although constables began to be paid publicly in England in 1829, their wages did not begin to compete with skilled labor until about 1890 (Martin and Wilson 1969, chap. 2). Today Indian constables are paid about as much as government peons, who are the runners and servants of Indian offices.

Recognizing that dating the existence of professional police will be imprecise and judgmental, the great age of professionalization is the nineteenth century. During the hundred years from 1815 to 1915, professionalization was confirmed among major countries in approximately the following order: Japan, France and Germany, Great Britain, India, the United States, and Russia. This does not mean that the quality of performance can be ranked in this order. It only indicates that problems of recruitment, training, pay, and supervision were explicitly addressed and systematically met. Priority is given to Japan because it not only professionalized as the European countries did, but it also pioneered in developing training schools for policemen of all ranks.[10] The tide of professionalization has been at the flood in the twentieth century, but ebbing is possible. Quite obviously it can occur when resources are stretched too thin. It can also occur due to changes in the auspices under which policing is undertaken. Private security forces are generally less professional than their public counterparts. Self-defense policing by voluntary organizations of citizens also inevitably reduces professionalism. This may be seen among neighborhood associations in western Europe, North America, and China and in the "People's Police" of Russia, East Europe, and Cuba. The future of professionalism may be less assured than experience in the past one hundred years would suggest.

THE CAUSES OF PROFESSIONALIZATION

Perceptible surges in professionalism historically occur after a change from private to public auspices in policing, in most cases after territorial communities have assumed responsibility. Professionalization occurs, therefore, when there is a need for reliable instruments of forceful regulation, either because constituent communities have lost their vitality or because the authority of a new polity is disputed. Perception of this need can occur in communities of varying size, both demographically and territorially. There appears to be no critical threshold.[11] Nor does the taxable wealth available to government affect professionalization. Quite unprepossessing police authorities, like American counties and English boroughs, professionalized in some measure without substantial wealth, though in the English case not until the national government undertook to pay some of the cost. (Philips 1977, chap 2; Tilly et al. 1974). France and Prussia, on the other hand, did not professionalize across all ranks until long after they had developed the capacity to tax, regulate commerce, administer justice, and raise armies. Though resource mobilization is required for professionalization, the amount of wealth available to government, above a small minimum level, is not a determining factor.

In the modern period, professionalization has been accepted as essential to efficient management. It was an axiom of progressive reform. Governments studied innovations made elsewhere and copied them at home. Prussia, Austria, and Russia studied the French experience closely in the eighteenth century. British and Americans knew about continental development and commented critically on the inefficiency of administration in their own countries. Japan borrowed self-consciously from Prussia and France, while European powers exported professionalism to their colonies. Professionalization promised to enhance effectiveness and reliability regardless of the nature of political systems. This explains why professionalization occurred during the nineteenth century in countries radically different both in terms of the character of their regimes and the national organization of the police. The United States, Britain, India, Prussia, Sweden, Japan, and the Netherlands all achieved minimal levels of professionalism at roughly the same time, despite the fact that they had little in common politically apart from a belief that territorial government should be responsible for law and order.

Pressure for enhancement of security under state auspices came from the middle class, as in England, but also from other influential social groups, such as aristocracies, artisans, commercial interests, and armies (Field 1981; Harring 1983; Lofland 1973, p. 65; Weinberger 1981). Response to this pressure was facilitated by traditions of administrative intervention by government. The French and Prussians were accustomed to professional state administration before they felt obligated to provide it in policing. The English, on the other hand, resisted doing so, because they believed that state intervention was dangerous to liberty (Langrod 1961, pp. 6–7). The administrative state, epitomized in France, was anathema to Englishmen, and they clung to amateurism even at the expense of security.

International learning, then, did not always produce emulation. However, once traditional inhibitions were removed with respect to the role government should play in policing, international learning caused professionalization to adhere to a common form.

Finally, professionalization does not ride on a wave of crime or violence. Although changes in policing of any sort are justified in terms of insecurity and turbulence, a causal link between crime and professionalism is difficult to show. Professionalization is too qualitative as well as too complex to follow directly from critical thresholds of criminality.

CONCLUSION

Policing in the modern world is dominated by organizations that are public, specialized, and professional. What is new about policing is the combination of these attributes rather than any of the attributes themselves. Public agency and specialization can be found in many places before the modern period; only professionalization is rare earlier, although even it is not unprecedented. Evolution toward this unique combination, which has been confirmed only in the past one hundred years, took place slowly over several centuries. Specialized police developed in England in the Middle Ages, but public agency did not become characteristic of English policing until seven hundred years later. France made policing public in the seventeenth and eighteenth centuries but did not specialize, as England had done, until the nineteenth. The United States had specialized and public police in the seventeenth century but delayed professionalization until the twentieth. Moreover, the order in which the three attributes were assembled varied from country to country, except that professionalization generally came after a shift to public auspices. There is no a priori reason why a nationwide system of professional police might not be created under private tutelage, even though historically it has not been done.

CHAPTER 3

The Structure of Policing

Any community that authorizes policing must organize coverage; it must create a structure for the exercise of command. Since the most important communities that organize policing today are nation-states, the description and analysis of police structure will focus on countries as the unit of analysis. The discussion will begin with an examination of how national structures can be described and will explore the range of variation in the world. Then patterns in the evolution of national structures of policing will be described, with a view particularly to determining whether long-range trends can be discerned. Finally, using both contemporary and historical materials, an attempt will be made to pinpoint the factors that critically influence the structure of public policing.

NATIONAL STRUCTURES DESCRIBED

In order to describe adequately the structure of national police systems, two dimensions of analysis must be distinguished: the centralization of command and the number of commands. These are often confused because the concepts of centralization and decentralization are used imprecisely. Great Britain has 43 autonomous police forces, each responsible for a designated area. It would seem to be a decentralized police system. Italy, like Britain, also has more than one police force, but the system is not decentralized. Italy's two forces are the Corps di Carabinieri and the Guardia di Pubblica Sicurezza, both of which are commanded from Rome.[1] Thus, Italy has multiple forces but centralized command. The Netherlands, too, has multiple forces, but one force is centralized and the other decentralized. Rural areas are covered by the *Rijkspolitie*, which is directed from the Hague, while 142 municipal areas have their own autonomous *Gemeetepolitie*. The point is that decentralization creates multiple forces, but multiple forces are not always decentralized. One reason, therefore, that some countries have multiple forces is because command is decentralized. Centralization of command and multiplicity of command are conceptually distinct, although centralization is one way in which multiplicity is brought about.

Using the two dimensions of analysis—centralization and number of commands—any national system may be characterized as belonging to one of three categories. (See Table 3.1.) Since a single decentralized police system is logically impossible, no countries will fit into that cell.

A country can be said to have a centralized police structure when operational direction can be given routinely to subunits from a single center of control. Conversely, independence of command in subunits is the indicator of decentralization. This test is de jure—that is, based on what *can be* done rather than what *is* done. France, for example, will be called a centralized system, even though command from Paris is rarely exercised with respect to day-to-day operations of departmental units (Crozier 1963, p. 225). The de jure test is easy to apply, but it injects an element of unreality into categorizations. The way to escape from this is to undertake studies of actual command relationships. Though there are clues to this in some writings, they are few and far between. Comparisons of formal and informal command relationships are urgently needed in studies of national police systems. Where custom is clear-cut with respect to the autonomy of local forces, even where centralization is formally established, I shall feel free to depart from the juridical test. In Norway, for example, the police were nationalized in 1936, but the central government has carefully refrained from giving operational orders to the fifty-four district forces (Kosberg 1978). Norway will, therefore, be designated a decentralized system. Sweden is the same (Becker ahd Hjelkmo 1976, pp. 75–76; Plantin 1979). By and large, however, categorization in terms of centralization and decentralization will err on the side of formal rules, eliminating for the most part judgments about practice.

Table 3.1
Typology of Police Structures

	Centralized	Decentralized
Singular	XXX	000
Multiple	XXX	XXX

France, Italy, Finland, Israel, Thailand, Taiwan, Ireland, and the Soviet Union are examples of centralized police systems. In France, control of the Police Nationale, which covers towns of more than ten thousand inhabitants, and the Gendarmerie, which polices rural areas and small towns, is exercised from the Ministry of the Interior in Paris (Bramshill Police College 1974). Italy's Guardia di Pubblica Sicurezza, organized into ninety-three provincial units, can be given orders through two chains of command, both originating in the Ministry of the Interior in Rome. One leads from the Ministry to the prefect, then to the *questore*—the provincial chief of police; the other, exclusively police, goes from the Ministry to the General Directorate of Public Security, then to the chief of the National Police, and ultimately to the *questore* (Bramshill Police College 1974). The Carabinieri, Italy's other major police force, is also commanded from Rome. In the Soviet Union centralization of command is more debatable, because the scale of the country limits effective command over far-flung operations. Moscow certainly has formal authority to direct both the Militzia and the KGB in every republic. The militia chain of command runs from the Ministry of Internal Affairs in Moscow to counterpart ministries in the republics; the KGB's chain of command involves Committees of State Security at each level (Hazard, Butler, and Maggs 1977, pp. 75–76).

In a general way, moderate and extreme degrees of decentralization can be distinguished, depending on how many autonomous units there are. Moderately decentralized systems would include Japan, which has given autonomy to 46 prefectures; Australia to 6 states; West Germany to 10 *Länder* and Berlin; Great Britain to 43 "police authorities;" and Brazil to 21 states (Rios 1977). Extremely decentralized structures appear in the United States with 25,000 units, Belgium with 2,359, and the Netherlands with 142 municipal forces.[2] So decentralized are the United States forces that no one is quite sure how many there are. Bruce Smith's figure of 40,000 separate police forces was widely accepted for many years, even though he did not explain where it came from (Smith 1940, p. 25). In the early 1970s the Law Enforcement Assistance Administration (LEAA) undertook a survey to determine how many forces there were. They decided that the appropriate figure was about 25,000.[3] Canada, too, is radically decentralized, having approximately 450 municipal police forces plus several provincial forces and the Royal Canadian Mounted Police (Stenning 1980).

Although it is possible to categorize countries by their degree of centralization, it is misleading to do so without providing other facts. Statements are frequently made that the extent of centralization affects important aspects of policing, such as efficiency, responsiveness to communities, public trust, accountability, and forcefulness. Such assertions are foolish unless the size of the unit being described is taken into account. The United States has more separate police forces than any country in the world, yet the average extent of command is quite large, about 176 square miles, which is much bigger than decentralized Belgium's 4.99 square miles and decentralized Switzerland's 5.3 square miles. France is more centralized than the United States, yet it is about four-fifths the size of Texas. The Netherlands has 142 police forces, making it much more centralized than the United States, but it is only half the size of West Virginia. Centralized Italy is smaller than decentralized Norway. Moderately centralized West Germany is about the size of Oregon. Clearly, a police system that is centralized in a small country may be smaller than one part of a decentralized system in a larger country. The dynamics of a police system depend not just on the degree of centralization but also on the scale of the community. Furthermore, the alleged linkage between centralization and police performance is even more tenuous when judgments about centralization are made, as they almost always are, on the basis of de jure rather than de facto criteria.

Because of the lack of international data, one cannot produce a definitive categorization of the world's police systems according to their degree of centralization. Standard reference books as well as specialized sources on the police provide information on structure for only a few countries. Putting available bits and pieces together, we can deduce that centralized systems are much more common than decentralized ones. This conclusion is based on my own study of police structures in a sample of forty-eight countries for which reliable information could be collected. Thirty-seven had centralized police systems—77 percent of the sample.

Turning to the multiplicity of forces, since describing structures exclusively as centralized or decentralized is inadequate, one finds that countries with a single police force tend to be small, such as Singapore, Sri Lanka, Poland, and Ireland (Becker 1973; Coatman 1959; Cramer

1964; Dorey and Swidler 1975). Smallness, however, does not necessarily produce singularity, as the Netherlands and Belgium show.

Multiple-force countries can be subdivided into two groups, based on whether jurisdictions overlap. A system is *multiple coordinated* when one force has jurisdiction over any area, even though there may be several forces in the country as a whole; a system is *multiple uncoordinated* when more than one force has authority over the same area. France, for example, has a multiple coordinated system. The Police Nationale covers towns with more than ten thousand inhabitants, the Gendarmerie all the rest (Bramshill Police College 1974). Finland and the Netherlands also have separate police for rural and urban areas. Canada has a multiple coordinated system, because in any one place policing is overwhelmingly the responsibility of a single force—though that force may be variously national, provincial, or municipal (Kelly and Kelly 1976, pp. 32, 35). When an area opts for self-policing, coverage by a more inclusive force—such as a provincial police—is removed. Similarly, when the Royal Canadian Mounted Police (RCMP) is hired on contract by municipalities or provinces to do their policing, it replaces other forces rather than overlaying them.[4] The fact that the RCMP has limited concurrent jurisdiction throughout Canada with respect to federal laws is a wrinkle that I will discuss later. Canada's system is extremely decentralized, but by and large it is carefully coordinated.

Multiple uncoordinated systems include Italy, Spain, Belgium, Switzerland, the Soviet Union, and the United States. In Italy the Carabinieri and the Guardia have joint jurisdiction everywhere. Indeed, there is intense competition between them, a situation that some Italians regard as an essential safeguard to freedom (Barzini, 1964, pp. 215–216). Spain's three parallel police are the Guardia Civil, the Policia Aramada, and the Policia Municipal. Switzerland has federal, cantonal, and municipal police, all with concurrent jurisdiction (Sherman 1977). The Soviet Union maintains two police establishments— the Militzia and the KGB. The most extreme case of multiple uncoordinated forces is the United States. Americans are subject to arrest usually by at least three different police agencies: the FBI, the county sheriff, and municipal or township police. If the police of a state have been given general authority, rather than acting primarily as traffic police, a fourth level is added.[5] Though the American system is always described as being decentralized, its multiplicity involves more than dispersal of command within a single kind of police, as has been done in Britain or Japan. In the United States police authority is vested in almost every level and unit of government. American police are not part of a designed overlapping system. They are not part of a system at all. The lack of coordination in the United States is the result of inadvertence traceable to constitutional permissiveness.

The proportion of national police systems that are multiple is not possible to estimate, both because worldwide information is lacking and because when systems are described, centralization and multiplicity are rarely distinguished. Though 77 percent of the systems sampled were centralized, indicating a tilt in the direction of singularity, some of them have multiple forces. Until a thorough country-by-country survey has been done, definitive generalizations about the number of forces in countries cannot be formulated.

Two major caveats must be added to this description of the structure of the world's police. First, national governments in decentralized as well as centralized systems always create police agencies with concurrent authority in order to meet enforcement responsibilities that transcend those of subordinate governmental units. The United States has the FBI, Canada the RCMP, India the Central Bureau of Investigation, Japan the National Police Agency, the Federal Republic of Germany the Bundeskriminalamt, and Brazil the Federal Police.[6] Strictly speaking, therefore, all multiple-force countries have uncoordinated forces.

When I describe countries as having multiple coordinated police systems, I have made a judgment that enforcement by the central government is relatively unimportant in the total view of policing. Central authority is curtailed in several ways: by limiting the scope of central authority, by delegating central enforcement functions to forces of subordinate levels of government, or by allowing central intervention only at the request of local police commands. West Germany, then, has been labeled as having a multiple coordinated system because the Bundeskriminalamt plays a very small part in policing, usually on the sufferance of *Länder* police forces (Romig 1977). The same is true for India and Japan. In the United States and Brazil, however, federal police establishments are large, active, and not required to obtain local approval to act (Rios 1977). Designating Canada as multiple coordinated or multiple uncoordinated is especially problematic. This is not because the national RCMP acts as a local force under the control of subnational authorities. That is simply a matter of decentralization. Doubts about coordination among the multiple forces arise from the fact that RCMP and local forces have joint authority to act under certain national statutes. Overlapping appears to be more extensive than in India and West Germany but much less than in the United States or Brazil (Government of Canada 1974).

Second, many countries establish specialized police attached to specific government undertakings. In terms of manpower, the most important are the various railway police, as in India, Canada, and West Germany. In the United States, one of the largest forces in the country is a specialized police of a local government agency—namely, the police of the New York Transit Authority.[7] Such forces have been excluded from consideration of national police systems because they supplement rather than supplant the major territorial forces.

The nearly universal existence of central police units with overlapping authority and of public police with specialized jurisdiction makes a descriptive categorization of the world's police very complex.

Table 3.2
World Classification of Types of Police Structures

		Centralized	Decentralized
Single		Sri Lanka	
		Singapore	
		Poland	
		Ireland	
		Israel	
Multiple	Coordinated	France	Great Britain
		Finland	The Netherlands
			Canada
			West Germany
			India
			Japan
	Uncoordinated	Italy	Belgium
		Soviet Union	Switzerland
			United States

Given the diversity of contemporary public police institutions, any categorization will be rough and ready, representing to some extent a simplification of reality. Table 3.2 shows the placement of some countries according to the classification scheme developed.

PATTERNS OF DEVELOPMENT

The structures of public national police systems display remarkable permanence over time. Structural characteristics have remained the same in most contemporary countries since they became recognizable as states. France has had centralized policing since the middle of the seventeenth century, when Louis XIII appointed *intendants* to administer the *generalités* into which France was divided. In 1667 lieutenants general of police, also servants of the king, began to be appointed in major cities. The French Revolution made only technical adjustments to this centralized system, transforming the lieutenant general of Paris into a prefect and creating *departements* out of *generalités*. As de Tocqueville noted, the revolution and Napoleonic aftermath only enhanced the conspicuousness and efficiency of *l'ancien régime* (Chapman 1953, chap. 1; de Tocqueville 1856 [1955], pp. 57, 195; Payne 1966, pp. 208–288). The centralized Soviet police system grew out of precedents also established in the seventeenth century, when administration was carried out by *prikazy*—departments of the Tsar's household. Peter I (1682–1725) adjusted administrative boundaries and regularized the system, creating district policy captains subordinate to centrally appointed provincial governors. In 1718 the post of police president was established in St. Petersburg, similar in function to the lieutenant general of police in France. Significantly, the secret police created by Nicholas I in 1826 was called the Third Department, referring to its location with the Tsar's personal staff, indicating again how close police command was to the font of all authority in Russia. In the 1860s, when the serfs were freed and the powers of feudal landlords abolished, an attempt was made to decentralize administration. It failed, as such attempts were to fail time and again in Russian history—after the 1905 revolution, during the early 1920s after the Bolshevik Revolution, and in the late 1950s and early 1960s (Abbott 1972, pp. 238–240; Starr 1970, sect. 4 and coda). Tension between local initiative and central control in Russia has always been resolved in favor of the latter.

Elsewhere in Europe the story is the same: the administrative practices established early in state histories persist, despite enormous changes in social structure, economic forms, and political character. Austria's centralized police system can be traced to the creation of a Police Ministry by Pergen in 1792 (Emerson 1968, chap. 1). Italy's dual centralized system was established after unification in 1871, growing out of Piedmontese practices originating in 1814 for the Carabinieri and 1848 for the Guardia (Fried 1963, pp. 40–41; Gregory 1976). In Britain command over the police has been in local hands since Frankpledge times. It evolved into the parish-constable system under direction of justices of the peace, then into county and borough commands, and finally into control by "police authorities." The reforms since the Middle Ages have changed the units of organization but have not centralized command (Webb and Webb 1963).

In the United States, the tradition of local autonomy in policing began with the original settlements in Virginia and Massachusetts in the early seventeenth century (Zuckerman 1970). The only dent in this tradition was made in the middle of the nineteenth century when state governments took control of policing in many of the country's largest cities. In every case the experiment was temporary (Richardson 1974, p. 172). Control remained local even when the state and national governments created substantial police forces responsible to themselves early in the twentieth century (Smith 1949, chap. 6). New tiers of policing were added but without abridging local autonomy. The opposite tradition exists in China, where the primacy of central authority is conceded in principle though often disputed in practice. Though the effectiveness of imperial control has fluctuated dramatically in Chinese history, the customary system involves national administration based on provinces (*hsien*) directed by appointed central officials. Central administration meshes with a complex array of more enduring local structures involving families, neighborhoods, villages, and, since 1949, the Communist Party (van der Sprenkle 1977). The vitality of central direction has depended on dynastic will and capacity (Li 1971; Li 1977, pp. 61–65). Finally, the police system of India is exactly the same today, a third of a century after independence, as it was in 1861 when the British created it (Bayley 1969, chap. 2).

This is not to deny that changes have occurred, but they have not been characterological. Moreover, the cumulative direction of change in national structures is by no means clear. In Canada, for example, there has been a gradual reduction in the number of separate police forces since 1920. Two national forces—the Dominion Police Force and the Royal North West Mounted Police—became the Royal Canadian Mounted Police. Most provinces abolished their own police and substituted the RCMP on contract. In addition, some municipalities gave up their own forces, either by amalgamating into a larger metropolitan force or by replacing their forces with the RCMP, which acted under contract locally or provincially.[8] In the United States, on the other hand, a wholly new level of policing has been added in the twentieth century, increasing the number of separate forces—namely, the several state police.[9] The national government, too, has become a prominent actor in law enforcement. The most famous addition has been the Federal Bureau of Investigation in 1924, but the process did not stop there. By 1977, 113 national government agencies had law enforcement power, one-third of them having developed since 1970 (Shane 1980, p. 157). Despite recommendations for consolidation from a host of government commissions, American policing is not becoming structurally more simple or more centralized (Walker 1977, p. 146).

In the Netherlands, too, the number of forces has increased, from 70 in 1945 to 142 in 1978. Any town with more than 25,000 inhabitants is allowed to form its own police. On the other hand, substantial consolidation has taken place in Britain, where the number of forces has declined from 239 in 1859 to 43 in 1978. Half of the decrease has taken place in the last twenty years.[10] Sweden has drastically reduced the number of its forces, though it has not centralized command. There were 1,621 police districts in 1944, 558 in 1965, and 118 in 1977 (Plantin 1979, Viirtanen 1979). Norway reduced the number of forces after nationalizing the police in 1936 but, like Britain, did not create a single national command (Kosberg 1978).

Probably the only case of characterological change in a national police structure has occurred in the Philippines, where the Integrated National Police replaced approximately fifteen hundred local forces and the rural Philippine Constabulary in 1975.[11] The Philippines moved from a decentralized, multiple coordinated system to a singular, centralized system.

On the basis of existing evidence, it would be presumptuous to argue that world police systems are becoming more monolithic, either through monopolization of policing by a single force or centralization. Because the countries that have achieved independence since the Second World War have tended to establish centralized, though not necessarily singular, police structures, the total number of centralized systems has undoubtedly increased. But it is not clear that the *proportion* of centralized systems has increased. Evidence is lacking to determine the point. For older countries, especially those in Europe, North America, and the Anglo-Saxon Commonwealth, centralization appears not to be the wave of the future.

Throughout the world, national governments are increasingly providing assistance to subnational police forces and coordinating and standardizing operations. This is sometimes mistaken for centralization. Almost everywhere, national governments have created criminal record files, forensic laboratories, and training facilities. Specialists are often made available to investigate crimes that local forces are unable to handle. Governments set up joint command centers and share operational personnel when criminal activity cuts across police jurisdictions. Standardization is also increasingly encouraged across jurisdictions in order to reduce disparities in performance. Britain's Inspectorate of Constabulary, for instance, examines local operations and submits recommendations for improvement to the Home Office. Since the national government pays half the cost of local police forces, Home Office leverage over local operations is considerable if government chooses to exercise it. In the United States many states have promulgated minimum standards for policing, though very few have provided enforcement power.[12] The Law Enforcement Assistance Administration was created by the federal government in 1969 to study law enforcement problems and assist local forces in meeting them. It did not increase the command of centralization. Decisions to accept LEAA largesse were made locally, ensuring that adherence to LEAA standards was discretionary. LEAA had been a facilitator of reform, but hardly an effective inquisitor. A much more important movement in the direction of centralization in the United States has come through the nationalization of certain crimes, especially since the mid-1960s. Pushed by a frightened public, Congress has passed legislation preempting local investigation of some crimes, such as kidnapping, bank robbery, rioting, and violent interruption of police and fire services. This development bears careful watching by people concerned with police centralization.

Though superordinate units of government throughout the world are increasingly assisting, coordinating, and standardizing police operations, this should not be construed as affecting the location of command. Indeed, paradoxically, it may strengthen the ability of local forces to resist future moves toward centralization. To the extent that centralization is a response to the ineptitude of local forces, increasing their capacity to work efficiently should reduce the attractiveness of a centralized command. Superordinate support may actually be a sound defense against centralization of command.[13]

DETERMINANTS OF STRUCTURE

What factors account for differences in the structure of police command among countries? My analysis will focus on command decentralization rather than multiplicity, because while multiplicity is conceptually distinct and needed for an adequate description, centralization largely determines the multiplicity of forces. In effect, I will be searching for factors that critically influence whether command over the police of a country is exercised from a single place or is dispersed over autonomous subnational jurisdictions.

The first factor that stands out is tradition. The persistence of structural characteristics over time in most countries indicates that tradition exerts an inertial weight that becomes more constraining the longer the system is in place. In short, the degree of centralization depends on traditions established at the time a public police force was initially developed. An appeal to tradition is often considered begging the question in social analysis. This is a mistake. It is true that invoking tradition does not explain why a phenomenon became established. The search for causes must be pushed back another step. But it is still informative to say that the longer a police structure lasts, the more likely that the influence of other factors will be attenuated. Though tradition requires explanation, it is a formative factor in its own right. To borrow from physics, custom acts like a constant in a mathematical equation. It displaces the effect of other factors in a particular direction.[14]

The most dramatic illustrations of the power of bureaucratic tradition come from Germany and Japan immediately after World War II. The occupying powers in both countries introduced the police structures with which they were familiar at home. In Germany, the British established in their zone of occupation police jurisdictions that were smaller than German states but larger than towns, directed by elected boards; the Americans insisted that every local government be made responsible for maintaining and directing policing; the French created tightly controlled state police forces directed by civil administrators immediately supervising professional police officers; and the Russians created a centralized police throughout their entire zone of occupation (Goedhard 1954; Jacob 1963, pp. 156–158). In Japan, MacArthur abolished the old Ministry of Home Affairs that had directed police operations throughout Japan and created 1,605 autonomous local forces (Sugai 1957; Supreme Commander for the Allied Powers, pp. 107ff.; Wildes 1953). In both countries as soon as the occupying powers withdrew, traditional structures reemerged. The German government recreated the police system of the Second Reich (1872–1918) and the Weimar Republic (1919–1933) in which responsibility for policing was given to the states (Länder), along with a few large cities. The Japanese rejected small local forces between 1951 and 1954, when community after community voted to disband local police. But Japan did not go all the way back to the prewar system; it created forty-five prefectural commands, with a central police headquarters providing an elite officer corps, training facilities, forensic laboratories, criminal records, and some financial resources. A genuine structural change did occur in Japan, a compromise between tradition and American instruction.

Accepting that tradition is important in explaining variations in command multiplicity, what circumstances account for the initial establishment of traditions? Using contemporary data from forty-eight countries whose systems could reliably be classified as to the degree of centralization, I found a strong association between centralization and the character of regimes. Authoritarian countries are more likely to have centralized police structure, nonauthoritarian to have decentralized structures.[15]

Although the connection between centralization and authoritarianism makes intuitive sense, it conflicts with the previous finding that structural characteristics change remarkably little over long periods of time. Governments in the older, established countries have certainly changed their character—sometimes permanently, sometimes episodically—during the last two hundred years. Yet their police structures have persisted despite these vicissitudes of political life. All continental European countries in the seventeenth and eighteenth centuries, during the so-called Age of Absolutism, had nondemocratic governments. Since police centralization was not universal in Europe, authoritarianism and centralization are not associated historically. Authoritarianism has not necessarily produced police centralization.[16]

The explanation for the contradiction appears to be related to the disparate nature of the evidence: cross-sectional analysis of contemporary countries for the linkage between centralization and authoritarianism, and longitudinal analysis for the permanence of structures. Both sets of evidence can be accepted only by assuming that the imperatives of rule are different as they affected police structures two centuries ago and as they influence them today. Effective rule did not require police centralization in earlier ages; today it apparently does. Only in modern times does the character of government establish traditions with respect to the amount of police centralization. Later in this chapter I will return to this point and suggest why this is so.

Because tradition is a partial rather than a complete explanation for centralization and the character of government bears an inconsistent relationship to police structure over time, circumstances attending the initial creation of contemporary structures must be examined carefully. The roots of traditions must be uncovered, and conditions that create centralization, as opposed to authoritarianism, must be disentangled. It is very important in this historical search not to confuse structural changes within units with structural changes resulting from the formation of new units. The reasons that lead a country to move from a centralized to a decentralized system may be different from the reasons that compel tribes with centralized systems to form a country with a decentralized system. In other words, if historical analysis of structural changes in policing are pursued across changes in political units, rather than exclusively within units, factors that influence police structure uniquely are confused with factors that lead to the development of new maximal political institutions. It should not be incumbent on an analysis of police structure to explain the development of new political units. Accordingly, I shall work backwards in time, trying to discover the conditions attendant on the emergence of police systems in countries recognizable today.

Referring exclusively to Europe and North America, the key factor that explains the initial impulse to centralize is violent resistance to the consolidation and assertion of state authority. The English government could tolerate decentralized institutions of policing because the unity of England under the crown was acknowledged as long ago as the tenth century (Strayer 1970, pp. 42–46). Though there was frequent political turmoil, it involved dynastic competition, as in the War of the Roses, but not disagreement over the unity of England. When civil war broke out in the middle of the seventeenth century, England experienced its only period of unitary policing in the form of Oliver Cromwell's Military Police. France, by contrast, was formed by conquest as kings in the Île de France extended sovereignty by force of arms. Powerful feudal lords and regional *parlements* resisted unitary institutions for years. Four hundred years after the Magna Charta in England set the seal on a political settlement between king and lords, the French landed aristocracy rose against the king in the Fronde (in 1648 and 1649). Louis XIII and Cardinal Richelieu, his chief minister, concluded that regional aristocracies could not be entrusted with government authority. So *intendants*, later assisted by lieutenants general of police, were appointed by the king to impose order as Paris required. At a time when members of the English landed gentry were entrusted by the king with administrative and judicial functions, especially as justices of the peace, members of the French aristocracy were expressly prohibited from becoming administrative officials (Barker 1944, pp. 23–38; Lowell 1914, pp. 48–50; Strayer 1970, pp. 45–56). The unity of England was achieved early and largely without violence; the unity of France was accomplished late and through conquest (Barker 1927, p. 148).

The explanation for the difference between England and France is not that traditions of local government were less strong in France than in England. All European countries had vigorous local government in the Middle Ages. What is different is that in the process of state consolidation, localism posed a persistent and violent threat in some places and not in others. England's kings could afford to govern through parliament and the squirearchy; French kings could not. While the ideology of absolutism was similar throughout Europe, the forms varied in accordance with circumstances, in particular to crises in the management of central institutions (Gruder 1968, pp. 5–10).

That violent resistance to central initiatives is crucial to police centralization is seen dramatically in the case of Prussia. In the early seventeenth century, government was in the hands of regional bodies composed of powerful landowners—the *Junkers*. When regional vitality became weakened as the result of the Thirty Years War, Frederick William I of Brandenburg appropriated the power to tax and maintain a large standing army throughout Prussia. In exchange, the Great Elector, as Frederick William became known, allowed local landowners to remain independent in other areas of administration, notably law enforcement. The *Junkers* became subservient to the House of Brandenburg in two functional areas but remained supreme locally in others. Even though Frederick William kept Prussia in a perpetual state of arms, the political settlement ensured that mobilization was not resisted (Rosenberg 1958, pp. 34–38). As a result, the nationalization of policing was not needed. French and Prussian absolutism, which are often compared, were very different with respect to the location of the state's power to coerce. Prussia was more like England, in fact, than like France. Unlike England, however, the cities of Prussia did fall under central police direction in the eighteenth century, as much because they represented political vacuums as because they offered resistance to the crown (Carsten 1954). When challenges to the regime arose in the nineteenth century, the power of the *Landrat* and *Steuerat*—crown-appointed administrators for rural and urban areas respectively—grew, though the police power of the *Junkers* in their own estates was not finally eliminated until 1872 (Jacob 1963, pp. 28–30, 55, 62). Curiously, the political settlement that Frederick William I used to unify Prussia was similar to the plan that Bismarck, another Prussian, adopted to create a united Germany three centuries later. Most internal administration, including policing, was left to the constituent states (*Länder*), while the central government in Berlin directed foreign affairs, imposed taxes, and maintained the army.

With the exception of the Hitler interlude, Germany, like Prussia before, has had decentralized policing despite effective central government control of foreign and military affairs, and for exactly the same reason: the absence of violent resistance by constituent territorial parts.

Police centralization in Italy is also traceable to strong regional resistance to a new state center. Italy had little natural feeling of fealty to Rome when it was unified in 1871. Rome, in fact, was declared the capital before it was liberated from the Austrians. *Risorgimento* was perceived in southern Italy especially as Piedmontese imperialism. Southern banks refused for some time to use currency issued by Rome through northern banks. Moreover, law and order was precarious in many parts of Italy throughout the late nineteenth century due to social dislocation, poverty, and traditions of violence. The government of Cairoli and Zanardelli fell in 1878 because of its inability to cope with widespread brigandage. In these circumstances, local self-government in policing meant at best inefficiency, at worst secession (Fried 1963, chap. 2; Lowell 1970, pp. 135–138). National government required unitary centralized administration.

Japanese history is similar in this respect, though less extreme. The statesmen of the Meiji Restoration in 1868 wanted to impel Japan into the modern world by the creation of an effective national government. Though fictively united under the emperor, some feudal kingdoms forcefully rebelled against the new unity. The political imperatives of modernization compelled the government to centralize administration, especially in education, taxation, and policing.

How different all this was from the history of the United States, which drew together, like England, without coercion to form a national union. During the colonial period, local communities acknowledged membership in the respective colonies and were left alone to regulate themselves largely as they saw fit. After independence, the constituent units did not violently challenge the national government until the Civil War. Reconstruction in the defeated South, meaning military occupation, involved centralization of policing in the hands of governors appointed by Washington. As soon as Reconstruction ended, traditions of local self-government in policing reasserted themselves.

The fundamental principle that emerges is this: traditions of police centralization will be created where state- and nation-building are accompanied by violent resistance. If the legitimacy of new state institutions is jeopardized, administrative resources of the state will be mobilized centrally in their defense. The principle may be expanded and stated more generally: if the formation of any new political community—not just states—is accompanied by violent resistance on the part of its members, policing will be dominated by agents of the new community.

This formulation is similar to Stein Rokkan's insightful thinking about European state-formation but with an important difference. Rokkan argues, as I do, that centralization depends on the relation between *centers* and *peripheries*—very useful terminology. If peripheries are weak, centralization will occur; if strong, decentralization. The key social actors determining peripheral strength as far as state-building is concerned are aristocracies and cities. Thus, centralization is strongest in Austria, Spain, Italy, and Prussia, which had weak cities and weak aristocracies, and is weakest in Switzerland, the Netherlands, England, and Sweden, which had strong cities and strong aristocracies. It is intermediate in France and Denmark, which had a mixture of strong and weak cities and aristocracies (Rokkan 1970). With respect to police administration, his placement of Prussia is mistaken, but that is a minor point. By and large, he ranks the countries as I do as far as centralization is concerned. The major quarrel I have with his theory is that it does not explain why peripheries are strong or weak. It appears as though weakness and strength are natural conditions, immutable historical givens. My argument is that centralization, especially with respect to the use of force within a new state, is a response to peripheral assertion of a violent sort. Peripheries are weak because of centralization imposed by force of arms; peripheries remain strong where unity is accepted. The balance between centers and peripheries, between centralization and decentralization in policing, is determined by the forcefulness of resistance by peripheries and the success that new centers have in subjugating them by force.

Because natural traditions with respect to structures of administration and political control exert a powerful influence on subsequent development, conditions attendant upon state-creation are particularly important. If state-creation requires forceful imposition of control, traditions of centralized policing are likely to be created. At the same time, changes in the degree of centralization can occur later; systems are not wholly shaped by initial conditions of the building of states or the creation of centers. But whenever centralization occurs, the formative element is the same: violent resistance to state demands. The principle already enunciated can again be expanded: police systems are more likely to be centralized if mobilization demands by the state are high and popular resistance of a violent sort is encountered.

While preserving the essential insight that resistance and centralization are linked, this formulation is not tied to initial acts of state-creation. By implication, states are now seen as mobilization events; that is, state-building is not accomplished all at once. Nor is it accomplished only in territorial terms, as Rokkan's argument also suggests. State-building is an additive process: it is accomplished along several functional dimensions, such as collecting taxes, maintaining armies, regulating business, and redistributing income. Policing is simply one of these dimensions. State-building does not inevitably involve the creation of centralized police institutions. Prussia, the Netherlands, England, and the United States are all examples of successful states without centralized police. Moreover, any expansion of state authority can generate popular resistance, whether of taxation, compulsory education, commercial regulation, moral prescription, or defense organization.

In states, the structure of police forces is shaped powerfully by initial conditions of territorial penetration by centers, but it continues to be influenced by the violence encountered whenever central attempts at mobilization, especially along new dimensions, encounter violent resistance. Government must then choose whether it will give up the venture, thus reducing the tendency to centralization, or persevere, thus raising the perceived utility of centralization. No mobilization action by a state necessarily brings police centralization. Similarly, no challenge to a state automatically brings police centralization. This is the problem with the argument that external threats to a state impel centralization, especially for the internal coercive apparatus of the state (Andrzejewski 1954, p. 92; Lasswell 1941). Prussian history shows that this is not so. Prussia was almost continuously at war from the middle of the seventeenth century to the middle of the eighteenth century. Nonetheless, policing remained decentralized. It is not the frequency of wars that produces centralization, but rather the response of the populace to demands made on them. Girding for war requires only some kinds of centralization. If the public accepts the requirements of defense—or of aggression—there is no need for police centralization. It is undoubtedly true that the more demanding mobilization is and the longer it lasts, the more likely resistance is to arise, encouraging centralization. But it is an oversimplification to argue that Britain is decentralized because the English Channel obviated the need for a large standing army or that the United States is decentralized because it was sheltered behind an ocean sturdily patrolled during the nineteenth century by the British navy. Between external threats and police centralization there is a crucial intervening variable: violent internal strife triggered by mobilization demands.

In sum, police structures are determined by political settlements and the traditions thus engendered. It follows that police structures are not affected by crime in general but only by one kind of crime: violent offenses perceived to threaten the political order. The more frequent they are and the more threatening they seem, the more likely it is that a country's police system will be centralized. Challenges to the political legitimacy of government are the most powerful facilitators of police centralization.

We can now explain the apparent contradiction between the findings that both authoritarianism and tradition shape police structures. Authoritarianism is more salient as a cause of police centralization in the modern world because the mobilization demands of state are now both greater and more ramified than before. Because the mantle of legitimacy must cover a wider ambit of state activity today, occasions for resistance are more numerous. Furthermore, state authority is more naked now than it used to be when it was supported by the aggregating capacity of feudal institutions and deferential class relations. Acquiescence, if not consensus, was easier to ensure in the face of mobilization demands when hereditary classes controlled resources. Police centralization is now part of the management of mass society, while hitherto it was only part of a political settlement among a fairly homogeneous elite. Authoritarianism was easier to maintain when states had less to do and populations were accustomed to being ruled by intimate surrogates for the state.

CONCLUSION

The argument presented here is that police structures depend on political settlements and resultant traditions plus the character of government. Centralization is explained in terms of political conditions. But can the argument be reversed? Does police centralization perhaps affect government? It is certainly clear from the historical cases we examined that police centralization is an instrument by which political centers impose political settlements. So perhaps centralization affects regime character as well. This real and important possibility will be examined in detail in Chapter 10. For the moment, let a word suffice. If the degree of police centralization is used to indicate political authoritarianism, then regime character and the structure of national policing will be related by definition. On the other hand, if regime character and police structure are kept conceptually distinct, then it is clear that decentralization, too, is compatible with repressive rule. Local governments are not necessarily less authoritarian than central ones. Serfs, slaves, dissenters, and nonconformists of all sorts have learned this lesson to their sorrow throughout history. Police structures should not be read as a symptom of governmental character, because identical command structures can accommodate regimes of vastly different types.

CHAPTER 4

Police Strength

Police forces are organizations whose variations in strength are an important matter of concern. People want to know how strong particular police agencies are relative either to others or their own past. This chapter will explore the issue of police strength, first by comparing contemporary national police forces and second by exploring changes in them over time. An attempt will be made to explain the patterns of variation found. That is, why are some police forces stronger than others, and why do particular forces grow in strength while others do not?

Unfortunately, differences in the strength of police forces are not easy to evaluate, for several reasons. First, strength is a meaningful concept only in relation to the capacity to accomplish objectives. One force may be particularly effective in deterring crime, another in controlling riots, another in capturing criminals, another in repressing political dissidents, and another in maintaining public decorum. It follows that unless there is agreement on the objectives of policing, a test of police "strength" comparatively cannot be carried out. Second, qualitative differences in police capacity may be related to various aspects of police organization, such as numbers of officers, budget, equipment, training, recruitment standards, strategic choices, honesty, accountability, and so forth. Two forces may be equally "strong" in terms of performance yet vary in many of these features. Conversely, two forces that share similar profiles in certain respects may be unequal in their capacity to do the same job due to a specific critical difference. Third, it is difficult to show empirically that any aspect of police performance is linked to results achieved, because effectiveness depends on many circumstances outside police control, such as literacy of the population, employment, economic well-being, technological development, and cultural values. Police forces may be strong or weak despite anything they do themselves.

Therefore, in order to compare the strength of police forces historically or contemporarily we must adopt a common measure that bears some presumptive relationship to capacity. The two most generally used are the number of personnel employed and the amount of money devoted to policing. Number of police is a relatively straightforward measure, easy to determine, even though problems arise in classifying functionaries as police. We explored these problems in Chapter 1. Expenditure on policing is not nearly as useful a yardstick for comparative purposes because of variations in purchasing power over time as well as from place to place. Actually, there is probably a close correlation between expenditures and numbers employed because most of the police resources throughout the world are expended on personnel.[1] In this discussion, numbers of police personnel will be used as the indicator of strength, recognizing that this expedient may obscure significant differences in police capacity.

In addition to data supplied from many other studies, the analysis will draw upon my own research in countries where I could obtain reasonably reliable information about police personnel over substantial periods of time. They were Great Britain, India, Japan, Norway, Singapore, Sri Lanka, and the United States. The countries represent targets of opportunity and not a scientific sample of the world. A capsule description of the forces studied in each of these countries is in the Appendix.

CONTEMPORARY POLICE STRENGTH

Except for a handful of countries, reliable information on police strength worldwide does not exist in any source available to the general public. The only comprehensive source, now quite outdated, is Charles L. Taylor and Michael C. Hudson's *World Handbook of Political and Social Indicators*, and it covers only 1950, 1955, 1960, and 1965.[2] The intelligence services of major powers probably collect comparative data, but that is small comfort to scholars, police officers, and the general public.[3]

The only way to develop current information on the strength of world police forces would be to undertake a country-by-country enumeration, using government documents and private access. Such a venture would be costly, enormously time-consuming, and very chancy unless undertaken by a prestigious international organization. The fact that data as elementary as the number of police personnel is unavailable internationally indicates how limited understanding is of policing and law enforcement in the world today. And the situation cannot be excused on the grounds of the political sensitivity of the topic. The strength of national military establishments is regularly published in authoritative sources (Dupuy, Hayes, and Andrews 1974; International Institute for Strategic Studies, yearly). Nor are the problems of classifying units as police more intractable than for the military. In fact, they are identical, because police and military shade into one another. The simple truth is that fewer people care about internal ordering than about external security.

Incredible as it may seem, an analysis of differences in strength among the police of contemporary countries founders for sheer lack of information. The best that one can do is to use Taylor and Hudson's data from 1965 covering 136 countries. Although this information is dated, it provides an impression of the range of variation in the contemporary world. The least policed country at that time was Tanzania, which had 7,789 people for each officer. The average for the world was 715 people per officer, exemplified in such different countries as Afghanistan, Bolivia, the Malagasy Republic, and the Netherlands.[4] By a wide margin, the least policed region of the world was Africa south of the Sahara, excluding South Africa (1,415 people per officer). The USSR and East Europe were the most heavily policed region (380 people per officer). In relation to territory, disparities in police strength were even greater. Singapore had the greatest density of police—one officer for every .077 square kilometers. Canada, Mali, Mauritania, and Tanzania had the least—one officer for every 1,000 square kilometers. The world average was one officer for every 2.5 square kilometers, as in Albania, Israel, and Japan.[5]

Using data available from 1965, it is difficult to explain international variations in police strength. (See Table 4.1.) Only economic development variables show association statistically with strength, and they show weak effects. Police strength tends to be higher in countries that are poor, illiterate, and underdeveloped. Another study that uses the same data has shown that police strength per unit of population is associated with differences in relative inequality among groups within countries, in education, professional employment, and income. The greater the inequality of these sorts, the larger the police force.[6] The

Table 4.1
Statistical Associations between Police Strength, 1965, and
Selected Variables: *r* values

(*N* = 136)

	1 Police per capita	2 Police per square km
Total Population	0.02 (.40)	−0.05 (.31)
Population in cities over 20,000	−0.43 (.04)*	0.84 (.01)*
Percentage of population literate	−0.30 (.01)*	0.15 (.07)*
GNP per capita	−0.20 (.01)*	0.02 (.40)
Energy consumption per capita	−0.17 (.03)*	−0.01 (.46)
Percentage GNP from agriculture	0.38 (.01)*	−0.24 (.02)*
Percentage male population in agriculture	0.35 (.02)*	−0.44 (.01)*
Total military manpower	−0.06 (.23)	0.83 (.01)*
Military manpower per capita	−0.05 (.30)	0.92 (.01)*
Ideological skewness (extremism)	−0.02 (.42)	−0.12 (.20)
Electoral irregularity score	−0.07 (.25)	0.003 (.49)
Index of press freedom	0.02 (.41)	0.09 (.22)

Source: Taylor & Hudson, *World Handbook of Political and Social Indicators* (Ann Arbor: Inter-University Consortium for Political Research, 1977).

Note: Significance levels are given in parentheses. Those that are significant at the 10 percent level are marked with asterisks.

inference would seem to be that inequalities generate social problems that require substantial police presence. When police strength is measured in relation to territory, the most powerful association is with the per-capita number of military personnel. Military manpower, both absolutely and relative to population, accounts for between 65 and 80 percent of the variance in police density. It is hard to understand why police strength per capita rather than per square kilometer would not also rise with military manpower, but it does not. The discrepancy suggests that the empirical dynamics of police strength, as well as perhaps of military strength, differ, depending on whether strength is measured in relation to population or territory.

There is also a strong correlation between police per unit of territory and the proportion of a country's population living in cities with more

than twenty thousand inhabitants. This is probably an artifactual relation that simply indicates that the greater the density of population, the
greater the density of police. The statistical analysis shows no association between police strength and three measures of the character of regime: ideological extremism, electoral irregularity, and freedom of the
press. None of these affects the number of police.

There are undoubtedly other factors that might affect police strength,
such as cultural heterogeneity, but testing these for an association with
variations in police strength should wait until more recent information
about police strength has again been constructed from an extensive
sample of countries.

One explanation for differences in police strength among countries
might be found in the respective amounts of criminality. Countries with
chronically high rates of crime could be expected to have more police,
other things being equal, than countries with low crime rates. This hypothesis cannot be tested because comparable data on crime is not
available for a substantial sample of the world's countries. Moreover,
the information that is available is by and large from reports to the police by victims. As I explained in Chapter 1, such information is too
unreliable to use. Victim surveys, which are much better measures of
the incidence of crime, have so far been done in only a few countries.
Until more studies are done, the relation between crime and police
strength cannot be determined internationally. It is of interest to note
that victim studies done in the United States do not show that police
and crime are related. According to the President's Commission on Law
Enforcement and the Administration of Justice (1967, p. 96), both
crime and police strength are related independently to the size of the
jurisdiction, character of the city, regional location within the country,
and the heterogeneity of the population. Another study did find a connection in thirty-five cities, but the incidence of crime was measured by
reports rather than by victim surveys.[7]

In the previous chapter we saw that one form of crime—collective
violence—did seem to exert an effect on the structure of policing. It
would be logical to expect that this might account for variations in police strength among countries, especially in light of the strong association found between police and military manpower. Surprisingly, this
does not appear to be the case. During the 1960s several careful studies
were made of the worldwide incidence of what was often called *inter-*

Table 4.2

Police Strength and Measures of Domestic Turmoil: r values

	1 Absolute Number of Police	2 Police per Capita	3 Police per km[a]
Rudolph J. Rummel[b]			
(a) Turmoil	0.24 (1%)	N.S.	N.S.
(b) Revolution	0.33 (1%)	N.S.	N.S.
(c) Subversion	N.S.	−0.24 (1%)	N.S.
Feierabend, et al.[a]			
(a) Homicide	N.S.	−0.18 (3%)	−0.17 (4%)
(b) Suicide	N.S.	N.S.	N.S.
(c) Conspiracy	N.S.	N.S.	N.S.
(d) Internal war	N.S.	N.S.	N.S.
(e) Turmoil	N.S.	N.S.	N.S.
(f) Total score	N.S.	N.S.	N.S.

Notes: Only values significant at 10 percent level presented. Level of significance appears in parentheses. The number of cases studied was 109.

[a] I. K. Feierabend, R. L. Feierabend, and T. R. Gurr (eds.), *Anger, Violence, and Politics* (Englewood Cliffs, N.J.: Prentice-Hall, Inc., 1972).

[b] *Dimensions of Conflict Behavior Within and Between Nations* (Evanston, Ill.: Northwestern University, 1963).

nal war. International scores on these indexes show only a small statistical association with Taylor and Hudson's figures on police strength in 1965. (See Table 4.2.) Moreover, the two informative correlations were with absolute numbers of police, not relative numbers. This could simply indicate that tumult and revolution were more likely in sizeable countries that had large police forces absolutely. The conclusion is that, using the best contemporary evidence, one cannot show that the strength of a country's police is related importantly to internal security needs, even those involving putative threats to regimes.[8]

In sum, then, variations in police strength among countries are explainable in terms of economic development and the strength of the military. Police strength is not related to domestic turmoil. Given the enormous methodological problems in generating reliable data of the sorts required, it may be premature to abandon these hypotheses.

At the same time, it would be presumptuous to place much faith in them without other empirical support.

CHANGES IN STRENGTH

Only a few studies have been done on police strength historically. They deal almost exclusively with Western countries, focusing very often only on cities. Estimates of police strength before the creation of public police are rarely attempted because of the lack of official records. Gurr and his colleagues concluded after painstaking research that there were more police relative to population in London, Stockholm, and Sidney immediately before the creation of a modern police system than after.[9] In Rome, too, there were more police per unit of population in the first century A.D. than in 1913 or 1975.[10] During the past 150 years, when modern police systems were being established, the absolute numbers of police have risen on a country basis. The increase is attributable to the rise of new cities, in effect to the filling in of rural areas previously not heavily policed. In relation to population, however, there has not been a uniform intensification of policing. Major cities in the United States, on the one hand, have experienced relative increases. In Boston, San Francisco, Chicago, Denver, New York, Philadelphia, and St. Louis the number of police has more than doubled in relation to population since the middle of the nineteenth century (Tilly et al. 1974). European cities, on the other hand, if Paris, London, and Stockholm are representative, declined in strength relative to population. In 1875 there were approximately 271 people per officer in Paris; in 1913, 336; and in 1980, 477 (Fosdick 1915 [1975]; Policie Nationale 1980). In London strength declined from 416 persons per officer in 1830 to 467 in 1970, and in Stockholm from 236 in 1850 to 304 in 1970.[11] In both Europe and the United States, the larger the city in terms of population, the greater the numbers of police, with the relative strength of police to population becoming constant after a certain threshold is achieved. Data is not available on enough cities historically to determine whether relative police strength was growing or declining up to that point.[12]

In terms of national territory covered, these increases mean that policing has intensified substantially over time. Given volumes of space throughout the world now contain more police than in the past. One effect is certainly to make police more visible to more people. Does it affect the capacity of police to accomplish objectives? It may, although the point cannot be proven. Capacity is probably related to the amount of territory covered by police; one officer can more easily accomplish objectives among five hundred persons on one block than among five hundred persons on ten blocks. This may account in part, for instance, for the remarkably lower crime rates in Japan than in the United States (Bayley 1976). The United States has more officers proportionate to its population than Japan—approximately 2.85 police officers per 1,000 people as opposed to 2.17. But Japan has vastly more police per unit of territory—0.59 square miles per officer as opposed to 5.44 (Government of Japan 1980). Studies of the relation between police strength and police effectiveness have neglected to consider the territorial density of police, concentrating instead on population density. Programs designed to enhance police performance have perhaps been playing the wrong numbers game.

Population growth clearly causes the number of police to increase, although the effect is not the same at all stages of increase. Wealth, too, probably shapes the rate of increase as population expands, but this is impossible to show with existing historical or cross-sectional data.[13] What of crime, whose suppression is considered the raison d'être of the police everywhere? The most exhaustive work has been done by Ted Gurr and his associates, who have shown that police increased in Great Britain and the United States in the late nineteenth and early twentieth centuries despite declining crime rates (Gurr 1979). Bordua and Haurek (1971) reached the same conclusion after studying American cities between 1902 and 1960.

My own analysis from eighteen jurisdictions in seven countries shows that changes in police strength and reported crime do not vary concomitantly in the period after World War II, even though both police strength and reported crime rose during the period in most places. I analyzed for strength against crime when data was available for murder, robbery, rape, and total crime for twenty-year periods. Because the implicit notion being tested was that changes in the incidence of crime caused policymakers to adjust the numbers of police, it was necessary to compare crime in a given year with police strength both for that year and for several subsequent years. Policy-making takes time, so that personnel changes may reflect previous rather than immediate fluctuations in crime. In order to allow for this, correlations were computed for crime and police strength in the same year as well as lagged by one and two years.

Because the character of police operations varies within countries, police jurisdictions were visited where there was substantial autonomy of command. Decisions about police manpower, especially, are usually made in relation to local needs and circumstances. Analysis of the relation between police strength and crime on a national basis, therefore, is unlikely to be informative. Unfortunately, information about trends in police strength and crime for subnational jurisdictions must usually be obtained locally, and appropriate data is not always available. So I sought information about police strength and crime for the period after 1945 in rural and urban locations in each of the nine countries selected for field research. The American data covers seven cities for which the Federal Bureau of Investigation had reliable time-series statistics. The analysis, while interesting, shows the limitations on international study, despite extensive fieldwork that provided access to local archival sources.

Both crime and police strength have increased steadily since World War II in most of the places studied. The statistical associations are very high. However, when we control for the trend and isolate the relationship between *changes* in crime and *changes* in police strength from year to year, we find hardly any association. In most jurisdictions where a computation could be made, changes in criminality are only marginally associated, if at all, with increases in police strength. (See Tables 4.3–4.6.) The Netherlands and Denver are the only important exceptions. The strongest predictor of increases in police strength was not crime, but rather the sheer passage of time. Time accounts for an overwhelming amount of the variance, changes in crime for very little. In a few places, indeed, crime and police strength moved in opposite directions. Police strength in Japan grew during the period surveyed even though crime fell; in Tamil Nadu police strength declined but crime rose; and in Boston police strength fluctuated while crime rose appreciably.

I should note that it is not inappropriate to correlate absolute changes between numbers of police and crime. Though such analysis makes no correction for changes in population, one cannot be sure whether policymakers consider this either. Often official statistics do not calculate

Table 4.3
Statistical Association between Changes in Police Strength
and Total Crime (*r* squares), based on Different Scores

Places	No Lag	One-Year Lag	Two-Year Lag
United States			
Denver 1946–75	0.41*	0.09	0.09
Chicago 1946–73	0.02	0	0.01
Boston 1957–76	0	0.02	0
Philadelphia 1957–76	0.09	0.07	0
Akron 1957–76	0.12	0.14	0.05
Cincinnati 1957–76	0.10	0.08	0.02
Los Angeles 1957–76	0.20*	0.01	0.04
Great Britain			
England, Wales 1946–75	0	0	0
London 1946–75	0.04	0.07	0.02
Norway			
National 1957–76	0.05	0.06	0
Oslo 1946–76	0.03	0	0.01
Rjukan 1957–76	0.05	0.03	0.01
The Netherlands			
State police 1956–77	0.58*	0.55*	0.53*
India			
Uttar Pradesh 1948–77	0.04	0.09	0.02
Tamil Nadu 1950–77	0	0	0.02
Orissa 1956–77	0.01	0	0.12
Karnataka 1956–77	0.03	0	0.15
Sri Lanka 1947–74	N.D.	N.D.	N.D.
Japan			
National 1946–76	0	0.01	0.01
Tokyo 1955–76	0	0.01	0.02

Notes: The correlation coefficient was computed for variations in differences from year to year in police strength as against crime; in effect, the data were "detrended" before the correlation was computed. Values significant at the 10 percent level are marked with an asterisk. N.D. means no data.

Table 4.4
Statistical Association between Changes in Police Strength
and Murder (r square), based on Differenced Scores

Places	No Lag	One-Year Lag	Two-Year Lag
United States			
Denver 1946–76	0.07	0	0.04
Chicago 1946–73	0.25*	0.03	0.10
Boston 1957–76	0.11	0	0.22*
Philadelphia 1957–76	0	0.10	0
Akron 1957–76	0.04	0.10	0.06
Cincinnati 1957–76	0.01	0.02	0.11
Los Angeles 1957–76	0.25*	0.02	0.13
Great Britain			
England, Wales 1946–75	0.04	0.01	0.02
London 1946–75	0.05	0	0
Norway			
National 1957–76	0.03	0.13	0.08
Oslo 1946–76	0	0.02	0.07
Rjukan 1957–76	0	0.02	0.43
The Netherlands			
State police 1956–77	0.15*	0.01	0
India			
Uttar Pradesh 1948–77	0.07	0	0.04
Tamil Nadu 1950–77	0.01	0	0
Orissa 1956–77	0.03	0	0.02
Karnataka 1956–77	0.24*	0.08	0
Sri Lanka 1947–74	0	0.17*	0.37*
Japan			
National 1946–76	0	0.06	0.05
Tokyo 1955–76	0.01	0.01	0.15*

Notes: The correlation coefficient was computed for variations in differences from year to year in police strength as against crime; in effect, the data were "detrended" before the correlation was computed. Values significant at the 10 percent level are marked with an asterisk.

Table 4.5
Statistical Association between Changes in Police Strength and Robbery (r square), based on Differenced Scores

Places	No Lag	One-Year Lag	Two-Year Lag
United States			
Denver 1946–76	0.30*	0.01	0
Chicago 1946–73	N.D.	N.D.	N.D.
Boston 1957–76	0.01	0.01	0.09
Philadelphia 1957–76	0	0	0
Akron 1957–76	0.07	0.22*	0.23*
Cincinnati 1957–76	0.14	0.15	0
Los Angeles 1957–76	0.22*	0.03	0.02
Great Britain			
England, Wales 1946–75	0.05	0.02	0.10*
London 1946–75	0.04	0.02	0.01
Norway			
National 1957–76	0.05*	0.24*	0.23*
Oslo 1946–76	0	0	0
Rjukan 1957–76	0.06	0	0.09
The Netherlands			
State police 1956–77	0.19*	0.10	0.03
India			
Uttar Pradesh 1948–77	0.16*	0.05	0.06
Tamil Nadu 1950–77	0	0.02	0.12*
Orissa 1956–77	0	0.01	0
Karnataka 1956–77	0.03	0.10	0
Sri Lanka 1947–74	0.12	0.15*	0.50*
Japan			
National 1946–76	0.06	0.11	0.02
Tokyo 1955–76	0.05	0	0.09

Notes: The correlation coefficient was computed for variations in differences from year to year in police strength as against crime; in effect, the data were "detrended" before the correlation was computed. Values significant at the 10 percent level are marked with an asterisk. N.D. means no data.

Table 4.6

Statistical Association between Changes in Police Strength
and Rape (*r* square), based on Differenced Scores

Places	No Lag	One-Year Lag	Two-Year Lag
United States			
Denver 1946–76	0	0.01	0.01
Chicago 1946–73	N.D.	N.D.	N.D.
Boston 1957–76	0.08	0	0.12
Philadelphia 1957–76	0.02	0.03	0.28*
Akron 1957–76	0.01	0.06	0.10
Cincinnati 1957–76	0.08	0	0.04
Los Angeles 1957–76	0	0.22*	0.29*
Great Britain			
England, Wales 1946–75	0.02	0.02	0
London 1946–75	0.10*	0	0.08
Norway			
National 1957–76	0.02	0.12	0.08
Oslo 1946–76	0	0.02	0
Rjukan 1957–76	0	0.05	0
The Netherlands			
State police 1956–77	0.61*	0.75*	0.63*
India			
Uttar Pradesh 1948–77	N.D.	N.D.	N.D.
Tamil Nadu 1950–77	N.D.	N.D.	N.D.
Orissa 1956–77	0	0.07	0.01
Karnataka 1956–77	N.D.	N.D.	N.D.
Sri Lanka 1947–74	0	0.32*	0.07
Japan			
National 1946–76	0.08	0.10	0
Tokyo 1955–76	0	0.14*	0

Notes: The correlation coefficient was computed for variations in differences from year to year in police strength as against crime; in effect, the data were "detrended" before the correlation was computed. Values significant at the 10 percent level are marked with an asterisk. N.D. means no data.

rates of police strength or crime to population, so that policymakers would have to make these calculations themselves. Without evidence about the information base used, it is as plausible to think that policymakers consider absolute changes as to think that they consider proportional ones (Jackson and Carroll 1981). Indeed, from the point of view of the police, policymakers should not do so; as long as the number of crimes rises, there is more work for the police to do even if the crime rate remains the same. The only compelling reason for using rates in statistical analysis is methodological: it prevents being misled by increases in police strength or crime that occur as a result of incorporating new territory within the boundaries of a jurisdiction. In any case, it was impossible to compute rates with any degree of reliability because population data was not always available for the locations and years sampled.

The international data show that there is a strong tendency for police strength to grow fairly automatically, probably because both population and crime are perceived to increase inevitably. In most countries, in fact, bureaucratic formulas have been established by which levels of police manpower are assessed. The major criterion is generally population, supplemented by considerations of territorial extent, crime, anticipated revenues, and specific law-and-order problems, such as the presence of military installations, port facilities, or antagonistic social groups. Government policymakers need some yardstick that allows them to respond with apparent rationality to demands for increased numbers of police. At the same time, they may perceive that crime and population are related, so that the strong associations found between increases in police strength and the passage of time reflect a connection made intellectually by people who make police staffing decisions. In sum, population growth appears to be controlling, but policymakers may not distinguish this clearly from criminality's likely increase.

One particular form of crime may play a particularly important part in bringing about increases in police strength: offenses against the social order, reflected especially in episodes of collective violence. This factor seemed to be important, as we saw in Chapters 2 and 3, in explaining the emergence and structure of modern policing. Police strength could be viewed, then, as a function of what governments decide to do for reasons of their own having nothing to do with the aggregate private needs of the individuals they govern. This theory can be formulated in terms of elites, but it need not be. The standard argument is that the ability to influence government is unevenly distributed in most societies, some groups and persons being more powerful than others. The interest of government, in such circumstances, is coincidental with the interest of an elite, which may be based variously on class, occupation, ascription, or force. Police strength grows, then, as elite domination is threatened.[14] But majorities too have collective interests that transcend those of individual members, and majoritarian governments have a political dispensation to protect, albeit a democratic one. Furthermore, majoritarian publics, like elites, may be more emotionally concerned about collective needs than about individual ones. While all members of the public suffer from crime, they do so individually. Offenses threatening the collective order may be more frightening precisely because the interest threatened is general. For both of these reasons, crimes against the political and social status quo could be connected uniquely to growth in police strength, regardless of the nature of the polity.

This theory, which is intuitively attractive, is not easy to test. It requires connecting changes in police strength, especially episodes of substantial expansion, with perceptions of collective danger by whatever social group determines policy—elite or majority. In addition to obtaining accurate data on police strength, we must distinguish changes in perceptions of collective threat. This could be done directly through surveys, but that approach would rule out historical research. Even contemporaneous surveys would be costly, because they would have to be done repeatedly on the same populations. Testimony from newspapers, speeches, legislative debates, memoirs, and private letters would be revealing but difficult to generalize from. Public opinion is variegated and individual impressions are quixotic. A more objective course would be to collect information about the incidence of the kind of events that presumably impel governments and their influential publics to decide that order is precarious. This would be similar to collecting information about crime, only more narrowly focused.

What kinds of events are commonly read as being threatening to the collective order? There are many possibilities: assassinations, kidnapping and intimidation of elite families, crippling strikes and boycotts, lawbreaking agitations, bombing of governmental property, and advocacy of the violent overthrow of government. People who study political instability have paid particular attention to one class of attacks against established order, namely, acts of violence committed by groups against political objects or with avowed political purpose. These have been referred to variously as "collective violence," "social violence," "civil strife," "popular disturbances," and "internal war." The most compelling evidence that increases in such events lead to surges in police strength comes from Ted Gurr and his colleagues. In London, Stockholm, Sidney, and Calcutta they discovered sixteen periods of unusually rapid growth in numbers of police relative to population between the middle of the nineteenth century and 1970 (Gurr, Grabosky, and Hula 1977, chap. 4). Eleven of them were associated with civil strife and collective violence; eight involved increases in crime generally. In Gurr's words, "we suggest that collective disorder is more threatening to elites than is crime, and this discrepancy has been sufficient to render elites more willing to invest additional resources in standby forces that can be used for crowd control than in manpower for crime control per se" (Gurr, Grabosky, and Hula 1977, p. 714).

The association between dramatic increases in police strength and collective violence have been noted in other countries as well. Canada doubled the strength of the Royal Canadian Mounted Police during 1919 and 1920 when the country was racked by labor agitation and strikes, seen by many as an attack on political institutions by the radical left (Brown and Brown 1973, chap. 3). Similar surges in manpower followed periods of collective violence in Spain from 1931 to 1933, in Ireland immediately after independence in 1922, in Singapore during 1955 and 1956 after the granting of partial self-government, in Malaysia during 1970 and 1971 with the threat of growing guerrilla terrorism, and in Sri Lanka in 1971 following an intense outbreak of communal violence in the north (Brenan 1943, chap. 11; Brady 1974, p. 105; Clutterbuck 1973, p. 101; private interviews). Indian officials generally agree that a rise in collective violence in the early 1970s caused a substantial expansion in the armed police of the states and of the Central Reserve Police. Analyzing police records in France, Charles Tilly discovered that police strength increased dramatically immediately after violent political threats or revolutions in the period from 1825 to 1900.[15]

It is worth noting again that cross-sectional analysis with countries as the units of analysis does not show an association between police

strength and several measures of domestic disorder generated by
Rudolph Rummel, the Feierabends, and Ted Gurr. Longitudinal and
cross-sectional analysis have produced contradictory results.

I have tried to test this hypothesis directly by collecting my own data
on police strength and riots during the last few years. The incidence of
riots is used as an indicator of the magnitude of civil violence. This is
convenient because figures on riots are often part of official crime returns and rioting is commonly defined as violence by groups. The dividing line between a riot and a nonriot, assuming similar levels of violence, varies from place to place, but always involves five or more
persons.[16] Whether violence has occurred is a matter of official judgment, but this is a problem with other categories of crime as well. Of
course, the occurrence of rioting is not an unambiguous sign that the
political status quo is threatened. Not all rioting, even by large numbers
of people, is politically threatening. Rioting and looting by thousands
of blacks in New York City in 1977 during an electrical outage was
viewed by many people as play—irresponsible and criminal, but not an
attack on the established order. Riots over food were common in France
throughout the eighteenth century, but they were politically innocent,
protesting specific grievances of local significance (Stead 1957, p. 155;
Tilly et al. 1974). England, too, well into the nineteenth century, had
"normative riots," as Allan Silver called them, that were not perceived
as attacks on the political order, but only as the venting of anger at particular states of affairs usually correctable by local administrative action (Rude 1964, chap. 1; Silver 1967; Tilly, Tilly, and Tilly 1975).
Some of the riots in India today against college examinations, train service, and food shortages are like this. They cause inconvenience but are
hardly revolutionary forays against political order.

The analysis shows that in three countries where data on rioting as
well as police strength could be collected over a minimum of twenty
years, increases in police strength cannot be attributed at all to an upsurge of rioting. (See Table 4.7.) The conclusion is that collective violence appears to be no more critical for police strength than other forms
of crime in the period after World War II. Neither the longitudinal
analysis from three countries nor the cross-sectional analysis of 112
countries from the 1960s supports the theory that episodes of collective
violence lead to increases in police strength.

There are three theoretical reasons, in addition to the methodologi-

Table 4.7
Statistical Association between Changes in Police Strength and Rioting (r square), based on Differenced Scores

Places	No Lag	One-Year Lag	Two-Year Lag
United States			
Denver 1946–76	N.D.	N.D.	N.D.
Chicago 1946–73	N.D.	N.D.	N.D.
Boston 1957–76	N.D.	N.D.	N.D.
Philadelphia 1957–76	N.D.	N.D.	N.D.
Akron 1957–76	N.D.	N.D.	N.D.
Cincinnati 1957–76	N.D.	N.D.	N.D.
Los Angeles 1957–76	N.D.	N.D.	N.D.
Great Britain			
England, Wales 1946–75	N.D.	N.D.	N.D.
London 1946–75	N.D.	N.D.	N.D.
Norway			
National 1957–76	N.D.	N.D.	N.D.
Oslo 1946–76	N.D.	N.D.	N.D.
Rjukan 1957–76	N.D.	N.D.	N.D.
The Netherlands			
State police 1956–77	N.D.	N.D.	N.D.
India			
Uttar Pradesh 1948–77	0.03	0.06	0.04
Tamil Nadu 1950–77	0	0.16*	0.04
Orissa 1956–77	0.05	0.03	0.01
Karnataka 1956–77	0.17	0.26*	0.04
Sri Lanka 1947–74	0	0.18*	0.06
Japan			
National 1946–76	0.01	0.30*	0.04
Tokyo 1955–76	N.D.	N.D.	N.D.

Notes: The correlation coefficient was computed for variations in differences from year to year in police strength as against crime; in effect, the data were "detrended" before the correlation was computed. Values significant at the 10 percent level are marked with an asterisk. N.D. means no data.

cal difficulties already discussed, why threats to regimes may not result in additional police manpower. First, governments faced with civil strife may increase internal security forces generally but not necessarily the police. Instead they may recruit special constables, mobilize the national guard, or create paramilitary forces. Second, frightened elites may doubt that official forces will be effective and will resort instead to private defense, as with the Ku Klux Klan (USA), Rashtriya Swayamsevak Sangh (India), Sturmabteilung (Germany), and, arguably, the Red Guards (China). Vigilantism often appears as the only practical option for people faced with widespread disorder and a government that they consider to be vacillating. Third, governments respond to political violence not only by expanding police but also by reforming them. Money is used instead for equipment, facilities, tactical training, redesigned command systems, and qualitative improvements in personnel. Police capacity does change, but not as a result of increased numbers of personnel. In effect, even though collective violence does not produce quantitative change in policing, it does produce qualitative change.

What is the evidence that collective violence may lead to qualitative reform of police? Some American historians have argued explicitly that full-time municipal police forces were created in Boston in 1834, New York in 1844, and Philadelphia in 1854 because existing police arrangements could not cope with rioting and collective disorder (Harring 1983; Lane 1967, chap. 12; Richardson 1970, pp. 28–29; Richardson 1974, chap 2). Voluntary part-time constables and watches could not contain the fighting that regularly broke out between proslave and proemancipation forces, between Protestants and Catholics, and between immigrants and the native-born (Bopp and Schultz 1972, p. 3; Lane 1967, pp. 6ff.). Harring argues that concern with public order prompted the development of the horse-drawn patrol wagon and the telegraphic signal system on police beats during the last two decades of the nineteenth century (1983, chap. 3). Much more recently, ghetto riots and anti–Vietnam War activity catapulted police to the forefront of national attention, resulting in a decade of unprecedented criticism, searching examination, and reform. National commissions painstakingly scrutinized law enforcement—the President's Commission on Law Enforcement and the Administration of Justice (1967), the National Advisory Commission on Civil Disorders (1967), the National Commission on the Causes and Prevention of Violence (1969), the National Advisory Commission on Criminal Justice Standards and Goals (1973), and the Senate Select Committee to Study Governmental Operations with Respect to Intelligence Activities (1976). With passage of the Omnibus Crime Control and Safe Streets Act of 1968, which created the Law Enforcement Assistance Administration, the national government for the first time in American history provided massive financial support to local police operations. Laws were also enacted that nationalized certain kinds of offenses related to collective violence, thereby permitting them to be investigated by the FBI.[17] At local levels, heavy weapons squads (SWAT teams) were developed to deal with rampaging crowds, concerted attacks on public buildings, and the holding of hostages. By no means all the changes during the period 1965 to 1975 were repressive. The reforms that they generated over the next decade, although uneven from place to place, made recruiting more careful and balanced, management more rational and farsighted, training more purposive, and policy formation more responsive to community opinion. By 1975 American police forces had become more self-conscious and sensitive.

Collective violence has prompted significant reform in other countries as well. According to Gurr and his colleagues, modern police in Stockholm arose out of the riots of 1848, in Sidney out of the "bushranging" and rioting in the goldfields of New South Wales in 1862, and in Calcutta out of the sepoy mutiny of 1857 (Gurr, Grabosky, and Hula 1977, p. 707). The Fronde in France, 1648/49, laid the foundation for the centralized police system that is still in place today. The *intendants* and lieutenants general of police who were created during the ensuing twenty years eventually became prefects and *commissaires*, respectively. Finally, Augustus Caesar created an effective public police for Rome under imperial direction in order to deal with violence associated with politics in the late Republic (Lintott 1968, chap. 11).

The most studied case of qualitative evolution is the British system during the nineteenth century. Yet it remains controversial precisely with respect to the formative influence of collective violence. The "New Police" who took to the streets on September 29, 1829, were England's first full-time, citywide, uniformed, preventive police. The force was created out of a mélange of watches, private guards, parish constables, and magisterial police paid by government.[18] The creation of the London Metropolitan Police marks a true historical watershed in Anglo-Saxon policing. Was it prompted by major episodes of strife and disorder?

The decade preceding 1829 was in fact remarkably peaceful compared with almost any time from 1760, certainly compared with the period 1810 to 1819. As Élie Halévy has remarked, "Never had the possibility of insurrection in England seemed more remote than at the time when the New Police Bill was carried" (1924 [1948], p. 288). As historians have noted, Sir Robert Peel never mentioned riots and public disorder as justification for introducing the Metropolitan Police Bill in 1828. Instead, he dwelled on recent increases in the number of committals for property crime (Bailey 1981, p. 13). At the same time, urban rioting and disorder were most certainly on the minds of politicians and the influential public. The urban mob had risen repeatedly during the preceding seventy years, paralyzing cities, inflicting heavy damage to property, and showing that parish constables were powerless against it. The army, supported by the militia, was garrisoned around major cities, especially in the industrial midlands. Military intervention was generally effective, but at a high cost in casualties to the public—a cost that often exacerbated feeling against authority. For these reasons the Duke of Wellington, leader of the House of Lords, supported the New Police Bill, hoping that it would save the army from demoralization and the contempt of the public. Furthermore, the character of rioting seemed to be undergoing a significant change. No longer focused on specific local issues, susceptible to administrative solution, it had become associated with diffuse demands for political power emanating largely from the rising commercial middle class. This movement was to culminate in the Reform Act of 1832, the first victory in a fifty-year struggle for universal male enfranchisement.[19] In sum, police reform did not spring unheralded from an era of peace; it came after a long period of turbulence that had prompted six parliamentary committees to investigate the state of London's police between 1770 and 1828, amid mounting pressures for expanded political enfranchisement.

The connection between police reform and collective violence in 1829 is obscured because reform was probably unnaturally delayed by foreign events. The ruling class in England had been terribly frightened by the French Revolution. The prolonged war against Napoleon confirmed their fear of Jacobinism; it also confirmed their distaste for any centralized French "system" of policing. France became an example both of the mob run wild and government unrestrained by law. If this seems inconsistent, it is instructive to remember that Americans have perceived Russia after 1918 in very much the same terms—as the embodiment of revolutionary upheaval and at the same time of the lawless state. The Cold War hardened these attitudes, as the Napoleonic wars did in England. And just as the English were prevented from profiting from French experience with respect to police institutions, so Americans have been unable to initiate social reforms that seemed socialistic regardless of their instrinsic merits (Moore 1967, pp. 443–444; Pringle n.d., p. 13). English police reform could not take place, despite the urgency of the need, until ideological fervor had cooled and Englishmen could approach police problems pragmatically. Finally, the moment came. Peel, whose ideas about policing had matured almost a decade before, introduced his bill without fanfare to a Parliament still exhausted after the bitter struggle of 1828 over Catholic emancipation (Reith 1948, p. 25; Critchley 1967, pp. 35–50; Gash 1961, pp. 487–507; Hart 1951, p. 27; Pringle n.d., pp. 205–206). With hardly any debate, the bill passed after Peel agreed to allow the City of London to remain independent in policing in exchange for Whig support of his measure.[20]

The creation of the London Metropolitan Police, which set the model for subsequent English police development, did not ride on a wave of collective violence, but it did occur after collective violence of an increasingly political sort had demonstrated to critical constituencies—merchants, the middle class, the army, landed gentry—that existing arrangements were ineffective and dangerous. Controlling tumultuous mobs was the issue of the day, however much it was downplayed in debate. One small fact confirms this interpretation nicely: the New Police were put in uniform, over the vigorous objections of many, precisely so that they would stand out in a crowd, the more effectively to deter violence (Radzinowicz 1957 p. 177).

But London reform was only the beginning of national reform. Expansion of the precedent to the rest of the country was slow and grudging, and its relation to the occurrence of collective violence is even less obvious. The County Police Act of 1839, the next major piece of legislative reform of the police, was passed just before the first wave of Chartist agitation. It was permissive, not requiring counties to establish police on the London model but only authorizing county magistrates to do so if they wished. During the 1830s and 1840s local governments did establish "new police," often inviting the London commissioners to send constables to form the nucleus of a reformed police (Field 1981; Jones 1970; Radzinowicz 1957, pp. 233; Reith 1948). Philips's historical research has shown that police reform in many counties was prompted in part throughout the 1830s and 1840s by concern with public disorder (Philips 1977, pp. 284). As we would expect, enormous unevenness in policing resulted. By 1856 twenty counties had no reformed police at all; twenty-four had a reformed unified force; and seven were a hodgepodge of reformed and unreformed forces (Hart 1951, pp. 31–33). The ratio of police to population varied greatly. London had one officer for every 450 persons; Liverpool one to 393; Manchester one to 540; St. Ives one to 6,500; and Rutland one to 11,491 (Critchley 1967, p. 123). In 1856 the County and Borough Police Act was passed, which obligated local governments to create reformed police and to place them under the supervision, though not direction, of the Home Office (Critchley 1967, chap. 4). The central government agreed to pay one-quarter of the cost of county police, provided crown inspectors of constabulary approved local management. The number of police personnel countrywide immediately jumped from 7,400 to approximately 13,000 (Critchley 1970, p. 143).

Once again, collective violence was certainly on the minds of many members of Parliament when they passed the County and Borough Police Act, as it had been on the minds of people in communities that had emulated London since 1829. Major riots had erupted over the Corn Law of 1846, and throughout the 1840s Chartism repeatedly brought gigantic crowds into the streets, especially during the presentation of the Great Charter in 1848 (Martin and Wilson 1969, pp. 7–8). Moreover, the wave of revolutionary violence that swept Europe in 1848 did not pass unnoticed in England. The *Edinburgh Review* could say in 1852 that it was "an axiom that you guard St. James by watching St. Giles" (Storch 1975, pp. 62–90). On the other hand, England was not Europe; its politics were less tempestuous and unpredictable. Compromise, not confrontation, was the instinctive response. Nor was Chartism revolution. So the expansion of reformed policing throughout England did not coincide with movements of dramatic turbulence, though it was nurtured in a general way by them. Actually, by the 1850s the heat had gone out of the police issue. London had showed that liberty and large-scale public policing were not incompatible. Reform now turned less on philosophical principle than on the willingness of the central government to help pay (Midwinter 1968, pp. 3–17; Field 1981; Tilly et al. 1974).

Examination of English police reform shows how difficult it is to argue conclusively that qualitative change is critically determined by collective violence. Qualitative change—reform—is really much too vague a concept to be useful in analysis. Since what is judged significant reform by one person may be thought of as routine adjustment by another, people can selectively link changes in policing with collective violence as they see fit. Furthermore, since people are motivated to support reform for a variety of reasons, the relative importance of their fear of collective violence is impossible to determine. Francis Place, for example, the so-called Radical of Charing Cross, supported creation of the London Metropolitan Police because he hoped they would control crowds less brutally than the army and militia, inhibiting radicalization of working-class politics and allowing moderate people such as himself to remain influential. Place, in fact, is credited with inventing the baton charge of the police that replaced the sabre charge of military dragoons (Radzinowicz 1957, p. 177).

Altogether, then, concern with collective violence has certainly been part of the climate of opinion when quantitative or qualitative change has occurred in the police. It has probably exerted a larger effect than concern with ordinary crime. A rigorous test of either effect is difficult to construct, though Gurr's and Tilly's evidence is persuasive, as is that from episodes in selected countries.

Collective violence is not, of course, the only factor that scholars have suggested to explain growth and reform of world police forces. Class conflict, for example, attendant upon industrialization, is another.[21] The rise of the middle class has also been thought to be important. A small hereditary aristocratic class can defend its interests through private means, but a numerous middle class needs the state in order to create the kind of public order that nourishes its manifold activities (Lofland 1973, p. 65). Public space needs to be rendered secure for everyone, not just for the wealthy with their armed retainers. Large police forces are needed for this (Spitzer and Scull 1977). Economic changes, such as industrialization, destroy older forms of social solidarity—village, guild, parish—and require new auspices for community protection. Changes in the normative climate may be important as well, raising expectations about safety and creating new rules about appropriate behavior in public places (Miller 1977, p. 6). All these arguments are plausible, but all are hard to sustain with evidence. They offer portmanteau causes, so general that they are as difficult to disconfirm as to relate directly to specific episodes of police reform. Furthermore, they have been derived largely from Western experience, so it is doubtful that they apply worldwide where growth and reform of police have also taken place during the last century.

CONCLUSION

Police forces have undoubtedly grown in numerical strength throughout the world during the last century or so. However, though the world is now more policed absolutely, it is not clear that there are more police relative to population. Public police forces may actually have replaced relatively more numerous nonpublic ones. The expansion of public police forces has produced a genuine increase in police capacity in two ways: through more intensive and coordinated coverage of territory and through qualitative upgrading of personnel.

Increases in public police strength are related to variations in population. They may be related as well to the incidence of ordinary crime, but statistical evidence is equivocal. Because population growth and crime are usually associated, we must get into the minds of decision-makers in order to determine the precise impetus to police growth. The number of police may be increased mechanistically, an act of faith without a clear relationship to general law-enforcement needs. Because collective violence affects the development of public policing itself as well as its structure, it is reasonable to expect it to underlie surges in police strength. Though there is considerable historical evidence to support this, rigorous statistical tests are difficult to construct. International comparisons contemporarily do not support the hypothesis. Collective violence perceived to be threatening to police regimes does, however, seem to be related to movements for qualitative reform. On balance, police strength seems more responsive to elite security needs than to those of the general public, but elites probably associate security needs of all sorts with growth in population, thus serving the public and themselves by concomitantly expanding police strength.

PART III
FUNCTION

CHAPTER 5

Police Work

The unique characteristic of police is that they are authorized to use physical force to regulate interpersonal relations in communities. This is a definition; it tells how to recognize police minimally. It is not a description of all that police do. Police are often given other responsibilities. Moreover, they do not always employ force in regulating interpersonal relations, even though they are authorized to do so. In terms of day-to-day activities, the work that police perform varies enormously around the world, despite the fact that the laws establishing police are remarkably alike in terms of obligations assigned. Modal patterns of behavior and formal authorization are not the same. In order to understand what police do, therefore, it is necessary to go behind definitions, laws, and perceived responsibilities and to examine behavior.[1]

This chapter examines the problems of describing accurately what police do. It stresses the importance of distinguishing different meanings of police "work" or "function" and evaluates the kinds of information that can be collected about them. A case is then made that in doing comparative work particular attention should be given to the kinds of situations that police encounter in dealing with members of the public. The following chapter demonstrates the sharp variations in the nature of police encounters in the contemporary world. For reasons that are explained, changes in police function historically are difficult to document. Using contemporary international data, an attempt is then made to construct a parsimonious theory that explains variations in the volume and nature of police encounters with the public.

Information about police work, apart from a few historical studies, comes largely from the contemporary Western world, mostly from Great Britain and the United States. Recognizing this parochialism, I undertook to collect data on police encounters with the public in a world sample of countries during the late 1970s. They were India, Japan, Singapore, Sri Lanka, France, Great Britain, the Netherlands, Norway, and the United States. The purpose was to determine the range of variation among police forces in the volume and nature of encounters. Though a worldwide sample meeting scientific criteria of representativeness was impossible to select due to limits on accessibility, these countries do provide more extensive coverage than any other study in terms of geography, culture, development, and political tradition. Police work also undoubtedly varies within countries, but determining representative subnational police forces is methodologically very difficult. All that could be done was to ensure that the forces selected in each country were not peculiar in some way. Apart from this criterion, the forces chosen for study were structured in order to contrast rural and urban locations, which were studied on the presumption that they might have sharply contrasting patterns of interaction between the police and the public. This intensive nine-country study enriches considerably the information available about police work in the modern world. It does not, I must repeat, allow for generalization about representative police work either globally or nationally.

THE NATURE OF POLICE WORK

Finding out what the police do is not a simple matter, not only because pervasive access is difficult to achieve, but for intellectual reasons as well. Three quite distinct ways of describing police activity may be used, each drawing on different sources of information. *Police work* can refer, first, to what police are assigned to do; second, to situations they become involved in handling; and third, to actions taken in dealing with situations.

Assignments are the organization's description of what personnel are doing—patrolling, investigating, directing traffic, counseling, and administering. Since staffing patterns are normally a matter of record, we can easily determine the proportion of personnel assigned to different activities. The greater the amount of formal specialization within police organizations, the easier such analysis becomes. At the same time, assignments are a very crude indicator of what police are doing. The assignment to which the largest proportion of personnel is devoted worldwide is patrolling, yet patrolling is a multifaceted activity. Patrol officers are jacks-of-all-trades. The British sensibly refer to them as "general duties officers." But officers on any assignment, not just patrol, may do things associated with other assignments: traffic police also patrol, patrol officers regulate traffic, detectives counsel juveniles, juvenile delinquency officers collect evidence about crimes, riot police guard public buildings, and everyone does a lot of administration (Martin and Wilson 1969, pp. 122–123). Information on assignments is important for management, but inferences to activity are tenuous.

Police work is also very commonly described in terms of the situations in which police become involved: crimes in progress, domestic disputes, lost children, auto accidents, suspicious persons, alleged housebreaking, public disturbances, and unnatural deaths. In this case, the nature of police work is revealed by what they are responsible for dealing with.

Finally, police work can be described in terms of actions taken by police in situations, such as arresting, reporting, reassuring, warning, giving first aid, counseling, mediating, interrupting, threatening, citing, and so forth. In this case, police work is what police do in situations that they encounter.

Assignments, situations, and outcomes are conceptually distinct indicators of what police do. Characterization of police work in a particular place can be significantly different depending on the focus adopted. Using different indicators in the same analysis is like comparing apples and oranges. Unless people recognize differences in operation, they talk at cross-purposes, disagreeing about the nature of police work without substantive justification. Furthermore, failure to distinguish the separate meanings of *police work* hampers the search for explanations for variations within it. The factors that cause varying proportions of police personnel to be assigned to patrol rather than criminal investigation are unlikely to be the same as the factors that account for a particular mix of situations being brought to police attention or the factors that influence how situations are handled. For example, it has been suggested that outcomes may be affected by the social distance between suspect and police officer (Black 1976). Social distance would hardly explain, however, why one force puts 20 percent of its officers in criminal investigation and another 40 percent. Similarly, the public may be encouraged to bring trivial matters to police attention if they believe they will receive sympathetic treatment, but a reputation for sympathy is unlikely to explain a pattern of either assignments or outcomes. Social distance and a reputation for sympathetic response are both possible explanations for differences in the composition of police work, but not for police work both as situations and as outcomes. At the same time, some factors may impinge on all three measures of police work. The national character of populations, for example, may affect what forces are prepared to do, what they become involved in frequently, and how they characteristically handle situations.[2]

Although assignments, situations, and outcomes are conceptually distinct, they are mutually interdependent. The structure of assignments affects the kinds of situations that police become involved in; situations influence the range of likely outcomes; outcomes shape the situations the public is encouraged to bring to the police; and situations help to determine formal assignments within a police organization. The conceptual and empirical points made with respect to the three aspects of police work are diagrammed in Figure 5.1.

This formulation of the alternative measures of police work assumes that descriptions of assignments, situations, and outcomes can be made independently—that the description of a situation does not affect the description of an outcome and so forth. This assumption is valid except in one instance. A police officer's characterization of a situation may be affected by the action he decides to take in handling it. Situations are sometimes described in ways that justify action taken. That is to say, situations are redefined for cosmetic purposes. For example, if police

Figure 5.1

TYPOLOGY OF ASSIGNMENTS, SITUATIONS, AND OUTCOMES

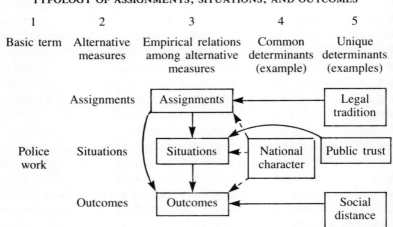

1	2	3	4	5
Basic term	Alternative measures	Empirical relations among alternative measures	Common determinants (example)	Unique determinants (examples)

officers subdue someone by force, they are more likely to describe the situation as "assaulting an officer" rather than "drunken behavior in public," even though objectively the latter is what occurred.[3] Officers are unlikely to describe a situation as involving a serious crime if they decide not to arrest the perpetrator. It will be called instead a "drunken fight" or a "family dispute." Thus, the validity of the distinction between situations and outcomes becomes questionable when the source of information about both is the responding police officer.

The variety of "work" within the categories of assignments, situations, and outcomes is very great. In order to make informative comparisons among forces, one must simplify description to concentrate on a few major differences within each category. Accordingly, I will describe administrative assignments in terms of patrol, criminal investigation, traffic regulation, internal administration, and auxiliary regulation. There are other functional specialties within many police forces, but they tend to involve relatively few personnel. The meanings of these terms are straightforward, except for *auxiliary regulation*. This refers to administrative tasks performed by police for the state that have nothing to do with their primary responsibilities; they could as well be performed by other government agencies.

The description of situations will be simplified even more radically for purposes of making comparative generalizations. This is essential, because the situations that police handle are as varied as the exigencies of human life.[4] Situations will be divided into those that involve violations of law and those that do not. In Michael Banton's useful terminology, police are sometimes called upon to act as "law officers" and sometimes as "peace officers" (1964, p. 608). Simplifying description so sharply is justified because law enforcement is a core function of police. If there are significant variations in the proportion of law-enforcement to non-law-enforcement situations encountered by police, something important has been discovered about the reality of policing. Obviously situations cannot always be neatly separated into those that are law-related and non-law-related. Particularly troublesome are situations that arise out of the anticipation of lawbreaking rather than the actual occurrence of it, as in the case of domestic disputes or drunkenness. The dichotomy is serviceable as long as the proportion of ambiguous cases is not very large.

Outcomes, too, will be divided for purposes of description into two categories—enforcement and nonenforcement—depending on whether or not police action constrains behavior physically. These categories are also responsive to fundamental notions of the role of police.

There is an important objection to this: because of the authorization given to police, a police presence is inherently constraining even when overt constraint is not applied. As Clifford Shearing says, "This context completely permeates, and thereby changes the meaning and significance of all the other resources at his disposal" (Shearing and Leon 1976). The point is well taken, but it does not destroy the value of the distinction. It makes an enormous difference to both police and public whether officers overtly constrain behavior or do so only indirectly. All sorts of people influence behavior by virtue of latent authority—teachers, parents, wives, priests—but police are unique in being authorized to limit freedom physically. Determining how frequently they do so in an explicit way is important for understanding what police work consists of.

In practice, of course, it may not be clear whether forceful constraint has been applied. For example, a great deal of police work involves physically interrupting behavior in order to avoid lawbreaking. Is it enforcement when boisterous drunks are sent home in taxis, when juveniles are told to leave the streets, or lovers are sent away from dangerous areas of public parks? Though laws have not been broken and official sanctions have not been applied, constraining orders have been given. Admonitions from police officers pose similar problems. When police warn people that they will be arrested if particular actions are continued, are they acting enforcingly or not? A warning can be interpreted as nonbinding advice or as a veiled threat. In Sri Lanka and the United States, officers often report "parties advised" as the action taken. This may mean that people were instructed about the law or that they were warned not to do something. The former would be nonenforcement, the latter enforcement. In Britain, police officers are authorized to "caution" suspects, meaning that they withhold arrest or citation in exchange for an admission of guilt, which becomes part of an official record. Cautioning is done commonly in connection with petty offenses committed by juveniles or first offenders. It poses a troublesome judgment in typing police actions. Japanese police are trained to stop people on the street and make them feel obliged to submit to questioning, even to coming along to police stations, in circumstances that do not justify an arrest. Officers deliberately use their latent authority to compel physical acquiescence (Bayley 1976, chap. 3). In Canada even arrests in law are ambiguous in fact. According to court decisions, arrests have occurred whenever people believe they could not have done other than what the police directed, even though the officers themselves did not intend to make an arrest (Ericson 1982, pp. 747–748). This extends the category of arrest over a very large range of police actions.

In summary, the nature of police work can be described variously in terms of assignments, situations, and outcomes. It is crucial to distinguish these measures of police work in order to make valid comparisons among police forces and to facilitate the search for determining factors. Given the complexity of each dimension, informative but simplified descriptive categories must be generated. With respect to assignments, formal designations of functional units within police organizations generally suffice. Important and generally meaningful comparisons can be made with respect to situations in terms of whether they are law-related or non-law-related and with respect to outcomes in terms of enforcement and nonenforcement.

ASSIGNMENTS

Information about the proportion of personnel assigned to different organizational specializations in police forces around the world consistently shows that patrol work is by far the most important assignment. A qualification to this generalization must be made for police forces in which separate formations of riot police are maintained, as in India, Pakistan, and Japan. In these circumstances, patrol will be the dominant assignment among personnel deployed for civil policing, which normally means among persons staffing police stations. Comparisons of personnel assignments among police forces are not particularly revealing about the nature of police work because the categories are so rough. They undoubtedly show the relative preoccupations of different forces, but they do not show the composition of police activity as work—that is, as things done (Manning 1977).

Because police are one of the most pervasive governmental institutions, expedience prompts giving them general administrative tasks. Police officials everywhere complain about this, arguing that it distracts them from carrying out law-and-order responsibilities. The French police, for example, issue identity cards, take applications for passports, act as a lost-and-found agency, register motor vehicles, issue drivers' licenses, and put seals on coffins being sent from one *departement* to another. The British police register aliens and until recently maintained records of livestock infected with communicable diseases. In Norway the police inspect the records that businessmen are required by law to keep (Kosberg 1978). In Japan they enforce environmental pollution laws. Canadian police enforce bylaws pertaining to public health, sanitation, and fire prevention (Kelly and Kelly 1976, p. 34). The Indian police impound stray animals in corrals that are attached to many police stations. The Royal Malaysian police record births and deaths; the Mali police collect some kinds of vending taxes (Hopkins 1967). And the Soviet police run detoxification centers as well as forced labor camps (Conquest 1968, p. 103; Juviler 1976, chap. 3).

Among police forces in Europe, North America, and the Anglo-Saxon Commonwealth, a gradual divestiture of auxiliary administrative functions appears to have occurred during the last century. This cannot be argued conclusively, because countries varied so much initially in the amount of such duties the police performed. In continental Europe, policing was originally coincidental with civil administration. *Police* denoted all functions of government that were not ecclesiastical (Fosdick 1915 [1975], pp. 12–24). In the eighteenth century, Prussia had field and forest police, cattle-disease police, hunting police, trade police, and health police. The French police, too, did almost everything, including ensuring adequate supplies of food for cities.[5] Through the nineteenth century, Russian police served as tax collectors, sanitary engineers, druggists, and inspectors of roads, buildings, industry, and public welfare (Starr 1970, pp. 493–494). Continental forces certainly seem to have contracted the range of their activity in the last hundred years, focusing more exclusively on criminal law enforcement. In Anglo-Saxon countries, on the other hand, police responsibilities have always been more narrowly conceived, a specialization within civil administration. Like European forces, they have probably reduced auxiliary administration, but the trend is harder to discern. As recently as 1953 the British government thought that the problem of auxiliary duties was sufficiently burdensome that it appointed a Committee on Police Extraneous Duties (Punch and Naylor 1973). There is some evidence that auxiliary administration may actually have grown in Britain since the middle of the nineteenth century, in line with the expansion of state responsibilities generally (Martin and Wilson 1969, pp. 25–26). In the United States, though new functional specialities have emerged, the police have given up conducting elections, providing food and lodging for indigents, and inspecting boilers, fire escapes, and weights and measures.[6] Altogether, a reasonably clear trend toward specialization in criminal law enforcement can be seen worldwide, although countries with less developed administrative systems and with traditions of making broad delegations of rule-making authority, as in Roman Law Countries, still tend to give the police a larger number of auxiliary administrative tasks.

Some wholly new assignments have emerged as formal specialties among world police forces during the past century, notably criminal investigation, traffic regulation, juvenile delinquency prevention, and internal administration. One must be careful, however, not to be misled by organizational specialization into thinking that police were unconcerned with such matters before. In the case of criminal investigation, specialization emerged earlier in France than Britain. The exact date when detectives were created in France is a matter of dispute. According to one authority, Cardinal Mazarin created one hundred detectives in 1645, although they were not organized into a separate unit until Fouche created the Sûreté in 1800 (Stead 1957, pp. 94–96). The Sûreté's existence was not revealed publicly until 1832/33, when funds for its operations were listed for the first time in the police budget. Another historian argues, from more detailed records, that specialization in criminal detection did not develop until 1740, when inspectors began to be assigned to the control and investigation of prostitution, sedition, activity of foreigners, murder, armed robbery, and theft (Williams 1979, pp. 99–104). Until the revolution, their number appears not to have exceeded twenty. The British created a formal detective unit within the London Metropolitan Police in 1842, consisting initially of two inspectors and six sergeants. Because of intense public suspicion of plainclothes police officers, the department was kept under wraps until 1878, when it became the Criminal Investigation Department (CID), staffed with 250 officers (Critchley 1967, pp. 160–162). But criminal investigation did not actually begin with the New Police. In fact, Sir Robert Peel wanted his Bobbies to emphasize crime prevention rather than thief-taking as had the Bow Street Runners and the Thames River Police. The creation of the CID in Britain marked a return to traditional preoccupations. American municipal police forces, like the British, also established formal detective units in the nineteenth century, but this did not reflect a change in organizational activity, since officers had historically stressed detection, often receiving fees for services rendered and property returned (Critchley 1967, pp. 12–62; Miller 1977, pp. 36–37).

Traffic regulation, too, was a concern of the police a long time before specialized units were set up in the twentieth century. In the narrow unpaved streets of Paris in the eighteenth century or London in the nineteenth, patrol officers unsnarled traffic, issued summonses to drivers of horse-drawn vehicles, stopped fights among drivers, and enforced regulations about where passengers could be picked up or discharged. Traffic was probably even less manageable than today because of its heterogeneity—carts and carriages, heavy and light wagons, riding horses, sedan chairs, handcarts, barrows, porters, runners, and endless streams of pedestrians, all clamoring for the right-of-way (Critchley 1967, p. 110; Coatman 1959, chap. 5; Richardson 1974, chap. 8). India is like this today--perhaps worse, because there are also motorized taxis, goods vans, scooters, and rickshaws.

The changes that have occurred in police assignments during the past century are traceable to several factors. First, new law-enforcement tasks have emerged. Juvenile delinquency is a case in point, as is environmental pollution. Second, the general administrative capacity of states has grown, creating new bureaucratic institutions to relieve the police of old work. Third, specialization in assignments has become a mark of progressive management, although it is always more pronounced in large forces than in small.[7] This has helped to dramatize the irrelevance of some traditional assignments. It has also created the appearance of change in police work that is not always reflected in day-to-day behavior.[8]

Police assignments have been described so far in this discussion according to managerial classifications of work performed. Assignments have another attribute, however, that is enormously important for understanding police work. Police assignments may be compared with respect to whether they are mainly state-directed or public-directed. Some assignments require police officers to respond almost exclusively to direction from senior command, others to be responsive to public solicitation. In criminal investigations and traffic duty, for example, instigation of activity lies with the police establishment. In patrolling, though, instigation is more commonly by the public, either in person or through radio dispatch. World police forces vary sharply in the proportion of state- to public-direction. In India, Pakistan, and Sri Lanka today, initiative belongs largely to the state. Very little of the aggregate time of police is available to the public. In Norway, Britain, and Canada, on the other hand, the bulk of police time is available to public initiative. Calculating the proportion of time commanded by the state and the public in different assignments reveals a great deal about the role of the police in any society.

In effect, the distinction between state-directed and public-directed assignments broadens the concept of proactive and reactive instigation to apply to police organizations as a whole. *Proactive instigation* describes a contact in which initiative was taken by the police, *reactive instigation* where initiative came from the public. Reactive instigation, then, can occur only with forces whose assignments are not monopolized by the state. While police response to public initiative is not automatic in any assignment, some assignments are inevitably proactive, such as protecting VIPs, guarding public buildings, and controlling crowds, where action is instigated by public authority exclusively.

SITUATIONS

Information about the nature of situations that police confront comes from four sources: observation of police officers at work, activity reports by individual officers, activity files maintained collectively by police units, and reports of calls for assistance from the public. The best of these is observation of police officers at work, because it is the most direct and the least self-interested. Observation is very expensive, however, requiring trained personnel to match officers work-hour for work-hour. Observers must also obtain total access to police operations. Not surprisingly, few studies worldwide of police work have been done based on systematic observation, and all of the ones that exist are in affluent, democratic countries such as Canada, Great Britain, Norway, and the United States.[9] To date, most of these studies have focused exclusively on patrol operations, neglecting all other specialized assignments. This is not unjustified. Patrolling is the most numerous assignment in all police forces, accounting for the vast majority of encounters with the public as well as the bulk of arrests. Patrolling is also the assignment that is most diverse in terms of situations encountered. Only a handful of studies have examined the daily activity of personnel assigned to criminal investigation, which is curious when one considers that the detective is generally considered to be the archetypal policeman (Ericson 1982; Greenwood and Petersilia 1975; Skolnick 1966).

Activity logs and diaries kept by individual officers provide firsthand information about situations, but they are not uniformly available among police forces. Even when they are available, the quality of individual reports varies considerably from force to force. The big problem is to get police officers to write down every occurrence in which they become involved. If a personal log is required at all, officers will generally record only those events that may create an official record and for which they are somehow responsible. The diaries of Indian police officers, for instance, are not true logs; they contain only a bare outline of comings and goings, as well as bits of information that might be needed for subsequent investigations.[10] The pocket notebooks of British officers, too, are primarily aids to memory, not a report of all activity (McCabe and Sutcliffe 1978). Personal logs are most complete when supervisors use them to evaluate the performance of an officer. In the United States, for example, some police forces calculate the amount of time that patrol officers are in contact with the public, as opposed to simply cruising the streets waiting for something to happen. Self-interest encourages officers to write down every activity that can be considered "work," no matter how trivial.

Reports of situations dealt with by officers may be kept by command units. This works well where the bulk of activity is initiated at a collective level of command, such as a police station or detective squad. Unit records are probably more complete in Western countries, where telephone solicitation and radio dispatch are more common, than in less developed countries. The development of command-and-control computer systems that link officers by personal radio has produced a quantum jump in the quality of information available about police work, especially patrol activities. At the same time, unit records may be relatively complete even without central dispatch if the proportion of officer-initiated activity is small, as in India, or where discipline with respect to reporting is strict.

Whatever the level at which activity is recorded—individual or command unit—the files reflect decisions by people about what is important to record. No recording system is automatic. Recording is work for someone. So the temptation always exists to omit events that are trivial, transitory, or without likely repercussions for police personnel. Another way to put this is that police records are always biased toward serious events, the bias being a function of the personal difficulty of creating a record and the workload of the officer.[11]

Information about police work obtained from both officer reports and unit files usually covers only patrol personnel and does not provide a picture of day-to-day situations encountered in other assignments. Internal reporting systems, in other words, focus routinely on patterns of initial interaction between police and public. Derivative police actions, such as criminal investigation, juvenile counseling, or internal administration, are not as well monitored.

The final source of information about police work as situations is records of public requests for police assistance. They do not show what the police actually encounter, but rather what the public thinks is happening. Calls for service reflect what the public thinks should generate a police response, regardless of whether the police agree. They reflect information only about those situations brought to police attention by public initiative—in the terms of the trade, only those encounters generated reactively rather than proactively.

The range of variation among world police forces with respect to the proportion of their work reactively and proactively generated is very great. The data I collected from rural and urban locations in several countries around the world show that the proportion of situations reactively instigated varied from 92.3 percent to 22.8 percent. (See Table 5.1.)

This data was collected as part of intensive fieldwork in nine countries that involved collecting reliable information from official records, rather than by observation, about the nature of situations that patrol personnel typically encountered. Because the volume of police work represented as situations was so enormous in most places, it was necessary to employ a sampling scheme. All data comes from the same sample of days from selected months—January, April, July, and Oc-

Table 5.1
Mode of Instigation

	Reactive	Proactive
United States		
Denver	55.4%	44.6%
Salida	63.7	35.4
Ft. Morgan City[a]	22.8	76.3
Chaffee County	33.3	8.3
Ft. Morgan County[a]	31.8	63.6
France		
Chilly-Mazarin	92.3	7.7
Lonjumeau	87.1	12.9
Norway		
Oslo	85.9	14.1
Rjukan	79.4	20.2
India		
Quaiserbagh, U.P.	76.6	23.4
Mall, U.P.	100	0
Mylapore, T.N.	51	49
Thiruporur, T.N.	37.5	56.3
Capital, P.S., Orissa	89.5	10.5
Bolagarh, Orissa	100	0
Sri Lanka		
Pettah	67.2	32.8
Kahataduwa	90.9	9.1
Singapore		
B Division	94.2	5.7
Rural West	81.8	18.2

[a]The high proportion of proaction was due to departmental policy concerning a unique traffic problem.

tober—covering all shifts during either 1976 or 1977. The sites are described briefly in the Appendix. With respect to determining modes of
instigation, the effort was successful only in the countries that appear
in Table 5.1.[12]

Other studies confirm that the range of variation is substantial: 93
percent reactive in Chicago, 83 percent in Salford and 74 percent in
Oxford, England, and 53 percent in Peel County, Ontario (Ericson
1982; McCabe and Sutcliffe 1978; Reiss 1971, p. 96). It is generally
supposed that the larger the proportion of encounters generated reactively, the more that calls-for-service data will overstate the proportion
of situations that are not crime-related. The reasoning is that the public's concerns that lead to encounters are more likely to involve noncriminal matters than are the concerns of the police that lead to encounters. Police are interested in a "good arrest"; the public has only a hazy
notion of when laws are violated and also feels it needs assistance in
many other situations. Proactive contacts have been shown to be overwhelmingly crime-related in the United States (Reiss 1971, chap. 2).
The international data cast serious doubt on this point. Statistical analysis of the association between mode of instigation and nature of the
situation—whether or not it was crime-related—shows that of the four-
teen jurisdictions where meaningful data was available, a positive relationship between proactive instigation and crime-related situations existed in only four of them. (See Table 5.2.) And in two of those cases
the effect was slight. Situations were coded in terms of eleven categories, which I will describe later. Situations were then grouped into
crime-related and non-crime-related groups. Situations that could not
be unambiguously assigned to one or the other group were omitted
from the analysis. The statistical results show that more times than not,
the manner of instigation had no effect on the nature of the situation
dealt with by the police.

Policemen believe that the proportion of situations instigated reactively rather than proactively is affected by the development of radio
and telephone networks. Police service thereby becomes easier to com-
mandeer, and policemen can be directed individually to particular
needs. International data does not support this line of thinking. Singapore, which has approximately 7 persons for every telephone, initiated 94 percent of police encounters reactively, while American cities,
which have almost as many phones as people, generated a smaller pro-

Table 5.2
Statistical Analysis of the Effect of Instigation
on the Nature of Situations Encountered (phi coefficient)

United States	
Denver	0.60 (690)*
Salida	0.06 (53)
Ft. Morgan City	0.28 (200)*
Chaffee County	—
Ft. Morgan County	0.26 (19)
France	
Chilly-Mazarin	0 (8)
Lonjumeau	0.17 (42)
Norway	
Oslo	0.08 (350)
Rjukan	0.15 (405)*
India	
Quaiserbagh, U.P.	0.09 (40)
Mall, U.P.	—
Mylapore, T.N.	0.04 (28)
Thiruporur, T.N.	—
Capital, P.S., Orissa	0.01 (42)
Bolagarh, Orissa	—
Sri Lanka	
Pettah	—
Kahataduwa	0.13 (19)
Singapore	
B Division	0.11 (735)*
Rural West	0.08 (269)

Notes: Values significant at 10 percent level are marked with an asterisk. A dash indicates calculation could not be made. Sample sizes are given in parentheses.

portion reactively. In India about three-quarters of all encounters were reactive, even though there was only one phone for every 336 people (Newspaper Enterprise Association 1978; U.S. Government, Bureau of the Census 1979). In the rural areas, moreover, where telephone communication was even less extensive, the proportion of reactive encounters was greater than in towns. In Sri Lanka, too, the reactive proportion of encounters was about 20 percent higher in rural than in urban areas. These data show that the relation between developments in communication facilities and police work must be rethought. Improved communications undoubtedly facilitate citizen direction of police. But primitive communications do not necessarily mean greater police initiative. Precisely because communications of all sorts, including roads, are not well developed, police may adopt a passive mode of deployment, waiting in station houses to be contacted by people who need assistance. In this way, police concentrate resources where they can be found by the public. Technological development, especially in communication facilities, does not necessarily affect the mode of instigation. Even when it does, one cannot make an inference about the impact on the composition of situations encountered.

Records of public requests for assistance, which are collected at unit command levels, vary enormously in quality. Central dispatch facilitates collection, but such records are only as complete as decisions by operators allow. Dispatchers around the world admit that they omit unimportant calls for service when the volume of work is large and they are tired. Where facilities exist for electronic tape recording, raw data on all telephone solicitations is available.[13] The problem here is to account for "walk-in" solicitations to supplement the telephone record. More commonly in the world, requests for police help are written down by hand by receiving officers at desks in police stations as people appear before them in person or call on the telephone. There is no a priori reason why such records are worse than computer-assisted ones. A rural police station in India with a low volume of requests and strict supervision by the ranking officer may produce scrupulously complete records. In fact, the station diaries in India usually fall far short of this, constituting, in the words of one experienced officer, the "minimum unavoidable record." The point is that no police record can be accepted at face value; only observation of recording behavior can allow reliable estimates to be made of the shortfall between requests and the official record.

Producing tabulations of the nature of calls for service from handwritten records, as is required most places in the world, is laborious. It means paging through voluminous files or bound registers. Police themselves rarely do so. Often there are several registers, depending on the nature of the solicitation, a process that leads to duplicate entries and the chance of multiple counting of the same event. In India, for example, each station has a station diary, which is supposed to contain a record of all that happens, including requests for service and deployment responses; petition registers for written requests, usually from government officials in other agencies and politicians; and first-information report registers for reports by victims of crimes. Police stations in Sri Lanka have a grave complaints information book, minor offences information book, minor complaints information book, traffic information book, accident information book, telephone register, and detective information book. These registers contain meticulous entries, often in copperplate handwriting reaching back into the late nineteenth century. They are fascinating in detail, but awkward to use to construct a summary of calls for service.

Even when records or requests for police assistance are reasonably complete, they do not provide an accurate picture of the situations that police encounter, because the public's characterization of situations may differ substantially from that of the responding police. A member of the public reports that an assault has taken place, while a police officer reports later that it was a domestic dispute. What the public perceives as the serious offense of "assault," the police perceive as "simple hurt," the distinction hinging on the nature of the injuries rather than on the intent of the assailant, let alone the fear of the victim. A request for medical assistance by a citizen becomes a case of criminal negligence; a report of criminal trespass is treated as reassurance to an elderly woman. In a careful comparison of public and police characterizations of the same incidents, Albert Reiss found that 58 percent were thought by citizens to be crimes, as opposed to 17 percent for responding officers (Reiss 1971). The public would appear to magnify the gravity of any situation, thinking perhaps that laws must be violated in order to justify calling the police. If this is indeed the case generally and not just in the United States, then records of calls for service may not distort the impression of police work as being non-law-related as much as has been thought. The key word, however, is *impression*. One must be careful not to presume that police reports about situations are more accurate than the public's. The perspective of the police, while apt to be better informed about points of law, is not necessarily more objective than the public's. Police officers, too, are interested parties, who may shape reports to fit bureaucratic processes or their own conceptions of what superiors want. Only independent observation can resolve disagreements in descriptions between these conflicting sources.

It should be obvious by now that obtaining complete and reliable information on the situations that police encounter is formidably difficult. Because sources of information about situations differ, comparisons among jurisdictions involve comparing calls for service, activity logs of officers, and unit compilations. Moreover, considering the unreliability of most of these sources, the only sensible conclusion is that comparisons, especially international ones, of the situations that police handle should be taken with a grain of salt. Elaborate statistical analysis is rarely justified, even among jurisdictions within countries, unless a system of quality control in the construction of police files is strictly applied. Though information about situations is critical for understanding the nature of police work, reliable description is barely possible with most of the data at hand.

In an attempt to document variations in the nature of police work, I succeeded in collecting data on situations that police encountered in twenty-three sites in seven countries. (See Table 5.3.) These are situations brought to police attention by the public or discovered by patrol officers. Specialized police work is not covered. Although all the data represent situations, the quality is extremely uneven. Information in Great Britain, for example, comes from a command-and-control computer; in India, from handwritten station diaries; and in the United States, from activity reports made by officers on each incident handled.[14]

Because the variety of situations that police deal with is so enormous, comparisons can only be done if they can be described by general types. The number and nature of the categories needed is a matter of judgment. The more categories, the less distortion from reality; the fewer categories, the harder it becomes to type each situation reliably

Table 5.3
Kinds of Situations Police Encounter

	1 Crime Emergency	2 Crime Invest.	3 Non-crime Emergency	4 Prevention
United States				
Denver (U)	17.2%	25.1%	4.0%	3.9%
Salida (R)	11.5	28.3	4.4	3.5
Ft. Morgan City (R)	5.1	25.7	3.7	0.2
Ft. Morgan County (R)	9.1	68.2	3.2	4.5
Dallas, Texas (U)	12.9	32.4	5.9	2.0
Great Britain				
Ipswich Town (U)	10.6	13.2	9.4	0.0
Stowmarket (R)	4.7	18.8	23.4	0.0
France				
Chilly-Mazarin (U)	0.0	30.8	0.0	0.0
Lonjumeau (U)	8.1	29.0	9.7	3.2
Norway				
Oslo (U)	0.0	28.3	2.8	0.2
Rjukan (R)	0.5	30.9	6.0	0.2
India				
Quaiserbagh, U.P. (U)	17.0	70.2	0.0	0.0
Mall, U.P. (R)	4.5	95.5	0.0	0.0
Mylapore, T.N. (U)	28.6	26.5	2.0	22.4
Thiruporur, T.N. (R)	25.0	18.8	0.0	31.3
Capital, Orissa (U)	10.5	45.6	0.0	1.8
Bolagarh, Orissa (R)	0.0	14.3	0.0	0.0
Sri Lanka				
Pettah (U)	2.3	73.4	0.0	0.8
Kahataduwa (R)	1.8	30.9	0.0	0.0
Singapore				
B Division (U)	7.2	30.2	21.2	2.3
Rural West (R)	0.0	36.4	0.0	10.2

5 In-capacitated	6 Dispute-Quarrel	7 Advice	8 Traffic	9 Crowd Control	10 Non-crime Invest.	11 Misc.
2.2%	5.8%	0.2%	36.1%	0.5%	2.5%	1.8%
1.8	3.5	0.0	31.9	0.0	0.0	0.9
0.7	2.2	0.0	59.3	0.0	1.5	0.4
0.0	0.0	0.0	0.0	0.0	0.0	9.1
2.0	14.7	1.0	13.7	2.0	13.7	0.0
12.9	3.4	0.0	6.2	0.0	29.3	14.4
0.0	7.8	0.0	3.1	0.0	26.6	15.6
7.7	0.0	7.7	30.8	0.0	15.4	7.7
4.8	4.8	1.6	19.4	0.0	14.5	4.8
25.1	9.6	8.1	10.9	0.0	10.7	4.3
7.0	7.4	7.4	19.7	0.0	19.7	1.4
0.0	0.0	0.0	10.6	0.0	2.1	0.0
0.0	0.0	0.0	0.0	0.0	0.0	0.0
0.0	14.3	0.0	4.1	2.0	0.0	0.0
0.0	12.5	0.0	12.5	0.0	0.0	0.0
3.5	14.0	0.0	8.8	0.0	15.8	0.0
0.0	71.4	0.0	0.0	0.0	14.3	0.0
0.0	23.4	0.0	0.0	0.0	0.0	0.0
0.0	63.6	0.0	1.8	0.0	1.8	0.0
4.7	0.6	24.9	1.7	0.0	6.8	0.4
0.0	0.0	51.7	0.0	0.0	0.6	1.1

(Banton 1964; J. Wilson 1968; Wycoff, Susmilch, and Eisenbart 1980).
After trial and error, I found that most situations could be allocated
relatively unambiguously to one of the following ten categories:

    1. crime emergency
    2. criminal complaint and investigation
    3. noncrime emergency
    4. crime prevention
    5. care of incapacitated/incompetent persons
    6. dispute or quarrel
    7. advising
    8. traffic
    9. crowd control
   10. noncrime investigation

Since I did all the categorizing of situations, the problem of intersub-
jective reliability was avoided.

Comparing the proportional incidence of each type of situation encountered—Table 5.3—it becomes obvious that police work is not uniform around the world. Not only does each kind of work display substantial range of variation, but a few are not undertaken at all in some
places. Police work has a distinctly different character in different
places. In the next chapter, the data will be analyzed to determine if
there are patterns to this variation and whether they are associated with
different social circumstances. For the moment, I shall try to capture
what is distinctive descriptively in police work by combining the categories into a smaller number of informative groups.

The format most commonly used by analysts distinguishes situations that involve violations of law from those that do not (Kelling and
Lewis 1979). Law enforcement is usually considered the central responsibility of the police, just as authorized constraint is their unique
defining characteristic. Referring to the list of categories, situations 1
and 2 are clearly crime-related; situations 3, 5, 7, and 10 are not. The
proportions of crime-related to non-crime-related work according to
this division are found in column 1 of Table 5.4. Situations 6 and 9—
quarrels and crowd control—may or may not be crime-related. Column
2 of Table 5.4 shows the results when they are not considered crime-
related, column 3 when they are treated as crime-related. Generally the
incidence of quarrels and crowd control are so small that categorizing
them as crime-related or non-crime-related makes only a slight differ-

Table 5.4

Proportion of Crime to Non-crime Situations

	1		2		3	
	Crime	Non-crime	Crime	Non-crime	Crime	Non-crime
United States						
Denver (U)	82.9%	17.0%	73.9%	26.0%	84.0%	15.2%
Salida (R)	86.5	15.5	80.3	19.6	87.5	12.5
Ft. Morgan City (R)	84.0	16.0	79.2	20.8	84.9	15.1
Ft. Morgan County (R)	88.9	11.1	88.9	11.1	88.9	11.1
Dallas, Texas (U)	66.7	33.3	53.4	46.4	73.2	26.8
Great Britain						
Ipswich Town (U)	31.5	68.5	30.2	69.8	34.4	65.6
Stowmarket (R)	31.9	68.1	28.8	71.2	38.5	61.5
France						
Evry-Corbeil (U)	60.9	39.1	55.1	44.9	64.6	35.4
Lonjumeau (U)	54.8	45.2	51.1	49.9	57.8	42.2
Chilly-Mazarin (U)	50.0	50.0	50.0	50.0	50.0	50.0
Norway						
Oslo (U)	38.8	61.2	33.4	66.6	29.6	70.4
Rjukan (R)	—	—	—	—	—	—
India						
Quaiserbagh, U.P. (U)	97.6	2.4	97.6	2.4	97.6	2.4
Mall, U.P. (R)	100.0	0.0	100.0	0.0	100.0	0.0
Mylapore, T.N. (U)	94.4	5.6	65.4	34.6	96.2	3.8
Thiruporur, T.N. (R)	100.0	0.0	77.8	22.2	100.0	0.0
Capital, Orissa (U)	74.4	25.6	62.7	37.3	78.4	21.6
Bolagarh, Orissa (R)	50.0	50.0	14.3	85.7	85.7	14.3
Sri Lanka						
Pettah (U)	100.0	0.0	76.4	23.6	100.0	0.0
Kahataduwa (R)	94.7	5.3	33.3	66.4	98.1	1.9
Singapore						
B Division (U)	39.3	60.7	39.0	61.0	39.6	60.4
Rural West (R)	41.0	59.0	41.0	59.0	41.0	59.0

Notes: Category 1 disregards quarrels and disputes and crowd control in measuring crime and noncrime. Category 2 counts quarrels, disputes, and crowd control as non-crime-related. Category 3 counts quarrels, disputes, and crowd control as crime-related.

ence to the proportions. Bologarh and Kahataduwa are the exceptions, being rural areas of India and Sri Lanka respectively. The small proportion of crowd-control situations is especially surprising for India, showing a defect in the sources used for documenting police work. Crowd control is a huge problem for the Indian police, but it is handled by specialized forces and does not show up as encounters in station diaries. Situation 4 (crime prevention) and situation 11 (miscellaneous) are impossible to categorize even in principle as being crime-related or non-crime-related. They have been omitted from the analysis. So has situation 8 (traffic). Traffic situations usually involve violations of law, almost always proactively instigated, but are technical rather than morally enjoined aspects of law enforcement.

The data show that except for Britain, Norway, and Singapore, police work is overwhelmingly law-related. If traffic enforcement is included, then the proportion that is law-related, not necessarily crime-related, rises even higher. In the United States, two-thirds to four-fifths of the situations that can be unambiguously classified are crime-related. In India and Sri Lanka the proportion is even higher. These findings, especially for the United States, are surprising. It has been considered proven that most of the situations that police encounter are not law-related.[15] Unfortunately, many of the studies are not comparable with mine because they are based on calls for service rather than police records of authenticated situations. Police can be expected to be more attentive in recording crime-related events than non-crime-related. At the same time, not all the American studies show a clear preponderance of non-crime-related situations. For example, the Police Executive Research Forum did an extensive study of calls for police service in Birmingham, Peoria, Hartford, and San Jose in 1977, discovering that about three-fifths, excluding traffic matters, involved crime control. The categorization was inexact, as all are, because some of the non-crime calls involved "peace maintenance," which included situations that might be found to be crime-related, such as disturbances, affrays, domestic disputes, and malicious mischief. In conclusion, given the problems of classification as well as the noncomparability of sources of information, it is too early, in my opinion, to be dogmatic about the character of police work, even in the United States.

For the rest of the world, there is even less independent documentation. My data for Suffolk County, Great Britain, show a clear preponderance of non-crime-related situations. Other studies, however, show equal proportions of law-enforcement and non-law-enforcement work.[16] With respect to Norway—the only other study of police work, undertaken in a rural jurisdiction similar to mine—also found that noncrime events dominated police work. In Japan and the Netherlands, the bulk of police work tends to be noncriminal. In Tokyo in recent years, crime has accounted for only about 12 percent of calls received through the police emergency number, traffic for about 25 percent, and noncrime matters, including fights and quarrels, for just over 60 percent (Tokyo Metropolitan Police Department 1979, p. 15). Responding to a survey, people in the Netherlands reported that 16 percent of their contact with the police in the preceding three years involved crime, 36 percent traffic, and 48 percent other matters (Junger-Tas 1978). The preponderance of world evidence would seem to support a conclusion that noncriminal matters dominate police work, although given the variety of information used and the clear indications of national variance, the issue of the nature of police work cannot be considered resolved.

OUTCOMES

The sources of information about outcomes are, with one exception, the same as for situations: reports of observers, activity logs of officers, and unit summaries. Unlike reporting on situations, the public is not a source of information about outcomes. Comparisons of patterns of outcomes among jurisdictions must surmount the same problems already discussed: disparate sources of information and the unreliability of each.

There is also a theoretical consideration that casts doubt on the value of comparing outcome data at all. A comparison of outcomes has no meaning unless the situations generating them are the same. It is not informative to discover, for example, that outcomes are 90 percent enforcement in one police force and 10 percent in another unless differences in the nature of situations are also known. In order to understand variations in police work, analysis of situations is logically antecedent to analysis of outcomes. On the other hand, determining that there are consistent differences in outcomes between police forces with similar compositions of situations is an important enterprise. It is probably the best way to make operational the vague concept of style in police work. A police style is represented by the proportion of outcomes from similar situations that are different. If outcomes are described dichotomously in this formulation as enforcement and nonenforcement, then style represents a gradient of enforcement. Other operationalizations of style are possible, depending on how outcomes are described, such as legality, rudeness, and forcefulness.

Many explanations for variations in outcomes have been suggested in the literature on police.[17] I do not propose to examine them here, because they are completely untested. No analysis of outcomes and, by extension, style has controlled for differences in the nature of the situations encountered.[18] Some of the larger observation studies would permit such analysis, but it would require painstaking reworking of original data. The point to reiterate is that empirical analysis of situations is necessary in order to interpret comparative data on outcomes meaningfully.

CONCLUSION

What the police do routinely from day to day varies substantially across time and space. Police work is by no means the same everywhere. The intellectual problem is to isolate meaningful differences despite the presence of alternative measures of police work—assignments, situations, outcomes—each of which rests upon a different evidentiary base. In my judgment, the most informative determinations that can be made about police work comparatively are the following:

What is the degree of functional specialization in terms of assignments?

What is the proportion of work-time subject to public direction as opposed to state direction?

What is the nature of situations encountered by police officers, with particular attention to the proportion that is law-related?

What is the manner in which situations are instigated?

What actions are taken by police in situations of the same kind, with delineations of the proportion involving enforcement being particularly important?

The study of police work is, obviously, not a simple undertaking. It can be made simpler if some of these dimensions of police work are more important than others. Can an argument be made that analysis should begin with one aspect of police work rather than another? I think it can. Situations are fundamental for several reasons. First, they are the most direct indicator of what police work involves. Assignments are not, nor are outcomes because they are derivative in meaning from situations. Second, situations reveal the ground on which encounters between police and public take place. They are the crucibles within which interaction occurs. Third, situations are empirically related to other features of police work. For example, if a police force is rationally managed, information on the nature and incidence of situations will affect the allocation of assignments. Furthermore, information about situations can easily be expanded to include the mode of instigation, thus getting at the public- or state-directedness of police activity. In other words, there are theoretical reasons for thinking that situations are the place to begin in understanding police work in all its complexity. The next step, then, is to provide a theory of police work based on situations. That is the task for the following chapter.

CHAPTER 6

A Theory of Encounters

In order to understand what police do, especially to describe variations in police work among forces, we must have information about the situations they confront. Situations are where public needs and police response intersect. As I explained in the previous chapter, situations are not only an indicator of the nature of police work; they are also empirically related to other measures of it, namely, organizational assignments and tactical decisions. This chapter will explore police work as situations in two ways. First, I will try to construct a theory that explains variations in the nature of the situations that police forces face. In other words, what factors determine the composition of the situations that police face? Second, I will describe contemporary variation in situational profiles confronted by police, based on information collected in several countries from around the world. This is original data, collected from rural and urban locations in Great Britain, India, Norway, Singapore, Sri Lanka, and the United States during 1977 and 1978. The data allow a very rudimentary test of certain parts of the theory put forth to explain variation in situations.

THE DETERMINANTS OF POLICE ENCOUNTERS

The situations that police handle depend on two major factors: public demand in the form of individual requests for assistance, and decisions that police make about priorities. Work supplied to the police is not the same as work handled by them. We must, therefore, examine factors that shape demand for police service and those that shape police selection.

PUBLIC DEMAND FOR POLICE SERVICE

It seems commonsensical to expect that public demand for police services is shaped by the public's needs and by their willingness to turn to the police to handle them. In other words, public demand reflects social conditions as well as the public's evaluation of the police. Let us explore each.

What social circumstances determine the need for police services? I suggest that calls for police service are related first to the character of interpersonal relations in society. Specifically, the perceived need for police service will rise in communities that cannot maintain social discipline and order through informal social processes. The reason for this is that where role relations are more impersonal (where a larger proportion of life's interactions occur outside primary social groups), the capacity of primary groups to maintain effective sanctions declines. People are forced to turn to formal institutions in order to resolve conflicts that were previously handled by informal groups. In most of the modern world, the primary locus of these institutions is the state. It would also follow that the nature of requests for police service would change with shifts in the character of interpersonal relations. Not only do intimate associations maintain discipline, but they also provide social services to their members. As informal relations erode, people must turn to the state for these services. Altogether, then, the volume of requests for police intervention and the proportion of enforcement to nonenforcement situations confronted by the police may vary directly with the quality of interpersonal relations in society. Two possible indicators of the vitality of informal social relations would be the extent to which role-playing is spatially segregated in the lives of individuals and the degree of impersonality with which roles are played.

This formulation leads to the conclusion that as societies become more industrial and urban and less agrarian and rural, police will deal with more service and fewer crime-related requests. This conclusion is counterintuitive; it is not what most people expect. Cities are supposed to be the great breeding grounds of crime; rural villages are more orderly and pacific. Therefore, police work would be more crime-oriented in cities than in farm communities. It is crucial to understand that I am not suggesting that there will be less crime in cities relative to population than in villages. The hypothesis explains the proportion of enforcement to nonenforcement requests. As societies develop modern economic systems and social structures, calls for service will increase relative to population, but the proportion of non-crime-related requests will become greater. Development produces both more crime absolutely and a larger proportion of service-related requests.[1]

This hypothesis rests on a rich theoretical foundation. Many sociologists have distinguished structural features of society—urbanization, industrialization, bureaucratization—from the interpersonal processes that vivify people's daily lives. Tönnies coined the terms *Gemeinschaft* and *Gesellschaft* to denote differences in the salience of face-to-face relations and the vitality of primary groups. A *Gemeinschaft* enmeshes the individual almost totally in groups of small scale; a *Gesellschaft* disperses role-playing among many groups and makes it impersonal (Tönnies 1957). Durkheim recognized the same dichotomy when he spoke of "mechanical" as opposed to "organic solidarity"; Redfield in the notion of a "folk-urban continuum"; and Sorokin in "familistic," "contractual," and "compulsory" social relations. Max Weber was speaking from the same insight when he said that what makes neighborhoods unique is the "reciprocal personal acquaintance of the inhabitants" (1968, p. 1212). Altogether, great voices have been raised in support of the idea that the character of interpersonal relations are crucial intervening variables between macroprocesses of change and institutional behavior. None, however, has specifically suggested their effect on the role of the police.

Turning to the literature on the police and law, one also finds supportive theories and some meager supporting evidence. Donald Black has argued that people will resort to law when the relational distance between them is very great. The more intimate they are in daily life, the less likely they are to invoke legal processes (Black 1976, pp. 40–46). When people are confronted with the illegal behavior of others, they involve the law more frequently when informal processes of accommodation do not exist (Black 1973). In Black's words, "we expect that mobilization of law will be infrequent in what Gluckman in his classic study of the Barotze of Zambia called 'multiplex relations,' meaning relations that are intimate in terms of duration, frequency of interaction, intensity, interdependence, and multiple-interactional dimensions" (1973, p. 134). Since police are one gateway to law, it is a short step to the proposition that people intimately associated with one another are less likely to take disputes to the police than are others. The gravity of problems will have to be greater to justify an appeal to the police when communities are close and personal relationships intense.

Michael Banton, one of the most insightful students in the comparative police field, has reasoned in exactly the same terms but has come to opposite conclusions. In *The Policeman in the Community* he argued that police work is related to "social density," meaning the closeness, intimacy, and "integration" of community life (1964, pp. 224–232). But Banton reverses the effect: where social density is high and people play multiple roles known to one another, the police are more likely to play a mediating, nonenforcement role; where social relations are more distant, as in cities, they will play a more enforcing role. This disagreement between Banton and myself is probably resolvable on theoretical grounds. It is not clear whether Banton is explaining police work as situations or outcomes. People in communities characterized by intimate social relations may want mediation more than enforcement in the same kind of situations that people in other social circumstances want police to handle through enforcement. If policemen are close to a community, they are less likely to act as enforcers, even though the proportion of enforcement requests is higher. Intimate communities provide proportionately more law-related situations, as I argue, and proportionately more nonenforcement actions, as Banton argues. Banton, in effect, is relating the nature of interpersonal relations to the enforcement proclivities of police organizations. In situations of the same kind, police in "integrated" communities would have a less enforcement-oriented style than police in impersonal societies. This is an important idea that deserves empirical testing.

I would note in passing that the idea seems to rest on the assumption that in intimate communities the police are close to people. This may be true in England and Scotland, but it is not always the case elsewhere. In India, for example, villages are very cohesive and "multiplex," to use Gluckman's word again, but the police are viewed as alien intruders. When policemen become integrated into communities, they may act as Banton says with respect to outcomes, but intimate communities do not necessarily have integrated policemen.

Arthur Niederhoffer and Graeme Newman have both argued explicitly that police work is related to the character of interpersonal relations in the manner suggested here, recognizing too that it is deducible from the thinking of Durkheim and Tönnies (Niederhoffer 1967, pp. 29–30; Newman n.d.). Niederhoffer supports his argument with American data showing that the proportion of arrests per police encounter are greater in rural than in urban areas; Newman shows, on the basis of a multinational comparison, that people in countries with more tightly knit communities are less likely to report criminal incidents to the police and more likely to report them to family and village. Though suggestive, neither set of data is appropriate for a direct test of the hypothesis. Arrests are an indicator of output from encounters and can vary independently of the situations that engender contact. Willingness to report criminal incidents may indeed be related to interpersonal relations but does not show that the proportion of situations of different kinds varies from place to place.

Another attempt to test this hypothesis has been made explicitly by Paul Shane (1980, chap. 4). Using comparative data from India, Israel, Great Britain, the Netherlands, and the United States, Shane showed that the proportion of nonenforcement to enforcement situations handled by the police is larger in socially disorganized communities. Police in India, for example, where the integrity of informal groups is still high, handle twice as many enforcement situations proportionately as police in other countries (Shane 1980, pp. 187–189). At the same time, the ratio of the volume of encounters to population in India is sharply lower than in the other countries, as the hypothesis would lead one to expect—2.2 encounters per 1,000 people in India, 6 per 1,000 in the Netherlands, 6 to 13 per 1,000 in Great Britain, 10.5 to 12.0 per 1,000 in Israel, and 40.2 per 1,000 in Baltimore. Shane's analysis of variations in the nature of situations within countries also supported the hypothesis. In Britain, the proportion of law-related calls was greater in rural than in urban areas (Shane 1980, p. 72). In Israel, differences in the nature of police encounters in Haifa and Jerusalem were associated, as expected, with measures of social disorganization in the lives of people seeking police assistance (Shane 1980, chap. 6).

Testing the proposition that differences in the character of interpersonal relations and the vitality of primary social groups affect both the volume and composition of demand for the police is not easy to do. Three problems have to be surmounted, as I discovered in my fieldwork in nine countries.

First, data collected by police departments about encounters are often not comparable. Sometimes they represent situations reported officially by police as having occurred, as in Britain and the United States; sometimes genuine calls for police service, as in Norway and France; and sometimes what might be called authenticated calls for service, where the police have had an opportunity to discuss the situation extensively with the complainant before responding, as in Sri Lanka and India. The obvious solution to the problem of incommensurate data is to observe how police receive and respond to public complaints in a variety of places, counting instances of different sorts. In this way, one can distinguish among requests, official descriptions, and outcomes. This strategy is very expensive, requiring a large staff.

Second, information about the character of interpersonal relations and the vitality of primary social groups is difficult to obtain unless, again, one undertakes direct observation. An alternate strategy is to look for proximate measures of interpersonal integration. The most obvious of these are residence changes, occupational mobility, distance between home and workplace, divorce rates, proportion of females in the work force, extent of public transportation, private ownership of motor vehicles, exposure to mass media, capacity of community health-care facilities, size of families and households, education and literacy, incidence of civil suits, and ethnic and linguistic heterogeneity. These are surrogate indicators of the state of interpersonal relations in communities. As one might expect, such an array of data is rarely available; where it does exist, its quality cannot be guaranteed.

Third, it is often impossible to match units of data collection between indicators of the nature of interpersonal relations and the nature of situations encountered by the police. Police jurisdictions are usually smaller than standard units for aggregating other sorts of data. Rarely, therefore, is it possible to avoid the ecological fallacy when associating situations with social determinants.

Given these difficulties, I conclude that a rigorous testing of the hypothesis that the volume and composition of demand for police services varies with the character of interpersonal social relations is possible only at considerable expense. This is a pity, because demonstrating a link between the nature of public demand for police services and macrosocial circumstances through the intervening variable of interpersonal relations would have important policy implications. Police administrators would then be able to anticipate the kind of work their personnel would confront as social conditions vary either as a result of historical processes of development or among areas of their jurisdiction with different social characters. Their strategic choices would be better informed, and discriminating in-service training could be provided for officers as they were moved from place to place.

Returning to the a priori exploration of factors that influence public demand for police service, changes in interpersonal relations leading to greater demands on the police, especially of a noncrime sort, may be offset to some extent by increases in personal wealth. Rich people can secure services for themselves through the marketplace—such as marriage counselors, lawyers, psychiatrists, doctors, and financial advisers—that are available to poor people only under public auspices. Thus, among groups with the same kind of interpersonal relations, those with more money will make fewer service requests of the police proportionately than those without money. Upper classes can be expected to have higher enforcement-to-service ratios than lower classes, even when both are similarly disorganized socially.[2] On the other hand, wealth might also act to encourage contact with the police, even in problematic areas. Wealth is usually associated with education and social standing, with the result that rich people are more likely to be confident and assertive in their relations with civil servants, such as the police. Generally, they expect to get what they ask for and to be treated respectfully when they do so. On balance, the effect of wealth on demands made of the police is probably ambiguous, so that variations in wealth either among individuals or societies are not likely to exercise an important effect.

If changes in interpersonal relations do affect the demand for police services, as suggested here, then processes of economic development and social change loosely captured by the label *modernization* affect police in two ways: by creating new tasks leading to new organizational assignments and by influencing social relations, thereby producing changes in the proportion of service-related to crime-related demands. Modernization processes do not affect the nature of individual demands for police service unless social relations change. If societies can preserve useful proximate groups in the face of modernization, the character of aggregate demand for police will not change.

Another factor, however, affects this relationship. All societies do not place the same value on cohesive, small-scale, informal interpersonal relations. Values, which belong to the domain of culture, cut across structural determinants. Therefore, if two societies undergo the same process of macrosocial change, the one that values more the vitality of proximate groups will make fewer service-related than crime-related requests proportionately. To the extent that culture inhibits the impact of macrosocial change on interpersonal relations, the shift in demand for police action of the service sort will be lessened.

In summary, then, citizens' demand for police services will be affected by the character of interpersonal relations, particularly the vitality of primary social groups; by the level and distribution of wealth; and by the cultural value placed on maintaining tight-knit proximate groups.

What the public actually takes to the police as requests for service depends not only on what they feel they need, but also on what they believe the police are willing to handle. In effect, there is a feedback relationship between demands made of the police and the selection decisions of the police: demands determine the range of choices that police have, but the responsiveness of the police when they make choices shapes public decisions about what matters to take to the police. A population that is reluctant to contact the police would do so only in overwhelming emergencies, especially those of a criminal sort. Populations not hesitant about contacting police would bring all manner of problems, many of them trivial and unrelated to crime. Thus, the greater the volume of calls for assistance per unit of population, the higher will be the proportion of service-related to crime-related requests.

There is another reason for arguing that the nature and volume of calls are related. As contact with police is facilitated, people would also be encouraged to bring less important matters to police attention. Inconvenience deters, as well as do perceptions of police unresponsiveness. If inconvenience in contacting the police is reduced, people are more likely to act on their inclination to seek help.[3] This should increase the proportion of nonserious calls to the police. Since convenience is to a large extent a function of communication, it follows that wealthier communities are more likely to have a higher proportion of service requests than poor communities. At the same time, one cannot always assume that a high volume of calls indicates a diverse demand. Volume may rise because crime needs have risen. Thus, although the volume of requests may be related to nature of requests, variation in volume is an imperfect indicator of differences in composition.

In summary, the situations that police handle are determined initially by the nature of public demand communicated to the police. The proportion of service-related to crime-related demands is affected by public willingness to contact police, which is traceable in turn to considerations of convenience as well as responsiveness of the police, and

Figure 6.1

SOCIAL DETERMINANTS OF POLICE WORK

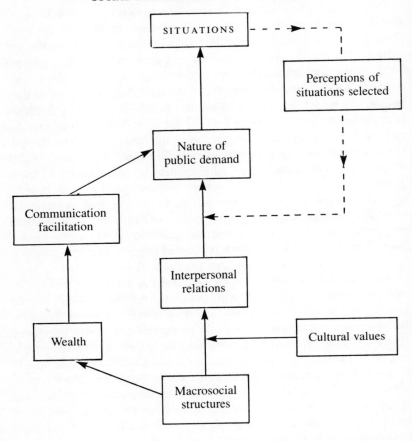

by the social integration of proximate groups, which is a function both of macrosocial structures and cultural values. These relations are illustrated in Figure 6.1.

SELECTION DECISIONS OF THE POLICE

The situations that police handle are affected not only by the requests made of them by the public but also by their own decisions about what is appropriate to do. Police selection decisions are affected by two factors: the volume of demand from the public and organizational priorities. I have already argued that as the willingness of the public to call the police rises, the proportion of service-related to crime-related demand also rises. However, if the police are unable to handle the aggregate demand, they will select in favor of crime-related calls. The greater the volume of calls in relation to police capacity, the more likely it will be that police will discriminate against service requests. Excess reactive capacity allows police to deal with more trivial requests. Therefore, the greater the number of police personnel per capita assigned to reactive roles, the greater will be the proportion of service calls selected.

In terms of operational practice, police select in favor of crime-related incidents in two ways. They establish priorities, dealing with the more serious calls first, and they increase their functional specialization as an organization by giving up responsibility for certain non-crime-related tasks. Radio-dispatched police forces commonly have codes that indicate the seriousness of situations. These assign priority. American police today are developing explicit "stacking" strategies whereby dispatchers determine the importance of calls and assign them accordingly (Farmer and Furstenburg 1979). In effect, criteria for the "postponability" of requests are developed. Police also develop referral procedures so that other agencies can be given responsibility for certain kinds of service clients. Police officers work closely, for example, with ambulance services, detoxification centers, juvenile shelters, and homes for battered women. Policemen are sometimes given pocket reference books that list agencies to which they can refer people with problems involving abortion, alcoholism, mental illness, marriage, unemployment, and drugs. Paradoxically, the development of improved referral ability may not solve the problem of high-level demand. Because the type of situations that police elect to handle affects the volume and nature of demand for police assistance, enhancing referral capacity may encourage more calls of the same type. The only advantage to the police is that they are relieved of follow-up responsibility.

One qualification should be made to the proposition that a low volume of requests increases the proportion of service-related to crime-related matters selected for handling by the police. Inactivity on the part of police officers leads to boredom and frustration, which often impels them to make work more exciting for themselves. They do this by searching harder for offenses, which usually means more stringently enforcing minor violations such as loitering, causing a nuisance, defects in motor vehicles, and traffic infractions. Therefore, while excess capacity encourages generous treatment of service requests, it can generate a countercurrent of enforcement discoveries. This is another reason for thinking that rural policemen, always less busy than their urban counterparts, become proportionately more involved with crime-related matters, especially those of a very minor nature. It is difficult to say how significant this contrary effect is. It is unlikely that the promptings of boredom in police forces with excess reactive capacity would cause officers to disregard service calls, but it probably means that the total mix of situations handled will be more skewed in the direction of law violations than the character of demand might suggest.

In addition to the volume of requests, selection decisions made by the police are affected by the priorities that police forces set. Priorities are expressed organizationally as assignments and individually as cues to performance within assignments. Certainly individual performance cues vary sharply from force to force. Some forces encourage sympathetic response to service situations, others a crime-control preoccupation. These cues occur, however, within a structure imposed by the nature of assignments. Some assignments, such as criminal investigation and traffic regulation, generate enforcement situations; others, such as juvenile counseling, generate services; and some, such as registering firearms and guarding VIPs, generate situations that cannot be labeled either service or crime. By and large, the more police assignments are monopolized by the state, the less available police are for handling service requests from the public. Furthermore, state-directed assignments that involve contact with the public tend to produce situations that require enforcement of law. This is true of auxiliary administrative tasks as well, if one considers regulation through compliance as enforcement.[4] Thus, the proportion of crime-related to service-related requests handled will increase as police are subjected increasingly to state direction. Where the amount of state-directed activity is large, as in the case of criminal investigation and auxiliary administration, police in reactive assignments will tend to disregard publicly generated requests for service in favor of crime-related ones. This point is tricky, because it involves distinguishing between the character of work performed by all police in a force and the character of work performed by

officers who are free to select among public demands individually articulated. In brief, selections from among public requests are influenced
by the capacity to respond, and this capacity is in turn influenced by the
extent to which assignments are monopolized by the state.

It has often been noted that actions of the police that are instigated
proactively within assignments, notably in patrol, favor crime-related
matters. This point can now be broadened. The greater the proportion
of directed activity by the police, whether by the state or by officers
individually, the lower will be the proportion of service requests from
the public that will be handled.

The argument I have made here is that organizational priorities expressed as assignments affect selection decisions made with respect to
public demand. Surely the converse is also true—that the volume of
service requests affects organizational assignments. This would seem
plausible provided that police, and more generally government, care
about satisfying public demand. Therefore, the likelihood of police organizations increasing responsive capacity in order to meet service demands depends on the character of government. This suggests that
more democratic governments will devote larger proportions of personnel to reactive assignments, social conditions being equal, than nondemocratic governments. A police organization might in some circumstances be more anxious to satisfy service demand than is the
government as a whole, but this would be unusual. Thus, police in
democratic countries will handle higher proportions of service-related
calls than in nondemocratic countries, provided police capacity and the
character of public demand are the same. Paradoxically, democratic responsiveness can produce selection away from servicing in the short
run. This happens when public anxiety about crime becomes intense
and politicians begin to make an issue of it. Then police shift their
operational priorities, increasing the amount of directed police activity.
This lowers the proportion of service-related to crime-related calls
handled. In a classic dilemma, the public's disaggregate demand for
service is frustrated by its collective demand for crime enforcement.
The police too become frustrated, finding themselves caught between
two equally legitimate sets of public demands, each articulated in a different way.

The explanation of police work as situations is now complete. Although the theory I have suggested is fairly straightforward in its parts,

Figure 6.2
A COMPLETE MODEL OF POLICE WORK

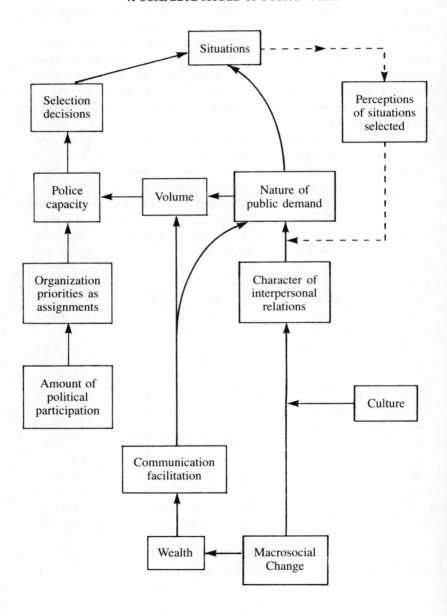

as a whole it does not provide a basis for predication. (See Figure 6.2.) There are too many independent variables (seven) plus a feedback loop. Moreover, some of the factors work in opposite directions. Increased heterogeneity in the nature of requests for police assistance are associated with an increase in the volume of calls, but an increase in volume decreases police capacity to respond to such variety. Economic development increases the demand for service calls through decay in the resourcefulness of informal social groups, unless offset by cultural norms, but development may also augment wealth, thereby providing the public with the means to obtain private assistance commercially. Finally, while economic development intensifies the public's need for servicing, it also generates new tasks—such as traffic regulation—that distract the police from both crime-fighting and responsive servicing. Altogether, unless most of the factors suggested prove in fact to be minor in importance, variations in the nature of police work as situations will prove to be unpredictable.

In the previous chapter I noted almost as an aside that assignments, situations, and outcomes—the three conceptually distinct ways that police work can be operationalized—were empirically related. The theory just elaborated shows the mechanisms through which this occurs. (See Figure 6.3.) Assignments affect the selection decisions that police make, directly through the work entailed and indirectly through reducing reactive capacity. Situations affect outcomes as they are filtered

Figure 6.3

EMPIRICAL RELATIONS AMONG ASSIGNMENTS, SITUATIONS, AND OUTCOMES

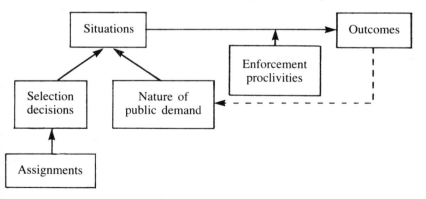

through the reaction philosophy of each force. Variations in outcomes can be attributed to situations only when the action proclivities are the same. Finally, the way police handle situations affects the public's willingness to contact the police, thus shaping situations through molding demand.

INTERNATIONAL PATTERNS OF POLICE WORK

The data collected internationally show clearly that both the volume and character of the situations that police handle vary from place to place. With respect to the volume of police work, it is not true on a worldwide basis that the number of situations handled proportionate to population is greater in urban than rural areas. (See Table 6.1.) Only in less developed parts of the world, such as India, Singapore, and Sri Lanka, do we find a greater proportion of calls in urban rather than rural areas. It is important to note that two sets of incidence figures have been computed: one for situations of all sorts, the other adjusted by eliminating traffic matters. The incidence of traffic encounters reflects technological development as well as explicit policies of police departments, the enforcement of traffic rules being almost wholly proactive and discretionary. Not surprisingly, the proportion of police work involving traffic is greater in the developed countries of the sample. Britain is not the exception that it appears. Information about encounters in Britain, as well as in Oslo, came from a command-and-control computer more than from the logs of events kept by officers. Though patrol personnel are supposed to record all encounters in the computer, they tend to file only reactive dispatches and consider reports of minor proactive encounters, such as traffic citations, too much of a bother.

However, even correcting for traffic situations, the volume per capita of situations that the police handle is sometimes greater, contrary to expectation, in rural areas. The areas outside of Denver, for example, had much greater volumes of police work per capita. Though it could be argued that both Salida and Fort Morgan City are towns, in fact county seats, they are hardly cities. Both Fort Morgan City and its surrounding hinterland have a higher incidence than metropolitan Denver after one corrects for traffic enforcement. In Norway, there may have been a unique reason for the much higher incidence in the rural than in the urban area. The Rjukan police station was located very close to a tavern that the police considered the bane of their existence because of the many fights that occurred there. The police were camped, as it were, on a perpetual law-and-order problem.

What these figures suggest is that "modernization" both increases convenience in mobilizing the police, especially for rural people, and at the same time breaks down disproportionately the reluctance of rural people to request help. In short, willingness and capacity to solicit assistance from the police becomes equal among large geographical areas. With modernization the rural-urban dichotomy ceases to structure the volume of police work. It would still be possible, of course, that per capita volume would be affected by other structural factors, such as class, ethnicity, and education. To determine this would require very discriminating analysis, involving comparison of the volume of police work among persons of different sorts, determined by keeping track of the character of people involved in all police encounters, either individually or according to the predominant sociological character of relatively homogeneous areas in which encounters occur.

Turning now to international variations in the kinds of situations that police handle, while there are marked differences from place to place, they do not occur between rural and urban locations. (See Table 6.2.) This conclusion is not affected by alternative operationalizations of crime and non-crime, built out of the ten categories used to describe all situations.[5] Although the locations do not constitute a statistical sample, we used a chi-square test for significant differences because it is robust and the variables were dichotomous. The plain fact is that police in urban areas in these six countries do not deal with a larger proportion of service-related as opposed to crime-related situations than do police in rural areas. In nine locations, differences significant at better than the 10 percent level showed up in only two of them. For the proportions of service-related to crime-related situations in each place, refer to Table 5.3. Examination of the ten categories used separately for describing situations also fails to show important differences between rural and urban areas. (See Table 6.3.) Because police records did not contain information about many categories, there were only two kinds of situations in which comparison could be made for more than half the paired locations: crime emergencies and criminal investigation. For crime emergencies there was only one difference signifi-

Table 6.1
Volume of Police Encounters and Population
in Selected International Locations

Place	Population	Volume of Situations for a Sample of Days per Year
United States		
Denver (U)	520,000	1,349
Salida (R)	4,500	113
Ft. Morgan City (R)	8,000	545
Ft. Morgan County (R)	12,105[a]	22
Great Britain		
Ipswich (U)	121,500	417
Stowmarket (R)	23,580	64
Norway		
Oslo (U)	465,337	467
Rjukan (R)	7,675	N.A.
Singapore		
B Division (U)	250,000	901
Rural West (R)	282,000	176
Sri Lanka		
Pettah (U)	65,000	128
Kahataduwa (R)	43,849	55
India		
Quaiserbagh (U)	110,000	47
Mall (R)	90,865	22
Mylapore (U)	108,000	49
Thiruporur (R)	129,790	16
Capital (U)	68,000	57
Bolagarh (R)	N.A.	7

[a]These figures are for the county population less the county seat.

Percentage of Traffic Situations	Estimated Yearly No. of Situations	Situations per 1,000 Population	Proportion After Correcting for Traffic
35.0	61,380	118	76.7
31.9	5,142	1,143	778.0
59.3	24,798	3,100	1,262.0
0.0	1,001 [a]	83	83.0
6.2	18,974	156	147.0
3.0	2,912	123	119.3
10.9	21,248	45.7	40.7
19.7	569	74.2	59.3
1.7	40,996	164.0	161.2
0.0	4,008	14.2	14.2
0.0	5,824	89.6	89.6
1.8	2,502	57.1	56.0
10.6	2,093	19.0	17.0
0.0	1,001	11.0	11.0
4.1	2,230	20.6	19.8
12.5	728	5.6	4.9
8.8	2,594	38.0	34.8
0.0	318	N.A.	N.A.

Table 6.2

Comparison of Differences in Situations Operationalized as Crime-
related and Non-crime-related between Rural and Urban Areas
(phi coefficients)

Countries	1	2	3
United States			
Denver / Ft. Morgan County	0	0	0
Ft. Morgan City /			
Ft. Morgan County	0	0	0
Great Britain			
Ipswich / Stowmarket	0	0	0
Norway			
Oslo / Rjukan	0	0	0
Singapore			
B Division / Rural West	0	0	0
India			
Quaiserbagh / Mall, U.P.	0.01 (68)	0.01 (68)	0.01 (68)
Mylapore / Thiruporur, T.N.	0.01 (35)	0	0.01 (45)
Capital / Bolagarh, Orissa	0.08 (45)	0.10 (58)*	0
Sri Lanka			
Pettah / Kahataduwa	0.04 (116)*	0.17 (181)*	0

Notes: Calculations significant at 10 percent level are marked with an asterisk.
Sample size is given in parenthesis. Category 1 disregards quarrels, disputes, and
crowd control. Category 2 counts quarrels, disputes, and crowd control as non-crime-
related. Category 3 counts quarrels, disputes, and crowd control as crime-related.

cant at better than the 10 percent level between rural and urban areas,
while for crime investigation slightly more than one-third of the comparisons showed significant differences. The proportions can be found
in Table 5.4. Taking all the categories together for all the sites where I
could collect information (54 out of 110 possibilites), one-third of the
computations showed significant rural-urban differences and two-thirds
did not. Moreover, the effect of location was generally weak, as the
contingency coefficients show. Finally, the few significant rural-urban
differences were scattered among the ten kinds of situations, so one
cannot say that one kind of situation was much more likely than others
to show rural-urban differences. The exceptions are crime investigation

and disputes and quarrels, but at most only three out of seven locations showed significant differences on any one of these.

This lack of significant differences in the composition of police work between rural and urban areas is remarkably consistent, considering the variety of countries studied and the enormous difference in the ambience between rural and urban areas in places like India, Norway, and the United States. One would have thought that we would have found differences somewhere. Instead, the composition of police work, determined from the same sources for rural-urban pairs within each country, appears to be the same within countries across a social division thought generally, and certainly by police officers, to be of great importance.

While the composition of police encounters with the public appears to be the same within countries, at least across the rural-urban gradient, there are striking and consistent differences among countries. Grouping Norway and Great Britain together as Europe and India and Sri Lanka as South Asia, one finds that the composition of police work varies among world regions roughly along a developmental dimension. (See Table 6.4.) The results are not affected by the scheme adopted for assigning situations to crime or non-crime categories. Furthermore, the strength of the association between world region and the composition of police work is substantial. Most of the contingency coefficients have values between 0.30 and 0.50.

With the exception of the United States, the richer and more developed the region, the more likely it is in both rural and urban areas that the police will handle a larger proportion of non-crime situations. Conversely, the poorer a country is, the more likely it is that the police will deal more exclusively with crime-related matters. (See Table 6.5.) This is true for Europe in relation to South Asia and Singapore as well as for South Asia in relation to Singapore. The United States provides the anomalous case. Although there are significant differences in the composition of police work between the United States and each of the other regions, encounters in the United States are proportionately *more crime-related*. In effect, even though the United States is more developed than the other locations—arguable in the case of Europe—its police deal consistently with more crime and less service than others. Singapore's police, for example, are in rural and urban areas always more preoccupied with non-crime matters than those in the United States. Com-

Table 6.3
Comparison of Differences in all Situations between Rural and Urban
Areas (chi-square calculations)

	1 Crime Emergency	2 Crime Invest.	3 Non-crime Emergency	4 Prevention
United States				
Denver / Salida	0.017	13.55* (CC 0.10)	1.50	0.48
Denver / Ft. Morgan City	51.4* (CC 0.16)	0.02	.014	19.88* (CC 0.10)
Denver / Ft. Morgan County	0.58	24.46* (CC 0.13)	1.7	0.05
Ft. Morgan City / Ft. Morgan County	0.86	22.9* (CC 0.20)	1.9	12.5* (CC 0.15)
Great Britain				
Ipswich / Stowmarket	2.17	1.52	11.47* (CC 0.16)	—
Norway				
Oslo / Rjukan	—	0.42	5.5	0.02
India				
Quaiserbagh / Mall	2.14	5.12* (CC 0.26)	—	—
Mylapore / Thiruporur	0.08	0.39	—	0.5
Capital / Bolagarh	—	2.51	—	—
Sri Lanka				
Pettah / Kahataduwa	0.05	28.9* (CC 0.37)	—	—
Singapore				
B Division / Rural West	—	2.9	—	29.7* (CC 0.12)
Total comparisons	11	11	11	11
Total computations	8	11	6	7
Number significant	1	4	1	3
Number not significant	7	7	5	4

Notes: Asterisk indicates significant chi-square value at the 10 percent level. CC
indicates the value of the contingency coefficient.

5 In-capacitated	6 Dispute/ Quarrel	7 Advice	8 Traffic	9 Crowd Control	10 Non-crime Invest.	N
0.13	0.81	—	19.1* (CC 0.12)	—	—	1,384
4.46	11.2* (CC 0.08)	—	84.96* (CC 0.21)	—	1.8	1,850
—	—	—	—	—	—	1,334
—	—	—	—	—	—	556
—	2.97	—	0.97	—	0.18	408
66.1* (CC 0.25)	86.0* (CC 0.28)	0.63	13.7* (CC 0.12)	—	14.2*	1,007
—	—	—	—	—	—	68
—	0.03	—	1.48	—	—	65
—	12.7* (CC 0.16)	—	—	—	0.01	64
—	27.1* (CC 0.36)	—	—	—	—	183
—	—	52.2*	—	—	0.55	1,070
11	11	11	11	11	11	110
3	7	2	5	0	5	54
1	4	1	3	0	1	19
2	3	1	2	0	4	35

Table 6.4
Significant Differences between Similar Areas for Proportions of Crime and Non-crime Situations for World Regions (chi square)

		Scheme 1	Scheme 2	Scheme 3
United States				
1. Europe {	Urban	293.4* (1518) CC 0.40	264.6* (1495) CC 0.39	304.5* (1515) CC 0.41
	Rural	119.7* (725) CC 0.36	126.3* (785) CC 0.37	105.1* (788) CC 0.34
2. S. Asia {	Urban	15.3* (902) CC 0.13	0.91 (1032)	17.7* (1031) CC 0.13
	Rural	4.87* (323) CC 0.12	28.5* (378) CC 0.26	10.8* (381) CC 0.17
3. Singapore {	Urban	172.2* (961) CC 0.39	106.2* (1050) CC 0.30	196.1* (1050) CC 0.40
	Rural	179.0* (980) CC 0.39	142.4* (1020) CC 0.35	194.1* (966) CC 0.40
Europe				
1. S. Asia {	Urban	199.0* (1036) CC 0.40	155.1* (975) CC 0.37	217.3* (994) CC 0.42
	Rural	44.35* (502) CC 0.28	5.68* (591) CC 0.10	77.3* (591) CC 0.34
2. Singapore {	Urban	0.02 (1095)	4.87* (993) CC 0.07	0.02 (1013)
	Rural	0.97 (1186)	0.00 (1233)	10.89* (1233) CC 0.09
S. Asia				
1. Singapore {	Urban	146.6* (479) CC 0.48	76.33* (530) CC 0.35	172.3* (529) CC 0.50
	Rural	30.0* (784) CC 0.19	6.05* (26) CC 0.43	114.8* (826) CC 0.35

Notes: Asterisks indicate chi-square calculations significant at the 10 percent level. CC is the contingency coefficient. The number of situations analyzed is given in parentheses.

Table 6.5
Percentage of Incidence of Crime/Non-crime Situations
for World Regions

		Scheme 1		Scheme 2		Scheme 3	
		Crime	Non-crime	Crime	Non-crime	Crime	Non-crime
United States	Urban	83%	17%	74%	26%	85%	15%
	Rural	84	16	80	20	85	15
Europe	Urban	40	60	32	68	42	58
	Rural	43	57	39	61	48	52
South Asia	Urban	94	7	77	23	95	5
	Rural	96	4	52	48	98	2
Singapore	Urban	40	60	39	61	41	59
	Rural	36	64	39	61	36	64

pared even with South Asia, the poorest region in the sample, American police work is either as crime-related or more crime-related.

It should be remembered that these data are from rural and urban places in each country and may or may not be representative. Though it is convenient to talk of Norwegian or Indian results, the fact is that these are results *from* Norway or India. One cannot correctly generalize about behavior in each country. The international comparisons suggest one very important hypothesis about police work that deserves further testing: countries generate unique patterns of action and reaction between police and public, regardless of location within the country, that largely shapes both what the public expects the police to do and what the police actually do. The analysis shows that variation in the nature of police work does not occur within countries but between them. There is a striking consistency in the absence of statistically significant differences between large urban areas and genuinely rural hinterlands, while at the same time rural and urban locations in each country show significant variations in the composition of police work when compared with similar locations in other countries. This is true for all six countries analyzed—countries that span three continents, Eastern and Western cultures, and developed and underdeveloped regions. The conclusion that it plainly suggests is that the nature of police work is idiosyncratic nationally. Although structural elements may be important to some extent in explaining police work, as the model indicates, factors belonging to the domain of culture and tradition may be much more important, possibly involving an interactional dynamic between police and public.

CONCLUSION

The hypothetical model presented here to explain police work, particularly the part dealing with public demand, can certainly not be considered supported by existing international evidence, despite the fact that it rests on a deep intellectual tradition. Moreover, rigorous testing will always be difficult because of the number of variables that it would seem reasonable to try to control.

Though provisional at the present time, the model does contain important implications with respect to the kind of work that police will be called upon to handle as societies change. First, as societies develop economically, requests for services unrelated to law violations may rise due to greater ease of physical communication with police and a decline in the supportive capacity of primary groups. Countries whose cultural values favor submersion of individuals in group networks will experience this shift less than others. Second, as long as the number of police assigned to reactive duties, meaning primarily patrol, is large relative to demand, police will be able to accommodate the rising proportion of service requests. This will occur more certainly in countries where bureaucratic tradition is against state monopolization of police activity, especially where the amount of auxiliary administration is small, and where public participation in government is extensive. Third, even if police succeed in fending off government demand for assistance in general administration, their work does not become more specialized as development proceeds. Rather, as the proportion of personnel assigned to reactive tasks increases, the demands made on them by the public increasingly divert them from narrow law enforcement.

The dilemma for police in modern, industrialized, urban societies is, therefore, that they may have to perform in a predominantly service role at the very time the need for law enforcement appears to be rising. The opportunity for exemplary enforcement, which is the foundation of deterrence, may actually decline in modern societies, contrary to public perceptions of what is needed. Even more peculiarly, the need for servicing is greatest among the most disadvantaged groups, the very groups that are considered at the same time to the be most disposed to criminal behavior. Modern police forces are often required to deal effectively with crime while simultaneously responding to a growing proportion of service requests. Aggregate and disaggregate demand work in contrary ways, and the police are caught squarely in between.

My international analysis, unlike Paul Shane's, fails to support the notion that differences in the type of work that police do is primarily attributable to differences in the character of interpersonal relations in communities. Within countries, rural and urban locations are not different in the composition of police work. And although police work varies along a developmental gradient for Europe, South Asia, and Singapore, it does not do so for the United States. Admittedly these measures of the character of interpersonal relations are presumptive; but given the difficulty of obtaining more direct indicators, they may be the best one can do. Actually, Shane's results are all the more impressive considering the complexity of interactions that determine police work as situations. Unless some of the factors that I have argued impinge on police encounters prove to be of small importance, the *cateris paribus* requirements for proving any single-causation hypothesis will prove to be unmanageable.

At the same time, the research presented here strongly suggests that the effect of structural variables on police work may vary according to a learned dynamic of police-public interaction. Referring to Figure 6.2, the controlling loop may be among situations, public perceptions of police selectivity and treatment, and the nature of public demand. If this is so, police and public create work between them. Moreover, the creative partner would seem to be the police, since within each country studied the kinds of people who brought problems to the police varied enormously in quite disparate social circumstances. Some factor, common to all locations within each country, appears to be creating similar profiles of public demand. This factor could, of course, be the cultural orientations shared by national publics; but it seems more likely that the common element is police culture, because police are the less numerous partner, are more authoritatively controlled, and are subject to systems of constraints nationally predicated, as other chapters have amply shown.

PART IV
POLITICS

CHAPTER 7
Control of the Police

The relation between police and society is reciprocal—society shapes what the police are, the police influence what society may become. This relationship may be explicit and purposive, as when courts are given power to punish police for erring actions and when police repress people opposed to government. It may also be diffuse and accidental, as when the intellectual capacity of recruits affects what police operations are like and when the communications requirements of police create demand for industrial products. The explicit and purposive interactions generally attract more attention. But one must bear in mind that they are but one part of a complicated, ramified interaction. The interactive effects of police and society that are not contrived may be vastly important in themselves, as well as conditioning the effects that are explicit and purposive.

The deliberated interactions between police and society belong to the domain of politics and occur primarily through government. They consist, on the one hand, of communities' attempts to direct and control the police and, on the other, of police impingement on political life. The first interaction embodies the issue of accountability, the second of political policing. They will be discussed respectively in this and the following chapter.

With respect to accountability, the most important question to answer is how successful different communities have been in achieving conformity between their wishes and police actions. Unfortunately, this is impossible to determine rigorously. In order to do so, it would be necessary to know both what communities want and what the police are doing. Considering how complex community sentiment is and how varied, subtle, and sometimes hidden police actions are, this is unlikely to be achieved. Moreover, police conformity to community wishes is not produced simply by formal mechanisms of accountability. Police behavior is constrained by all the soft influences of culture, education, and conscience. As a result, the police of one community could have an enviable record of correct behavior, yet have hardly any formal mechanisms of accountability, while the police of another could have an atrocious record but tight formal constraints. So, unfortunately for policymaking, it must be recognized at the outset that the question of the effectiveness of community control must be begged.

At the same time, there is still a role for empirical analysis. What we can do is examine the manner in which countries have approached the task of controlling the police. We can accomplish this by looking at the mechanisms designed to achieve control and the changes that have occurred in them. To this end, the first section of this chapter explores the variety of control mechanisms employed in the world. The second section determines whether countries display characteristic patterns of control. On the basis of this empirical groundwork, it is possible to discuss strategies for achieving responsible police. The third section discusses the interactive dynamic among different forms of control. The final section presents an explanation for distinctive strategies of control in various countries.

MECHANISMS OF CONTROL

The words *control* and *accountability* will be used interchangeably in this discussion. Both refer to the achievement of conformity between police behavior and community objectives. Sometimes a distinction is made between controlling the policy of a police force and controlling the behavior of individual members. The former is then referred to as *accountability*. In my opinion, this is a distinction without a difference. Institutional action is manifest in what members do; control of institutions does not exist if the behavior of members is unaffected. Accountability implies control and control achieves accountability. Both should be understood to refer to processes whereby the behavior of police is brought into conformity with the requirements of the encapsulating society.

Control over police behavior is exerted by mechanisms located both inside and outside the police. Judicial review of the propriety of shooting into a rampaging mob is an instance of external control; demotion in rank of a subinspector by a superintendent is an instance of internal control. Distinguishing between internal and external mechanisms depends on being able to determine the location of control in relation to the police institution. This seems straightforward in principle, but there are difficulties in practice. For example, is the minister of the interior in France inside or outside the police? We may ask similar questions about Police Authorities in Great Britain, managers of public safety in the United States, or police commissions in Japan. One must determine the boundaries of the institution that specializes in police work. In bureaucratic environments, which all modern police forces have, there are various presumptive signs of an institution of policing: the wearing of uniforms, a career service, and a promotion hierarchy. When police institutions are not organizationally specialized, the distinction between external and internal control will not apply.

External mechanisms of control differ from one another in the exclusiveness of their attention to the police. Civilian review boards in the United States, for example, deal single-mindedly with police; police are their exclusive charge. Legislatures, on the other hand, regulate the police as part of a larger mandate to regulate governmental processes generally. They are inclusive rather than exclusive mechanisms of control located externally to the police. The best way to describe this difference would be in terms of the degree of specialization exhibited by a control mechanism with respect to the police. Since *specialization* has already been used in another context, not without difficulty, it might be confusing to reintroduce it here. I shall, therefore, categorize external control mechanisms as being *exclusive* or *inclusive*.

It would be neat theoretically if internal control devices could also be subdivided into exclusive and inclusive sets. Then one would have the usual fourfold typology. This is not possible. By definition, any internal control device applies exclusively to police. But another distinction can and should be made about control within police organizations. Not all internal control is exerted through mechanisms that exclusively control. Some processes within the police are designed explicitly for control; others assist in controlling, but that is not their primary function. I shall refer to these respective internal processes of control as being explicit or implicit. Accordingly, devices for achieving control of the police will be described in terms of four categories: external-exclusive, external-inclusive, internal-explicit, and internal-implicit. I will pay particular attention to the exclusive and explicit subsets, because they reflect self-conscious concern with the need to regulate the police.

EXTERNAL-EXCLUSIVE

The location of external, exclusive control over the police varies enormously among countries. The great division is between countries that put it within government and those that put it outside in ad hoc bodies. In the United States, for example, accountability is exercised by mainline government, usually by officials of the executive branch such as mayors, governors, and the president. On the European continent it is by officials in the ministries of the interior and justice. In Indonesia and Sri Lanka the ministry of defense is in charge. Ministries of defense are also influential in France and Italy with respect to the Gendarmerie and Carabinieri. In other countries, however, control has been shifted outside of government, though it still resides in an official body. In Japan, accountability is exercised through national as well as prefectural police commissions. Members of these commissions are appointed for fixed though renewable terms from among persons who have not held elected or appointed positions in government during the preceding five years (Bayley 1976b). Legislatures define police tasks, establish conditions of service, and provide financial resources, but the public safety commissions supervise all operations, from hiring, promotion, and discipline to deployment, equipment, and procedures. The same is true in Canada, where there are municipal and provincial police commissions, mostly in Ontario and the western provinces.[1] In Britain, all police, except those of the City of London, are supervised by a Police Authority, a statutory body outside local or national government that chooses the chief constable, raises and maintains the force, makes disciplinary decisions, and generally oversees all aspects of operation.[2] The primary purpose of all these external bodies is to ensure competent supervision that is not identified with ongoing political or bureaucratic interest.

Civilian review boards responsible for receiving and investigating complaints about police misbehavior are another form of ad hoc external, exclusive control. Briefly popular in the United States in the 1960s, they have gone out of business in every case (Walker 1977, p. 173). At the same time, there are a few boards of appointed police commissioners that receive complaints as part of their supervisory responsibilites, such as in Detroit and Los Angeles. In addition, there are complaints agencies in other countries with governmentwide jurisdiction, such as ombudsmen in Scandinavia.

When control over the police is exercised from within government, it is by no means always unitary, located at a single place. In Europe, the practice of dividing control has in fact been institutionalized. Routine order-maintenance operations are supervised by one ministry and criminal investigation by another. Control is functionally divided. In the Netherlands the municipal police are responsible to the Burgomeister for all police work except criminal investigations. For the latter they report to the Ministry of Justice. In Norway, police are organized into two divisions: one for order work, supervised by the Ministry of Justice; and one for investigation, supervised by the director of the State Prosecution Authority, a body responsible to the king in council rather than the cabinet. Bifurcated systems are also common throughout Latin America and the Middle East. In Anglo-Saxon countries, by and large, external control is not parceled out functionally among different agencies. At the same time, there may be more than one control agency. Britain's Police Authorities have primary responsibility for supervising police, but the Home Office, through the Inspectorate of Constabulary, exerts important influence. Provincial and municipal forces in Canada, excluding the RCMP working on contract, may be jointly supervised by public safety commissions and provincial attorneys general.

There is also considerable variation in the nature of personnel who supervise on behalf of mainline government agencies. In some places supervision is by elected politicians, in others by appointed civil servants. In France, for example, the line of control, apart from criminal investigation, runs through appointed prefects in each *departement* and then to bureaus in the Ministry of the Interior. A similar system exists in Italy and West Germany (Coatman 1959, pp. 78–92). Political supervision is buffered by a redoubtable layer of bureaucrats. In Russia, control over the ordinary police—the Militzia—is heavily bureaucratized within ministries. Control over the KGB, however, is subject to close political direction through the Communist Party. By and large, this is the continental tradition. In Anglo-Saxon countries, control tends to be more political. In the United States, for example, elected officials exercise fairly immediate control—mayors over chiefs of police, governors over the head of the state patrol, and the president over the director of the FBI. In larger cities, managers of public safety sometimes coordinate supervision as appointed subordinates to mayors, but this post represents only a single layer of bureaucratic separation. In India, control is exerted directly by state and national ministers. It is interesting to note that during the last decade the chief ministers of every Indian state have taken over the direction of the Ministry of Home Affairs. This is a dramatic indication of the importance of the police in political life in contemporary India. Contrast this with the relative positions of the home secretary and the chancellor of the exchequer in Britain or comparable positions in Canada and the United States, where money is much more important than law enforcement in politics.

Finally, in a development that bears watching, some countries are experimenting with local consultative committees of citizens that do not have formal powers of control. They provide a bridge between operational personnel and the populace. Consultative committees can be found in Sweden and Denmark, as well as in several cities in the United States. They are one solution to the problem of enhancing community input without changing formal patterns of control, and are often suggested to appease demands for structural decentralization.

In sum, external exclusive control of the police may be located within government or outside, may be unitary or multiple, and may be carried out by politicians, bureaucrats, or a mixture. Some ad hoc bodies have complete authority over police operations; others review only disciplinary matters; and some are purely advisory.

Because each of the four forms of control contains several features, as we have just seen for external-exclusive, the reader should refer to the summary on page 170 as the discussion progresses.

EXTERNAL-INCLUSIVE

Outside the formal police establishment are a host of institutions that control the police but do so intermittently or indirectly. The most obvious are courts. In many countries, courts are empowered to punish officers for criminal offenses committed in the line of duty; in a smaller number of others, they may award civil damages. Both kinds of sanctions are allowed in Great Britain and the United States. Until the Police Act of 1964, civil damages were paid by British officers from their own pockets rather than by the state. Private responsibility is the rule in most jurisdictions in the United States. Some countries, however, expressly prohibit criminal or civil prosecution of police through the ordinary courts. Instead, as in France, redress may exist through a special set of administrative courts. Special juridical status for police officers, as well as for other civil servants, seems dangerous to people raised in the common law tradition, but administrative courts have unique advantages. Not only may they provide redress to individuals, as courts do in common law countries, but they also have the power to compel changes in operating procedures with a view to eliminating recurrent patterns of error (Langrod 1961, pp. 42–51). They may make administrative rules. Anglo-Saxon courts cannot do this, although their determinations about the legality of police actions may cause far-reaching changes in procedure, as in the case of the Miranda warnings in the United States.[3]

Successful judicial intervention depends in large measure on whether police officers are readily identifiable to civilians. Some countries facilitate this; others do not. In the United States policemen have been required to wear nameplates or badges with numbers since about the middle of the nineteenth century.[4] British police began wearing numbers in 1829. French police, however, still have no individual identifying marks, nor do the Japanese. In order to determine on a worldwide basis the possibility of citizen control over the police through legal remedies, it would be important to chart where identifying marks exist.

Legislatures are also crucial inclusive agencies of control, exercising influence in three primary ways: by creating conditions of service favorable to responsible behavior—such as pay and qualifications for appointment; by subjecting police activity to public scrutiny through questions and investigations; and by withholding resources if conduct does not meet minimal levels of effectiveness or rectitude. Neither the capacity nor the willingness of legislatures to control the police is the same from place to place. In the Netherlands, for example, because budgets are mandated by the Ministry of Justice, municipal councils can investigate police conduct but cannot refuse to provide resources. American legislatures have almost unlimited authority over the police, but they tend to be reactive in interest and unsystematic in evaluation. They rarely develop coherent philosophies of enforcement to help guide the police.

Political parties sometimes directly supervise police, especially when a single party is dominant. This is especially likely to happen if the dominant party is dedicated to radical social transformation, usually as part of an ideological vision of the good society. The Cultural Revolution in China during the late 1960s is the kind of party-inspired event that can dramatically affect policing. Similar influence was exerted by the churches in seventeenth-century Puritan Massachusetts and is exerted today by councils of imams and mullahs in Islamic countries. The Soviet Union, interestingly, although revolutionary ideologically, has not consistently provided for party control of police. The law-and-order police (Militzia), as distinct from the secret police, has by and large been directed by bureaucratic structures of government. Local *soviets* have some directing influence, but since they are only consultative and membership in the Communist Party is not required for participation, party authority cannot be considered strong through them (Karpets 1977; Hazard, Butler, and Maggs 1977, pp. 75–76). Supervision of the police in the Soviet Union, the secret police excepted, is bureaucratic like France rather than political like either the United States or China.

The mass media are certainly one of the most important inclusive mechanisms of control over the police. At least they are potentially so. Their efficacy depends altogether on the general character of political life, especially on whether they are free to inquire about and publicize official actions. In Britain, Canada, and the United States, their influence is enormous. Police forces consider carefully the impact of their actions on public opinion. Sometimes, of course, this leads them to take strenuous action to mislead the public. In countries where the media are not free, they may be used to mold public opinion and behavior so as to conform to the requirements of police operation. Certainly it is a rare government, of any political stripe, that does not earnestly gauge the impact of media presentations of the police on public opinion.

Scandinavian countries have pioneered the development of a unique external-inclusive control device: the ombudsman, who is empowered to receive and investigate complaints about any government official.[5] Like French administrative courts, he can recommend corrections of a programmatic nature.

Finally, many countries have created special institutions to administer personnel policies. Commonly called public or civil service commissions, they may be responsible for recruiting police, discharging them, determining promotions and salary increments, and overseeing disciplinary processes.

INTERNAL-EXPLICIT

A description of control mechanisms within police institutions must focus on processes rather than structures. Most police organizations, especially large ones, have the same kind of differentiated structures. The important question is whether the parts operate in ways conducive to producing conformity between police behavior and community wishes. Five explicit features of internal control are particularly important: the extent of disciplinary power possessed by the organization, the closeness of supervision, the nature of disciplinary processes, the vitality of collegial responsibility, and socialization in rectitude.

The ability of a police organization to control itself depends initially on the extent to which it is allowed to do so. Some forces, such as the Japanese, are virtually sovereign with respect to internal control. Though public safety commissions oversee management, the police themselves, within the scope of law, appoint, dismiss, transfer, promote, and discipline personnel. In Canada, disciplinary decisions within the Royal Canadian Mounted Police are not subject to court review. And the commissioner may award without trial up to thirty days' imprisonment to erring officers (L. Brown and C. Brown 1973, p. 3–6). In the United States, by contrast, senior officers argue that discipline has become problematic because they have lost control of promotion, pay awards, and disciplinary sanctions. Authority in these areas has been effectively transferred to civil service commissions, courts, and police unions. Though such claims cannot be accepted at face value, the fact remains that the authority of senior officers to manage varies considerably from place to place.

Even when the police are allowed to exercise effective control, they may not choose to do so. There are many reasons for this. Supervisory officers may be too busy to attend as they should. This can occur when the ratio of supervisors to line personnel is too low. For example, senior officers in the United States have nearly twice as many lower ranks to supervise as Japanese officers (Bayley 1976b). Or the climate of opinion may be against close supervision. American officers consider police work to be solitary by its nature (Rubinstein 1973, p. 122 and intro.), requiring the development of individual initiative. They hesitate, therefore, to blunt the enthusiasm and sense of responsibility of line personnel by supervising too closely.[6] Japanese officers, on the other hand, stress errorless performance and insist that most enforcement decisions be referred to higher ranks (Bayley 1976b, chaps. 3 and 4). In India the power to enforce law is unevenly distributed through the police rank structure. Constables, in particular, are prohibited from undertaking certain actions. Supervision is so strict over anything they do that they have been relegated to the role of spear carriers in the police drama.

The efficacy of internal control also depends on the disciplinary processes set down. This is a complex topic. Some departments may have written disciplinary codes; others may not. The codes may be specific or general, extensive or limited, petty or substantial. Moreover, effective control depends on the sureness, speed, and strictness with which sanctions can be brought to bear. These in turn are affected by many things, such as the existence of specialized investigatory personnel, the nature of procedures for determining culpability, the presence of legal protections against self-incrimination and for the right to counsel, and agreement to disclose income as a condition for continued employment. The problem of research into these matters is, of course, that police forces jealously guard knowledge of internal disciplinary proceedings. Yet the relative efficacy of such internal processes can only be determined through close inspection.

Control may be considerably augmented within police organizations if collegial responsibility for actions is explicitly developed. Formal command procedures can be supplemented by the willingness of personnel to discipline one another informally. For example, Japanese police officers almost always work in pairs, with the understanding that one officer is responsible for ensuring the propriety of the other's behavior. American officers more commonly work alone and even when working with others are reluctant to be overtly critical. This is not to say that preferences and evaluations are not communicated, but doing so is much less acceptable in the United States than in Japan. In India, too, constables almost always work in groups, but the ethos is against assumption of mutual responsibility. An around-the-world assessment of the readiness of peers to assume informal responsibility for one another's conduct is difficult to make and will always be impressionistic. It seems to me that the Japanese capacity in this regard is greater than the American, the British greater than the Indian, and the Singaporean greater than the Italian. Since peer supervision is closer and better informed than that of senior officers, it is a crucial aspect of internal regulation. It is also one of the most neglected.

Finally, internal control is affected by the kind of training in propriety that police organizations explicitly undertake. Some forces give a great deal of attention to moral instruction, others only passing attention or none at all. Exhortations about doing right are ubiquitous in Japanese policing. Though unremarked by the Japanese, the atmosphere created seems to an American very much like that of a Boy Scout troop or a Rotarian luncheon (Bayley 1976b, chap. 4). Training in rectitude is neglected in American policing. Though troubled by recurring scandals, American officers are much less comfortable than Japanese in speaking to their subordinates about the moral requirements of policing.

INTERNAL-IMPLICIT

Police organizations also affect internal control indirectly, through mechanisms designed for other purposes. Four illustrations will suffice. First, police personnel may be organized into associations, such as unions, brotherhoods, and professional societies. Some develop standards of responsible performance and support organizational efforts to enforce them. Others are defensive in orientation, deliberately working to attenuate organizational control, shielding members from disciplinary sanctions.

Second, control over personnel is powerfully influenced by the vocational sense that personnel bring to their work. If policing is just a job, selected because of its pay and retirement benefits, discipline will probably be looser than where it is considered a calling, drawing upon motivations of community service. Japan and Britain, for example, seem to have developed a greater sense of vocation than the United States or India.

Third, rewards such as promotion, pay, and postings can be given automatically or in recognition of superior performance. They can be used in close connection with considerations of control or not.

Fourth, the extensiveness of social contact encouraged between police and the civilian community can have a significant effect on police behavior. American police believe they should be closely integrated socially with the public, although they have moved more hesitantly to do so in job-related settings. Japanese police act conversely: they are relatively isolated socially from the civilian population but are deployed on the job so as to make regular interaction unavoidable. Throughout the world senior officers are convinced that community contact affects accountability, but they are not sure in what direction. Indian officers worry about poorly paid lower ranks being corrupted by contact; British officers are more concerned that lack of contact will make police personnel ingrown and distant. Clearly the appropriateness of enhancing community contact, professionally and socially, depends on the extent of contact already existing, the nature of the community with which contact is expected, and the proclivities of the police themselves.

This review has shown that there is a complex array of mechanisms by which control over the police is obtained. The major types are as follows:

I. EXTERNAL-EXCLUSIVE
   1. Governmental–ad hoc
   2. Unitary-multiple
   3. Political-bureaucratic
   4. Authoritative-advisory
II. EXTERNAL-INCLUSIVE
   1. Courts
   2. Prosecutors
   3. Legislatures
   4. Political parties
   5. Media
   6. Ombudsmen
III. INTERNAL-EXPLICIT
   1. Hierarchical supervision
   2. Organizational disciplinary proceedings
   3. Peer responsibility
   4. Socialization
IV. INTERNAL-IMPLICIT
   1. Unions and associations
   2. Vocational commitment

3. Reward criteria

4. Community contact

In practice, communities will rely on several types at the same time. They will have distinctive mixtures of the same mechanisms. To give one example, in Great Britain the primary external mechanism dealing exclusively with police are the Police Authorities, which are ad hoc bodies made up of a combination of political and bureaucratic people. Their control is supplemented by Home Office supervision exercised through the Inspectorate of Constabulary and based on the threat to withhold central government funds. External supervision more inclusively comes from a rich variety of attentive institutions characteristic of democratic societies. Parliament, the courts, and the press are most important. Internal explicit control is tight by world standards, the degree of organizational autonomy in matters of discipline high, disciplinary procedures codified, collegial responsibility relatively high, and socialization in rectitude fairly extensive. Within the organization, professional association does not appear to be antithetical to discipline; vocational dedication is reasonably high; reward criteria stress merit; and there is extensive community contact both on and off the job. Note that many of these characterizations are judgmental and are relative to practice elsewhere. Control mechanisms cannot be described adequately without reference to a baseline of comparison.

Considering how important the subject of control is to both police practitioners and social analysts, it is striking that so little attention has been given to mapping patterns comparatively. There are a few studies of particular sorts of control—usually the external-exclusive variety—in particular countries. But there are no general comparative studies, not even lists of countries that use one device rather than another. Formal description, of course, is only the first step. It is necessary to go further and determine whether mechanisms in place are actually used. For example, Japan has nonpartisan police commissions with full authority over the police, but they rarely take initiative in control. Their control is more passive than active (Bayley 1976b, chap. 4). In England, some Police Authorities are more assertive than others (Banton 1975). One Police Authority, for instance, tried to avoid any disagreement with the police, allowed the chief constable to fix the agenda, accepted unquestioningly police recommendations for additional personnel, and repeatedly refused to investigate problems of police-community interaction (Brogden 1977). The same variability in practice has been found among Canadian police commissions (Stenning 1980). In Sweden so-called lay witnesses, who are appointed to observe activities in police stations in order to protect the rights of citizens, have been accused of being coopted by the police, too readily taking the police side. Studies of police control must start, not stop, with descriptions of mechanisms. They must describe actual operation.

NATIONAL PATTERNS OF CONTROL

One can easily confuse patterns of accountability with the structure of national policing, that is, the way in which policing is organized within a country. Americans, for example, commonly assume that decentralization in command assures popular control. Americans have a deeply ingrained fear that centralization in command will bring nonrepresentative control. This is by no means always the case. Decentralized structures of command are compatible with bureaucratic as well as relatively inattentive control mechanisms. Norway would be a case in point. Conversely, centralized systems may be characterized by close and partisan political supervision. This is the case in the several states of India, many of which are larger in both population and territory than European countries. The fact is that the scale and multiplicity of commands are independent of the nature of control over the police, although one caveat should be added. It is probably true that the larger the scale of the political community directly controlling the police, the more likely it is that supervision will be bureaucratic rather than political. Increasing scale makes supervision more difficult to accomplish without delegating authority to civil servants. The American suspicion of centralization on the grounds of unrepresentative control is conceptually confused, but it is founded on a sure instinct. To the extent that centralization involves supervision over jurisdictions of large scale, bureaucratic dominance will become more prevalent. Scale, not command structure, is the key determinant.

At the same time, there is a relation between the location of control mechanisms—not their nature—and the structure of police systems. Police command tends to be concentrated in a political community at those places where accountability is exercised. There is a coincidence worldwide between the organization of political power and the structure of the police. Police command is decentralized in the United States because local communities are powerful politically, at least relative to local communities in places like France and India. Police command is relatively centralized in Italy and Russia because political power is concentrated centrally. The direction of causation is from the organization of political power to the structure of the police. And, except for the caveat previously mentioned, both are independent of the way in which accountability is achieved.

Perhaps even more surprising, the character of government in terms of the openness of political participation does not appear to be related to the way in which external-exclusive control over the police is exercised. Among democratic countries, for example, accountability is achieved variously. France, Germany, and Norway rely primarily on bureaucratic supervision; Great Britain and the United States stress the political. The United States and western European nations tend to use mainline government institutions; Japan and Great Britain have created ad hoc supervisory authorities. Greater autonomy is given to police institutions in matters of discipline in Japan and Canada than in India or the United States. Democracy is clearly compatible with a variety of control strategies. On the other hand, authoritarian regimes may have ubiquitous political oversight as well as bureaucratic supervision. Control by political persons is especially likely where there are dominant parties wedded to a revolutionary ideal or where regimes represent only a part of a heterogeneous and divided population. Even more confusing, it is not clear that bureaucratic control is necessarily less responsive to community wishes than political ones. The American spoils system of the nineteenth century, whereby victorious political parties remade police departments as they pleased, was certainly democratic, but one may question whether it was responsible. Partisanship can undermine an equitable rule of law. For just this reason, expansion of political participation in the Western world has led concomitantly to the development of mechanisms for eliminating partisan control. These have usually taken the form of nonelected public boards, as in Japan and Canada.

Historical evidence, too, for the lack of connection between the character of government and the nature of mechanisms of control over the police, is incontrovertible. Despite enormous changes in the political character of government in most countries during the last century and a half, external-exclusive control over the police is exerted in much the same way in each. By and large, the same kind of mechanisms continue to be used in each country, and the balance between external and internal control is unchanged. French police, for example, have been supervised by bureaucratic officials responsible to ministries in Paris for four hundred years. Even across the momentous divide of the French Revolution, the only change that occurred in control was replacement of the *intendant* by the prefect and the lieutenant general of police by the *commissaire*. Although police forces in communities with fewer than ten thousand inhabitants were taken over by the central government in 1941, the change in control was more apparent than real. The local mayor, whose authority over the police was abolished, had been supervised all along by the prefect in all matters related to public safety (Fossaert and Blanc 1972, p. 10). What has been remarked about the government as a whole is certainly true of the police, namely, that France has for a long time combined "the organization of an empire with the forms of a republic" (Lowell 1914, p. 10).

The control system in West Germany, despite the reforms of three occupying powers after the Second World War, is virtually the same as that of the Second Reich, 1872 to 1933. Though political authority now emanates from legislatures rather than the crown, supervision over the police continues to be exercised by constituent state governments operating through appointed officials. Bureaucracy continues to buffer direct political contact with the police. In the Soviet Union, too, the system of control is clearly that of nineteenth-century Russia, though now vastly expanded to cover the several "autonomous republics." Control is centralized and bureaucratic, apart from the secret police, whose supervision remains in the hands of the paramount political authority— the tsar before 1918, the Communist Party after. Local input is achieved through the *soviet*s, which are communism's version of the nineteenth-century *zemstro*s now made ideologically pure by replacement of gentry with workers and peasants. Their power is still only consultative (Abbott 1973; Florinsky 1953, chap. 14; Seton-Watson 1967, pp. 238–240; Squire 1968, chaps. 1 and 2; Starr 1970, sec. 5 and coda).

India, which might have been expected to transform the organization of police radically after independence, has kept exactly the same system that the British created in 1861. Police power is concentrated at state levels, formerly provinces, and is responsible to political ministers. One change is the attenuation of bureaucratic control represented in the decline in power of the Indian Administrative Service, formerly the Indian Civil Serivce, over the police relative to these political masters. Still, the modern Indian police are accountable to state-level cabinet officials, as the colonial police were responsible to provincial-level cabinet officials. The control mechanisms of the British raj have survived, invigorated by a new political dispensation.

The system of control that exists today in Britain was put in place gradually from 1829 to 1888.[7] It is characterized by local control supplemented by the supervision of the home secretary, who may withhold central government funds in cases of inadequate performance. Not only has local control remained preeminent, but the balance between bureaucratic and political representation remains virtually unchanged, even though the number of forces has been dramatically reduced since 1829. The Joint-Standing Committees that supervised police in the counties in the nineteenth century were composed half of elected persons and half of appointed magistrates. The Watch Committees of the boroughs, however, were completely political. Upon enactment of the Police Act in 1964, all jurisdictions, based for the most part on counties, were given Police Authorities, which are composed two-thirds of elected politicians from local councils and one-third of judicial magistrates.[8] Thus the Police Authorities are both political and bureaucratic, just as the Joint-Standing Committees had been before. In effect, a compromise has been made between county and borough precedents. It should also be remarked that the power of the home secretary over forces outside the metropolis has grown de facto since 1829, while discipline, which continues to be strict, remains primarily in the hands of professional officers (Critchley 1967, p. 197; Fosdick 1915 [1975], p. 50; Reith 1948, chap. 17; Royal Commission 1962).

During the past century in the United States, great changes have occurred in the mechanisms of police accountability—from the partisanship of the spoils system to the professionalism of commissions, managers of public safety, police chiefs chosen for fixed terms, nonelected chiefs, and civil service management. At the same time, remarkable similarities still exist. Though the layer of appointed officials supervising police has thickened, it is still thin by international standards. By and large, control is exercised through mainline government in the persons of elected officials. Managerial autonomy of police chiefs, especially concerning discipline, remains problematic. Police are subject to a host of intrusive pressures from outside. While Americans have become disenchanted with partisan control, they have not been converted to accepting a significantly larger measure of self-regulation on the part of police. Nor are police themselves appreciably more willing to discipline themselves than a century ago. Close supervision by senior officers is resented, with peers uniting defensively against discipline rather than facilitating it. In comparative descriptive terms, American forms of control have changed very little. The significant developments, which have material impacts on the quality of control by the community, have concerned the way in which the external political system operates. The demise of big-city political machines is a dramatic example (Carte and Carte 1975; Fogelson 1977; Walker 1977).

The point is that traditions of police control have enormous inertial weight. Characteristic forms of accountability persist in countries despite major political and social upheavals. This suggests that identical formal control systems can accommodate enormous variations in performance. Control systems in themselves do not determine conformity between police behavior and community wishes. Formal structures are less important than living procedures, an insight that is especially true for mechanisms of accountability located outside the institutions they are supposed to control. Mechanisms are passive; they may be infused with whatever spirit the polity generates. A determined regime, for example, can get what it wants from almost any set of mechanisms. It follows that reform with respect to mechanisms of control is less important for instrumental effects than symbolic ones. That is, the mechanisms eventually adopted in any effort at improvement in police responsiveness are not as important as the messages generated about what the community wants. And these messages are to be understood in terms of current practices in specific places. Institutional reforms of the same sort do not have the same effect everywhere.

As far as future developments are concerned worldwide, two forms of control will probably become more common. First, nonpartisan commissions of control are being established to shift authority over the police outside of ordinary government. Public safety commissions, as they are often called, exist in Canada, Malaysia, Great Britain, and

Japan, as well as in several cities in the United States. The recent National Police Commission in India carefully considered the advisability of establishing them there. As I have already noted, increased political participation does not seem to produce a shift toward accountability structures of a more political sort. Widened electorates seem to be more concerned with fairness and equity in control than in direct participation. By and large, direct political influence is considered beneficial only in countries riven by uncompromising social divisions often of an ascriptive sort, or where ideological fervor is high.

Second, grassroots consultative committees are becoming increasingly popular. While governments everywhere give lip service to the need for police to be responsive to local conditions, they are reluctant to devolve supervisory authority onto local bodies. Consultative committees are the device often suggested to balance a greater measure of local autonomy with existing patterns of control. These bodies take various forms, such as crime councils in the United States, crime prevention associations in Japan, Rukun Tetangga in Malaysia, and People's Police in the Soviet Union.

THE DYNAMICS OF ACCOUNTABILITY

Communities interested in controlling their police more closely have complex choices to make, as we have already seen. Are there any principles that should guide these decisions so that police behavior can be made more assuredly conformable to community standards? Is one set of controls likely to be more effective than another?

The most fateful choice, in my opinion, involves the relative reliance placed on external as opposed to internal controls. In principle, internal processes are to be preferred, for at least three reasons. First, internal regulation can be better informed than external. A determined police can hide almost anything it wants from outside inspection, certainly sufficiently so as to make outside supervision haphazard. Second, internal regulation can be more thorough and extensive. It can focus on the whole gamut of police activities, not simply on the more dramatic and visible aberrations. Third, internal regulation can be more varied, subtle, and discriminating than external. It can use informal as well as formal mechanisms that are omnipresent in the professional lives of police personnel. Altogether, then, a police force that is willing to make its behavior conform to community standards is much more likely to be effective than an unwilling police force required to conform under threat of external regulation.

The problem that arises, however, is that external and internal regulation, while conceptually distinct, may be empirically related. To begin with, communities that rely on external supervision probably doubt the utility of internal control, while communities that stress internal regulation have less perceived need for regulation of any sort. Communities tempted to expand external control have probably already given up on internal regulation. They do not have a free choice. More importantly, however, opting for external supervision may actually reduce the capacity for active internal self-regulation. The efficacy of internal self-discipline may be related to reliance on external supervision. If this is true, then the preferred strategy for making police accountable—responsible self-discipline—can be undermined by external controls designed to achieve the same purpose. This formulation contradicts an assumption widely accepted, notably among Americans, that increasing external regulation is a way of increasing internal discipline. There are no trade-offs, in effect, between these forms of control. Clearly this is a momentous issue to resolve.

On a priori grounds, the proposition that external regulation impinges on internal processes of regulation is plausible. External control is exerted when police institutions are thought to have failed to meet their responsibilities. External control reflects suspicion both of police behavior and of the institution's inclination to set it right. Read by the police as an indictment, external regulation impinges on police pride and self-esteem and confirms their impression that the public does not respect them. Persistent intrusion by agencies outside the police also threatens organizational autonomy. The natural inclination on the part of the police is to begin to dissemble, covering up mistakes and putting appearances before discipline. In these circumstances, senior officers often find regulation of subordinates very difficult. In order not to be considered outsiders themselves, losing the leverage that comes from solidarity, they turn a blind eye to misdeeds. Gradually, the capacity of the institution for self-discipline—by peers or supervisors—is undermined. Defensiveness, riding on embitterment, destroys effective self-regulation. Unfortunately, the cycle is self-perpetuating. As discipline declines, impropriety increases and the public becomes even more distrustful. As the need for reassurance increases, external control becomes more attractive. The tragic part of this interaction is that a reinforcing downward spiral is created. Public belief that discipline is lax leads to an insistence on heightened external control. External control diminishes police self-esteem and command solidarity. Declining capacity for self-regulation weakens restraints on discipline. And the weakening bonds of individual dedication, peer responsibility, and supervisory legitimacy lead to new instances of indiscipline. Through this dynamic, external regulation achieves less in accountability than it might, though there are instances when it is the only likely recourse.

This is not all conjecture; there is some evidence, albeit impressionistic, to support the theory. In the United States, suspicion about police misbehavior is common, and people are inclined to believe the worst. As a result, external disciplinary intrusion is common, emanating from a variety of sources. At the same time, police pride and morale are low, and policemen display defensive solidarity against the civilian community, often denying the legitimacy both of external control as well as the standards brought to bear by outsiders. Internal regulation, on the other hand, is formalistic, cumbersome, and suspect in the eyes of policemen. Finally, of course, the record of scandal and impropriety in American policing is dramatic (Goldstein 1977; Reiss 1971, pp. 128–129; J. Wilson 1968, pp. 231–232). Japan is the mirror image of the United States in all these respects: the public thinks police behavior is exemplary; external interference, especially with respect to discipline, is both strict and legitimate; and police misbehavior is remarkably rare by world standards.

Though a wider test of this theory is not possible with the data at hand, some corroboration comes from diverse intellectual sources. First, external regulation of the police is a form of control through deterrence, exactly analogous to the actions of criminal law with respect to deviants generally. For a variety of reasons, criminologists doubt the efficacy of deterrence, especially what is called general deterrence. They tend to believe that self-imposed control or control informally exerted is much more effective than formal sanctions. If this is true for criminal behavior generally, it may be no less true for potentially non-conforming policemen.

Second, police officers themselves, especially in the United States, seem to have perceived the relation between pride and self-regulation. The persistent talk in police circles for almost fifty years about "professionalism" indicates that they want to be considered as conscientiously responsible as members of other professions. "Professionalism" is a plea for respect, the kind of respect that comes from being trusted.

Third, there is one psychological study that has demonstrated a relation between pride and the acceptance of discipline, although the study was not conducted among policemen (Day and Hamblin 1964).

If the reasoning presented here is correct, we must give careful attention to the mix of external and internal controls over the police. It may be a mistake for some countries reflexively to increase external intrusions when the behavior of the police is discovered to be poor. Such actions may merely make a bad situation worse. Japanese experience shows that the cycle of reinforcement can spiral upwards, if only the chain of interaction can be broken at some point and reforged. Doing this, however, requires an extraordinary act of faith on the part of the communities involved, since they must decide in the face of perceived bad performance that the police can be trusted to put their house in order. For many countries such a move would defy cherished political and cultural traditions, as will be discussed shortly. Americans, notably, would be instinctively opposed, and not without reason, since the imposition of informal controls by peers, while inevitable to some extent, is often considered oppressive and improper.

In the search for mechanisms for achieving conformity between police activity and community wishes, three principles should, I believe, be borne in mind. First, because only policemen can really know what other policemen are doing, the most effective form of control is internal, especially that which emanates from peers. Second, too great a reliance on external supervision can be counterproductive, weakening active and responsible regulation by police officers over one another. Third, it follows that the primary value of external mechanisms of control may not be instrumental. That is, external supervision is not so important for its direct and specific effects as for the reassurance it gives the public that someone is watching on their behalf and that in cases of default by the police there is a second line of defense.

DETERMINANTS OF CONTROL

How can differences in forms and processes of control among contemporary countries be explained? Since the array of devices in most countries is large, an exhaustive analysis would be very elaborate. I propose to narrow the question by examining only the relative reliance that different countries place on external as opposed to internal regulation in achieving responsible police behavior. The balance struck from place to place between these sources of accountability indicates the relative autonomy of the police as well as the state of public regard. Moreover, there is a dynamic between external and internal control, as I have just argued, that affects the likelihood that meaningful accountability will be achieved. Reasons of policy, as well as of parsimony, lead to an examination of the determinants of this balance.

Obviously, the reliance that communities place on external supervision is related to the preferences communities have for it. But this, in turn, is shaped by the perceived success of internal controls. External intervention is more likely to be used when internal regulation is thought to be ineffective. If police can be counted on to keep their own house in order, then civilian oversight can afford to be relaxed. Public perceptions of the correctness of police performance may, of course, be mistaken. But barring misreading, the less successful the internal control, the greater the tilt is likely to be in favor of external regulation.

Macrosocial factors—such as economic development, urbanization, technological innovation, and mass education—would not seem to be important determinants of the balance between external and internal control. If they were, control strategies for countries would not have been so stable historically. The fact is that great social changes have occurred around the world in the last century or so, but characteristic patterns of control have been largely undisturbed. It seems much more reasonable, therefore, to expect that the explanation for national differences in control is to be found in the domain of culture, meaning learned sets of preferences and behaviors. This would be borne out if countries that rely on external control and have weak processes of internal supervision share with one another general orientations toward government and authority and vice versa. There is evidence that this is the case.

The United States relies as exclusively on external mechanisms of control as any country in the world. Americans do not trust the police to regulate themselves. In order to assure conformity to community wishes, Americans put their faith in external scrutiny and correction by politicians, civil service boards, ad hoc commissions, courts, complaints committees, and private organizations such as the American Civil Liberties Union and the National Association for the Advancement of Colored People (Haller 1976). Americans believe with Thomas Jefferson that the price of liberty is eternal vigilance, implying unrelenting watchfulness over all processes of government. Indians in South Asia, sharing the view that disinterested administration is uncommon, also stress external supervision of bureaucracy, usually through political parties. At the other end of the spectrum, the Japanese police are expected to discipline themselves. Though Japan has the same array of external mechanisms as the United States, they are not used as actively. By and large, the Japanese police anticipate disciplinary problems, conscientiously trying to avoid actions that would affront the public. There is a strong preference in Japan for informal group regulation rather than stern external supervision. Other countries fit somewhere between these two extremes. Canada and Great Britain appear to occupy a middle position, their people having greater faith than Americans in professional self-regulation but being more willing than the Japanese to authorize external penetration of the police. I judge Norway, France, and Germany to be located more toward the Japanese end of the continuum.

With respect to the vitality of internal control, Japanese tend to believe that enhancement of professional dedication and group responsibility obviates the need for external supervision. Japanese police assist in maintaining exacting standards of discipline. In every work group, even two-person patrols, someone is recognized as being senior, hence responsible for the behavior of others. Hierarchy, one might say, is so pervasive as to eliminate peers. Even when Japanese police socialize off duty, the senior person present, which may be only by virtue of length of service, can be held responsible for the misbehavior of the others. In the United States, on the other hand, junior officers unite defensively in a "conspiracy of silence" to frustrate supervision that might result in punishment of a colleague (Bayley 1976b, chap. 4; Rubinstein 1973; Sherman 1981). Great Britain occupies an intermediate position once again—closer control from superiors and peers than in the United States but less than in Japan.[9] Canada is more like Britain than the United States. My information on the internal regulatory vitality of other countries is too meager for me to place them along this continuum.[10]

Accepting the necessity of external control and a diminished capacity for self-regulation appear to me to be part of two larger cultural orientations. The first of these is an orientation toward government. This dimension consists essentially of two contrasting positions, which I shall refer to as *contractual* and *statist*. Societies with contractual orientations toward government rely more extensively on the external regulation of the police; societies with statist orientations rely more on internal regulation.

People in countries that rely on external controls, like Americans, are more distrustful of bureaucracy generally than people in countries that do not, like Japanese or Germans. They exhibit much less deference customarily to government officials. Government service is not considered an especially high calling, but an occupation that honest amateurs might do well enough if they had a mind to. Americans, and to a lesser extent the British, also tend to doubt the benevolence of government; they think, therefore, that its authority must be strictly limited. Government should be allowed to do only what people specifically require rather than paternalistically doing what might be in everyone's interest. As a result, broad grants of administrative authority are discouraged; bureaucratic discretion is limited by law, which is not to argue that it may not be very great in specific instances (Bayley 1976*b*, chap. 7; Goldstein 1977, pp. 72–73). Countries that rely more extensively on external checks also have stronger traditions of individual self-help and assertiveness. People are expected to defend their own rights. The government helps those who help themselves, the corollary being that government cannot be trusted not to abuse power. Personal influence, lobbying, and politics are not just activities guaranteed by law; they are what prudence requires of any citizen. Respect for the institution of law as such, therefore, is not great. Law is an instrument; it is important for what can be achieved through it. Finally, reform of government in these same countries is unlikely to be programmatic. Specific problems require specific solutions, making reform both reactive and ad hoc (C. Robinson 1970; J. Wilson 1968, pp. 233–234). It is

preferable, because it is more practical, to provide for avenues of redress for specific problems rather than try to enhance the capacity of
the police for autonomous and responsible self-regulation.

Altogether, countries that stress external more than internal control
in policing have traditions of individual self-help, laissez-faire government, distrust of bureaucracy, nonelite civil services, relatively narrow
grants of administrative authority, and law viewed as being useful but
not sacrosanct. Countries at the other end of the spectrum have opposite traditions: subservience, paternalism, elite civil services, respect for bureaucracy, broader grants of administrative authority, and
deference to law.

The second general cultural orientation that appears to determine
the balance between external and internal regulation is the psychological capacity of people for group self-regulation. Described dichotomously again, the dimension is bounded by societies whose people are
communitarian and those that are *individualistic*. Communitarian societies encourage group self-regulation; individualistic ones hamper it.

Japanese police, for example, display great pride and sense of vocation. Being a policeman is not simply a job; it is a way of life, with
gratification derived simply from belonging. As a result, proper behavior is encouraged by stressing the importance of maintaining the reputation of the force rather than by threatening individuals with punishment
for misdeeds (Van Maanen 1974). Discipline has a positive rather than
a negative character. The acceptance of authority and acknowledgment
of dependent membership is greater, too. By contrast, the psychic grati-
fications of being a policeman in the United States are very mixed.
Membership is a curse as well as a benefit (Bayley and Mendelson
1969, chap. 2). Indeed, discipline itself is a threat, not a source of
pride. Taught to stick up for their rights, American officers do not accept the legitimacy of disciplinary sanctions; they often try to subvert
them, just as civilians do legal restrictions on them. In the face of error,
the customary attitude of American officers is not shame and contri-
tion, as in Japan, but truculence and defense. More largely, officers do
not work collaboratively to prevent abuses (Bayley 1976b, chap. 4;
Walker 1977, pp. 55–56; Wambaugh 1974). The person who assists
superiors in maintaining discipline is regarded instead as a "stool pi-
geon," "squealer," or "fink."

The readiness of police to accept discipline and to identify personal interests with organizational ones is shown by whether appeals against departmental judgments are allowed. Countries with weak internal control tend to allow officers to use politicians, lawyers, the courts, or unions to protect themselves against their own institutions. Like their compatriots in contractual societies, they too are distrustful of paternal bureaucracies, even their own. The United States and India have very nearly hamstrung effective internal regulation by the prevalence of outside appeals. Japan, and to a lesser extent Britain, have been much more careful.

Internal discipline may also be facilitated by a structural feature of police organizations. Effectively self-regulating forces tend to have greater tolerance for stratified recruitment to higher ranks. Senior positions are not automatically filled by persons promoted from the ranks. Supervisors are, therefore, less likely to share the subculture of the lower ranks and to have close social relations with them (Chevigny 1969, chap. 14; Hahn 1971). A marked exception is India, where there are three separately recruited cadres: rank and file, noncommissioned officers, and gazetted officers. The chasm socially between officers and rank and file is so great, trust so uninstinctive, that effective supervision is severely compromised. Even speech patterns are affected, so that officers are addressed by subordinates in the third person, as in "Will the Superintendent like to take tea?" The Indian example suggests that the relation between social distance among ranks within the police and effective supervision may describe a U-shaped curve: up to a point, increases in social distance may enhance internal control, allowing senior officers to put organizational interests above the promptings of camaraderie, but beyond that point it may become counterproductive, cutting senior officers off from informative interaction.

There are, then, two general intellectual-cum-psychological orientations that may be associated with the balance between external and internal control of the police: an orientation toward government and an orientation toward social relations. The relation between each of them and control strategies may be formulated in two hypotheses: *First*, reliance on external supervision with respect to the police will be greater in contractual than in statist societies. *Second*, reliance on external supervision will be greater in individualistic than in communitarian societies, because the former will be relatively ineffective in achieving appropriate police behavior through internal self-regulation.

The argument developed here asserts implicitly that formal structures of control over the police are shaped by modal attitudes of individuals in society. Moreover, what people believe to be proper in terms of formal mechanisms of control over institutions is related to what they will tolerate individually in terms of discipline. Americans rely on external modes of control with respect to police. They are suspicious of government and know instinctively that meaningful internal discipline is problematic. Japanese, on the other hand, rely more on internal regulation because they are more respectful of authority and know that internal controls would work if they were themselves involved.[11]

It is tempting to speculate that the political and cultural orientations specified here are themselves empirically related—statist political philosophy with a communitarian orientation toward society, contractual political philosophy with an individualistic orientation toward society. While I am inclined to believe that communitarian societies will tend to be statist, the converse is not true—individualistic societies are not necessarily contractual. The relationship between these two orientations takes the discussion far afield, so I shall leave the resolution of it to others.

Finally, inspection of the groupings of countries' cultural orientations suggests that there may be one structural factor that affects strategies of control. Countries that rely on external accountability, like India and the United States, are extremely heterogeneous socially. Japan and Great Britain, which emphasize more internal regulation, are less so. This suggests that where social cleavages are sharp, especially as related to ascriptive criteria such as race, caste, religion, and ethnicity, authoritative institutions are not trusted to regulate themselves; they must be closely watched, carefully controlled, and deliberately counterbalanced lest they fall into the hands of antagonists. Trust in government and regulatory processes is less where groups feel the need to mobilize in explicit self-defense. Americans in the nineteenth century, it has been said, "were much less afraid of the idea of police in the abstract than they were afraid of what their political opponents would do with such a force" (Walker 1977, p. 6). The British, on the other hand, did not view police as an instrument of partisan advantage, although sometimes of class conflict, but feared public policing as a threat to everyone's liberties (Silver 1967). The general implication is that heterogeneous societies are more likely than homogeneous societies to view

Figure 7.1

FACTORS SHAPING THE BALANCE
BETWEEN EXTERNAL AND INTERNAL CONTROL OF THE POLICE

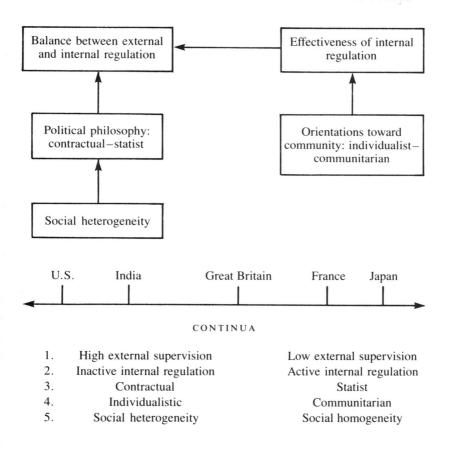

CONTINUA

1.	High external supervision	Low external supervision
2.	Inactive internal regulation	Active internal regulation
3.	Contractual	Statist
4.	Individualistic	Communitarian
5.	Social heterogeneity	Social homogeneity

government and politics instrumentally and thus are more likely to be contractual in political culture.

In sum, I have suggested that three factors shape the mixture of external and internal controls with respect to the police. They are political philosophy (contractual/statist), normative orientations toward social relations (individualism/communitarianism), and social heterogeneity. Figure 7.1 shows the patterns of association and the placement of several countries with respect to both the modes of control and the determining factors.

CHAPTER 8

Police in Political Life

The role that police play in the political life of countries has probably attracted more attention than any other topic in comparative police studies. The reasons are obvious. The police are to government as the edge is to the knife. The character of government and police action are virtually indistinguishable. A government is recognized as being authoritarian if its police are repressive, democratic if its police are restrained. It is not an accident that dictatorial regimes are referred to as "police states." Police activity is crucial for defining the practical extent of human freedom. Furthermore, the maintenance of social control is fundamentally a political question. Not only does it powerfully shape what a society may become, but it is a matter in which governments feel a vital stake, for they know that their own existence depends upon it. For all these reasons, the police are in politics, whether they recognize it or not.

While identification of the police with government lends excitement to the study of the police, putting them at the center of politics, it also creates a significant intellectual problem. If the character of police activity is a crucial indicator of the nature of regimes, then the role that the police play politically cannot be explained in terms of regime character. It is tautological to say that a repressive police role in politics is caused by the existence of a nondemocratic government, when one knows that the regime is nondemocratic because the police are playing a repressive role in politics. Great care must be taken to avoid this kind of circularity. For the same reason, attempting to explain variations in police impingement on politics is audacious, because unless one is careful, it amounts to accounting for the nature of the government, which has been the classic question of political analysis since Aristotle. On the other hand, when the character of government is distinguished without reference to police actions, but instead by the extent of participation, structure, social representativeness, and so forth, it is perilously easy to conclude that the police do whatever governments require. The only escape from this truism is to take on, once again, the intellectual burden of explaining the differences in the imperatives that drive regimes. The reciprocal relations between governments and the police is too important a topic to ignore, but it represents a logical thicket that impedes dramatic generalization.

This chapter will explore first the ways in which police impinge on political life, searching especially for patterns of involvement that persist historically in different places. Attention will then be given to discovering circumstances that encourage police intrusion, avoiding easy inferences from regime character to police action.

FORMS OF POLICE IMPINGEMENT

The police affect political life in six general ways, each containing several variations. First, police often determine who can participate in politics by their decisions with respect to arrest, detention, and exile. Such practices may be directed at political opponents systematically, as in the Soviet Union, or haphazardly, as in Pakistan. More subtly, the criminal law may be used simply to harass and frustrate opponents. Opposition politicians in many countries frequently claim that police file false charges and enforce minor laws more strictly against them, thus encumbering their money and time in lengthy defense. A ramified criminal law in the hands of a determined police can make life very difficult for law-abiding citizens.

Second, the police in many countries are given explicit authority to regulate political processes. This takes several forms. During the nineteenth century, American police were often in charge of balloting. Since they were controlled by political parties, they sometimes turned a blind eye to repeat voting or intimidated people into not voting (Richardson 1970, p. 36). The Spanish police during the 1930s screened would-be voters on a crude class basis by turning people away whose shirts did not have collars (Brenan 1943, p. 30). The Japanese police today are responsible for enforcing laws regulating electioneering, such as the use of loudspeakers in public places, the distribution of campaign materials, and solicitation and expenditure of campaign funds. Though enforcement has been scrupulously evenhanded, such powers would be easy to abuse.

Since police everywhere have authority to regulate conduct in public places in the interest of safety and order, political meetings, parades, and demonstrations fall under police scrutiny. Organizers are commonly required to notify the police and obtain approval. The police may routinely give permission, as in Denmark where only one rally has been banned since 1938, or they may precipitate endless delays or outright rejection, as in the Philippines (Great Britain, Police College 1974). Italian prefects and *questores*—provincial chiefs of police— throughout the late nineteenth and early twentieth centuries closed meetings, banned parades, confiscated posters, and arrested demonstrators in order to assure the dominance of the governing party (Adams and Barile 1961, pp. 217–218; Fried 1963, chap. 3). In imperial Germany all clubs and societies were required to file copies of their constitutions as well as lists of officers with the police. The police had to be notified twenty-four hours in advance of all public meetings on political subjects (Fosdick 1915 [1975], p. 76). Police regulation is not always restrictive. In Great Britain and the United States, police have protected unpopular groups, such as Nazi parties, in the exercise of their right to hold public meetings. In India and elsewhere they have defended the rights of strikers to picket, placing themselves squarely against the interests of powerful groups.

Freedom not only to associate but also to speak and write is essential to open political competition. Regulation of these processes through censorship is often entrusted to the police. It is in Russia today, following immemorial tradition; it was in imperial Germany after 1872, where copies of all newspapers and periodicals had to be submitted to the police. They could confiscate without trial any publication whose contents urged disobedience of the law, incited class hatred, threatened public order, or showed disrespect to the emperor or the prince of a *Land* (Fosdick 1915 [1975], p. 76).

Police affect political processes not only by what they do but also by what they do not do. When opposing groups use force against one another, the police may decide the issue by standing aside and allowing the stronger to win. Many politicians in India hire thugs known as *goonda*s to disrupt meetings, intimidate opponents, and deface campaign advertisements. In the 1840s the New York City police allowed Mike Walsh's Spartan Band and Isaian Rynder's Empire Club to prevent supporters of political opponents to vote on election day (Richardson 1970, p. 36). Because the Communist Rotfront repeatedly assaulted the police during the Weimar Republic, 1918–1933, while the Nazi Sturm-abteilung (S.A.) did not, the police began to view the Nazis as their friends. As a result, during the climactic events of the early 1930s they let the Nazis fight the Communists to the finish, confident that a Nazi victory was in the interests of order (Liang 1970, pp. 94–95). Acts of omission can have as deadly an effect as acts of commission, but they are much harder to substantiate.

Finally, the police influence political processes by giving material aid in open contests for political power. Especially in less developed countries, they sometimes provide transportation to politicians, bring voters to polling places, and distribute campaign material. Even in developed countries, police have been used to marshal electoral support for governments, issues, or persons. Because the police represent a large, ready-made, and pervasive network, the temptation to use them, especially by incumbent governments, is often irresistible.

Third, when governments are faced with concerted violent opposition, police action may decide whether they stand or fall. At the onset of the revolution in France in 1789, the police offered no resistance to the urban mobs and simply took off their uniforms and faded away. In 1851, when Napoleon III overthrew the existing government, the police played the opposite role, engineering a bloodless coup that has been described as "an intensified police action, made possible by the army" (Bramstedt 1945, p. 37). During the liberation of Paris in August 1944, the prefecture of police became a strongpoint of organized resistance as the police fought pitched battles with the retreating Germans. The Berlin police have been irresolute against revolutionary activity at several crucial periods in German history. In 1848 they initially defended the revolution but quickly changed sides when the army intervened on behalf of the government. When the Kaiser was overthrown in November 1918, police rank and file defied direct orders to defend the regime (Liang 1970, pp. 27ff.). By the early 1930s, suffering from what has been described as "political exhaustion," the result of being caught between Communists and Nazis for almost a decade, the police allowed Nazi intimidation to create a tide that swept Hitler to power and the world into war (Liang 1970, pp. 93–95).

The Italian Carabinieri generally failed to resist Mussolini's Squadrista, partly out of sympathy with Mussolini and partly because the government vacillated. As in Germany, the populace began to look to the Fascists to save them from the turmoil the Fascists had deliberately created. In Spain in 1931, the commander of the Guardia Civil caused the collapse of the dictatorship of Primo de Rivera and the establishment of a republic when he decisively withheld support for the king (Brenan 1943, p. 241). Police performance was inconsistent in the civil war: where local commanders were loyal, the police stood by the republic and against the generals; where they were not, the Guardia sided with the army (Brenan 1943, p. 216; Carr 1966, p. 655).

Considering that the police are the first line of defense against attempts to overthrow regimes by force, it is curious how few studies there are of them at critical watersheds in political history. There are certainly many fewer than of the military. This relative neglect probably stems from the fact that police action is rarely dramatic; it is too much a part of routine processes of governing. Climactic turning points arise to some extent because the police have had their turn and failed. To use a military metaphor, police are committed piecemeal to political struggles. By the time choice with respect to forceful involvement can be determinative, their cohesiveness has often been destroyed, their loyalty compromised, and their effectiveness eroded.

Fourth, the police influence politics by clandestine activities such as spying and provocation. Probably the most notorious of the forms of police intervention in politics, these practices are the hallmark of "police states."

Unfortunately, the terminology used to describe such operations is clumsy and inaccurate. *Secret police* and *political police* are pejorative phrases commonly used to describe agents of government who clandestinely influence political outcomes. The first problem with these terms is that police are not the only agents of government that secretly spy and disrupt political activities. The French Renseignement Genereaux, Britain's MI 5 and Special Branch, Russia's KGB, and the United States' Federal Bureau of Investigation and Central Intelligence Agency are often labeled "secret" or "political" police. Though they all operate secretly to some extent and are often directed at political objects too, they are not all police. A secret police, following the discussion in Chapter 1, is an agency authorized to use physical constraints within a community and does so covertly. The Central Intelligence Agency of the United States, therefore, was not designed to be either a secret or a political police, though it became one during the 1960s and 1970s when it did forceful counterespionage in the United States in violation of its charter. The FBI, however, is clearly both—a police agency working secretly to monitor and sometimes change political outcomes. Secret political police, properly called, may be created by entrusting existing police agencies with the responsibility for clandestine activity in politics or by creating covert organizations for use in politics whose members also have authority to apply physical constraint. The root of the terminological problem is that there is no word to describe covert political agents of government who are not police. Neither "spy" nor "agent provocateur" are apposite. On the other hand, just as not all secret political agents are police, not all secret police operatives intrude into politics. The joint federal, state, and local "strike forces" in the United States, which have been created to investigate and prosecute "organized" crimes, are an example. Finally, "political police" are not necessarily "secret police." Police often operate quite openly, as we have seen, to affect political processes. In short, then, the attributes of being political, secret, and police do not always go together in any combination. In particular, the custom of associating secrecy and a political object with police is damaging to an understanding of both policing and political manipulation.

American police at all levels act as secret political police. In order to prevent violent actions that are politically motivated, they routinely collect information secretly about political activity. An indication of the scope of this activity was revealed by congressional investigators who found that by the early 1970s the FBI had collected over a half-million intelligence files, each representing an individual or group; had investigated 740,000 subversive targets in the preceding twenty years; and had 7,482 "ghetto" and 1,200 "domestic intelligence" informants to whom it paid $7.4 million per year.[1] Even more disturbing to public opinion, the FBI had infiltrated a large number of organizations they considered subversive—including the civil rights movement, black and white racist organizations, antiwar groups, and the radical left—in order to disrupt their activities. They would use their access to sow dissension, urge unwise actions, and obstruct routine functioning. They also spread misinformation about people and groups in order to destroy their reputations and hence their efficacy as political advocates (International Association of Chiefs of Police 1976, chap. 8). In the most celebrated case, the FBI attempted to blackmail Martin Luther King,

Jr. (Halperin et al. 1976, pp. 111–115). Under the intense public pressure generated by the congressional investigation, the FBI ordered provocative, as opposed to passive, penetration of political groups stopped in the mid-1970s (J. Wilson 1980).

Russia has had specialized, secret, and centralized political police for centuries. Ever since Ivan I created the Oprichnina in the early seventeenth century, Russian governments have given enormous enforcement powers to special operatives centrally directed to collect information on public opinion, spy out dissent, and neutralize threats to the regime. They have worked independently of the ordinary public police and, except for brief periods, have been responsible to paramount political authority rather than to bureaucratic ministries. The model is the secret police of Nicholas I, known as the Third Section. Created in 1826, its name refers to a unit within the imperial chancery (Monas 1961, p. 62; Squire 1968, pp. 48–62, 228–230). The Bolshevik Revolution in 1918 did not change these traditions. In the Soviet Union the secret police, now referred to as the KGB, has been directed by the Politburo, the supreme leadership council of the Communist Party, except for one year immediately after the fall of Lavrenti Beria, when control was transferred to the Ministry of the Interior.[2]

The Sicherheitspolizei of imperial and Weimar Germany and the Geheimstaatspolizei (GESTAPO) of the Hitler period were both secret police. They were branches of the police given responsibility for active and passive operations directed at political persons and processes. While both were located within the Ministry of Interior in Berlin, the Sicherheitspolizei had authority only in the state of Prussia, while the GESTAPO had power throughout Germany (Goedhard 1954).

The secret and systematic monitoring of public opinion and political activity has been a core function of French policing for centuries. It is carried out by the Renseignement Genereaux, which is part of the National Police. Control is exercised directly from Paris, bypassing the normal chain of command through commissioner and prefect. The British, on the other hand, did not develop a secret political police until 1884, when the Special Branch was created within the London Metropolitan Police (Critchley 1967, p. 161). Though spying both at home and abroad has been documented from Tudor times in the late fifteenth century, such agents were not given enforcement powers. That lay with magistrates.[3] When the British did combine police power and covert political surveillance in a bureaucratic way, they placed them within an accountable police organization. They did not create a separate force, as did Russia and Nazi Germany. The Home Office's MI 5 also collects and collates intelligence of a political sort, but if constraint is required, it requests the ordinary police to carry it out. MI 5, then, although secret and political, is not police. Special Branch detectives, too, even though they are police officers, traditionally defer to overt personnel if offensive actions are necessary (Clayton 1967, chap. 3).

The fact is that all governments develop some capacity for monitoring and intruding secretly into political life. But it is enormously misleading to say that all governments have secret and/or political police. Governments differ a great deal in the powers authorized, the extent of secrecy, the range and scale of operations, and the location of such operations with respect to police organizations.

Fifth, police affect politics directly by becoming protagonists in policy-making within governments. In some countries, like the Soviet Union, police power is acknowledged through representation in high councils of government—for the KGB in the Politburo, for the Militzia in the Councils of Ministers at the center and in the republics. In other countries, senior professional police personnel are expressly excluded from general policy councils. This is true in the United States, Britain, India, and Japan. Though they have ready access to top leadership, they do not participate in the development of policy that does not touch their narrow competence. Of course, police may also be powerful within government in informal ways. Napoleon, Hitler, and Stalin depended on their chief policemen—Fouché, Himmler, and Beria, respectively— for wide-ranging information, support, and advice. This kind of secret access is easy to abuse as police play on the fears of political leaders for their own purposes (Radzinowicz 1957, pp. 561–562). Most unscrupulous of all, police can affect policy by using secret intelligence to blackmail politicians and officials into supporting police positions. J. Edgar Hoover, first director of the FBI, was believed to have extensive files potentially damaging to many public people. He even shared some of this titillating information with presidents.[4] Belief in the existence of such information, whether it existed or not, may have caused people to mute their disagreement with the FBI, even though the threat was never made explicit.

Police occasionally enter the political arena as avowed spokesmen for particular issues. In the United States, for example, they have introduced referenda against civil review boards, mobilizing support so successfully that in every case the boards were eliminated (Walker 1977, p. 173). In Britain the Police Federation has outspokenly opposed homosexuality, abortion, and the abolition of capital punishment (Reiner 1980). Police favor is wooed because in democratic countries they can mobilize a bloc vote that may determine election outcomes. Police exchange electoral support for solidarity with them on "law-and-order" issues.[5]

Sixth, police have considerable latent power with respect to all policy that requires law enforcement as part of implementation. If police are unwilling to apply appropriate constraint, the programs may be undermined. This has been the case for dowry limitation in India, alcoholic prohibition in the United States, and land reform in parts of Latin America. Even the intimation that police support is problematic may be enough to discourage policy initiatives. At the other extreme, police can undermine policies through too scrupulous enforcement, applying the law so mechanically that public anger is aroused. Though rare, this has happened, as in the case of traffic enforcement policies in the United States.

In summary, the police can affect political life in six important ways: by determining the players, regulating competitive processes, defending or not defending regimes from violent attack, covertly monitoring and manipulating political groups, advocating policy inside and outside government, and providing material aid. These modes of impingement do not, however, exhaust the subject. These are the major modes of direct influence, that is, where a political objective is consciously pursued. But the police influence politics in indirect ways as well. Though these are rarely recognized and still less often calculated, their effect may be profound. Let us examine several forms of indirect influence.

First, because police are government incarnate, they are society's most pervasive teachers about civic values. An American study found that government is personified for primary school children by the president and the policeman (Easton and Denis 1969, chap. 10). Later the saliency of policemen declines as children learn more about the impersonal workings of government. Children coming from sections of the population with pronounced negative views toward the police, like black and Hispanic children in the United States, may develop significantly different orientations toward government than children from sections more favorably disposed (Bayley and Mendelsohn 1969).

Some authors have even argued that police are formative actors in the determination of national character. Charles Reith has attributed the vaunted British traits of orderliness, courtesy, and respect for law to the police (1948, pp. 83–89). The British public was by no means always law-abiding and peaceable. On the contrary, until the nineteenth century it was violent, disorderly, and tumultuous. It changed, Reith argues, as a result of the forbearance, impartiality, and stolid good humor shown by Peel's New Police after 1829. Geoffrey Gorer, too, believes that the British internalized the norms of the Bobby. This occurred because national character is modified by "the selection of personnel for institutions that are in constant contact with the mass of the population . . . and in a position of authority" (Gorer 1955). A Canadian study even purports to have tested this theory. Skagway and Dawson were raw frontier towns on the Yukon River in the late nineteenth century, the former in American Alaska, the latter in the Northwest Territories of Canada. Although both were inhabited by the same kind of violent, migratory, questing people, Dawson was recognized at the time as being considerably more law-abiding and orderly. The difference is attributed to the disciplined example set by the Northwest Canadian Mounted Police (Morrison 1974).

It is revealing that the two countries where the police are supposed to have exerted the most beneficial effects on the public—Britain and Canada—are the only two countries that use policemen as symbols representing quintessential qualities of national character (L. Brown and C. Brown 1973, p. 1,927). What is rarely considered is that other police forces are having as great an effect, both on natives and foreigners, but not in nearly so favorable a manner. Very few countries have grasped the lesson that what the police do reinforces or subverts the values of the larger political system. One case is Japan, which used the police, army, and schools consciously during the Meiji period to foster a modern set of orientations toward the nation. Another is contemporary Malaysia, where the police are constantly pressed to exemplify a new moral awareness that will serve to educate the populace at large.

Second, the police are in a position to influence powerfully the legitimacy of government and its attendant processes. Their use of force particularly can be momentous in the lives of individuals and can shape political movements. If the police are habitually brutal, hostility is kindled toward themselves and the government they represent. Francis Place, the "Radical of Charring Cross," noticed that police brutality in handling demonstrators played into the hands of extremists and tilted control of working-class movements away from moderates such as himself. In what would otherwise seem paradoxical, he is credited with inventing the baton charge by foot officers as a substitute for sabre-wielding cavalry (Reith 1948, chap. 9). Moderation appears to have worked, since the battle between police and demonstrators at Coldbath Field in 1833 was the last time a mob came out expressly to discredit the police. Restrained handling of Chartist demonstrations in 1839 and 1842 again confirmed moderate leadership (Radzinowicz 1957, p. 251). On the other hand, repeated acts of brutality by the Guardia Civil in Spain during the nineteenth and early twentieth centuries brought contempt upon themselves and the government, almost always generating vengeful counterattacks. Ferocious police repression in the 1890s, especially in connection with the anarchist bombings of the Lido Theater and Corpus Christi procession in Barcelona, triggered reprisals that included the assassination of three prime ministers during the ensuing twenty years. Liberal Europe reacted to police barbarity with anger and contempt, rekindling memories of the "Black Legend" of Spain during the Inquisition (Carr 1966, p. 441; Brenan 1943, p. 74). Political extremism became inevitable in a situation where police dealt with trade unionists in three ways: drawing up a "hit" list and paying to have them shot, arresting them and shooting them for allegedly trying to escape, and releasing them from jail and having them killed by *pistoleros* before they could regain the safety of working-class neighborhoods (Brenan 1943, chap. 4). The legitimacy of the republican government was severely undermined in 1933 when the Guardia razed the village of Casas Viejas by airborne bombing and executed twenty-five peasants. The incident began when peasants on a large *latifundia* in Andalusia, thinking that the millennium had arrived with the establishment of a republic, went to a local Guardia station to invite policemen to join them in tilling the fields. The police became frightened and responded with shots. Enraged, the peasants besieged the police station (Brenan 1943, p. 247). Two years later Guardia personnel were hacked to death in Oviedo in explicit retaliation for the Guardia's overreaction at Casas Viejas. In circumstances like these, which have not been confined to Spain, suspicion between government and populace becomes ingrained and trust appears naive.

Third, police indirectly affect politics because, due to their unusual visibility, they are a kind of demonstration project for the problems and potentials of the nation—integration or division among classes, castes, races, or religion; merit or ascription in employment; honesty or venality in public life; and equality or inequality before the law (Potholm 1969).

Fourth, the police contribute to the economic development of a country. They may do so by contributions of labor, as in Indonesia, or physical equipment, as in Africa. They also affect development by the demand they generate for literate personnel, educated leadership, technical skills, improved roads and electronic communication networks, and equipment and scientific hardware. Generally, police are forward-looking developmentally, anxious to utilize what is new so as to compare favorably with their professional counterparts in other countries.

It should be apparent by now that police have considerable influence on politics whether they choose to use it or whether they even recognize it. The ways in which they impact politics are much more varied than is generally supposed, as the summary list in the following outline indicates.

I. MODES OF DIRECT INFLUENCE
  A. Open
    1. On persons
      (a) by arrest
      (b) by detention
      (c) by exile
    2. On processes
      (a) by election supervision
      (b) by regulation of public meetings
      (c) by censorship
      (d) by acquiescence in intimidation
      (e) by physical support
    3. On regime under attack
    4. On policy
      (a) by formal participation
      (b) by influence through privileged access

    (c) by threats of nonsupport
    (d) by political mobilization
  B. Secret
    1. by surveillance
    2. by manipulation
II. MODES OF INDIRECT INFLUENCE
  A. By socialization of the public
  B. By legitimization of government
  C. By demonstration-effect
  D. By participation in development

In all of this discussion, I have not mentioned the core contribution of the police, namely, maintaining orderly, predictable processes of community life. Public safety—a tarnished but useful phrase—is the bedrock on which all social processes rest. The quality of life and the consequent demands people make on government are shaped by judgments that police make about such seemingly technical matters as priorities in law enforcement, the emphasis given to crime prevention as opposed to investigation, and the manner in which any police activity is undertaken.

TOWARD COMPARATIVE JUDGMENTS

Making judgments about the relative role of the police in politics among countries, or among communities of any kind, is important. Indeed, it is unavoidable among politically sensitive people. But judgments are difficult to make for several reasons.

First, reliable information is lacking, especially in precisely those communities where the police role is largest.

Second, comparative description must deal with multiple dimensions of impingement. Intrusion takes place in many ways, not all of them immediately obvious. If people keep score on different dimensions, disagreement about the police role is inevitable. Even when similar matters are assessed, overall judgments may vary as greater importance is placed on one form of intervention than another. What does one say by way of summary of the police role in politics in country A, which has systematic clandestine surveillance but no overt assistance to incumbents, and country B, which forbids secret manipulation of political outcomes but installs police in the paramount councils of government? When multiple dimensions of analysis are present, some system of weighting each is necessary when making an overall judgment.

Third, qualitative judgments must be made about the nature of police intrusion. France in the time of Napoleon III and the Soviet Union under Stalin have both been called "police states" (Payne 1966; Bramstedt 1945). Both had elaborate networks of spies, public opinion was closely monitored by government, and competition for political power was exceedingly limited. But the French people in the mid-nineteenth century were not generally punished for their beliefs, concentration camps were unknown, and letters were rarely opened. Surely there is a world of difference between the "police states" of the Napoleons and the commissars.

Fourth, the enterprise of making accurate comparative judgments is encumbered by disagreements over the morality, necessity, and justifiability of similar practices in different places. People raised in the Western liberal tradition assume that police should not be involved in determining political outcomes; they have been taught to believe that the police should be neutral. The police serve the law, not regimes; institutions, not persons. Accordingly, almost any intrusion into political life is condemned. From this perspective even mild amounts of intervention are regarded with horror. But objections to neutrality can be raised on two grounds—ideological and situational. And both may be used to discount police intervention in one place where it would not be countenanced in another. Substantive notions of justice or of the just society often require that certain kinds of people be excluded from political influence. Governments in Russia, China, and Cuba make this case against large landlords, ascriptive aristocracies, and capitalists. Other governments single out different targets, like adherents of certain religions, castes, tribes, or national communities. Police neutrality is acceptable when the procedures of politics can be counted on to serve the dominant vision of justice. When this is not so, a community may feel that partisan intrusion by the police into politics is required. Situational factors also undermine the value of neutrality. What should the police do if, for example, a community is confronted with an onslaught of terrorist violence committed by people dedicated to curtailing political competition? The Italian government faced this with the Fascist militia, the Malaysian government with the Communist Party, and the Weimar Republic with both Nazis and Communists. Justice may require what looks like a partisan intrusion into politics. The same question might be asked with respect to the IRA in Britain, the PLO in Israel, the RSS in India, and the Ku Klux Klan in the United States. The need to protect innocent people rather than passively awaiting criminal outrage tempts the police into secret and sometimes preemptive action. Neutrality can be terribly expensive, in terms not only of political outcomes but also of human life. Unfortunately, the limits on neutrality are rarely discussed carefully. Even less often are they made matters of public directive. The result, in countries of very different political stripe, is that the police frequently take action uninstructed except by their own sense of what needs to be done.

In order to analyze comparatively the reasons for differences in the police role in politics from place to place, we must be able to characterize that role accurately. Analysis faces a choice: either to proceed disaggregately, separately treating each dimension of impingement, or to simplify description, either through summing the various readings or focusing on a few to the exclusion of the rest. The latter strategy is clearly the simplest and the one that will be adopted here. Three modes of impingement I consider particularly revealing, as well as easy to obtain general impressions about, are the extensiveness with which the police overtly constrain processes of political competition; their thoroughness in monitoring politics clandestinely; and the salience of their presence formally in the councils of government. Countries can be recognized, I believe, as having distinctive traditions in each area. The task of analysis will be to explain them in terms of contextual factors.

DETERMINANTS OF POLICE INTERVENTION

What conditions are associated with traditions of police intrusion in politics, as indicated by persistent and extensive activity of the three kinds stipulated? Some ciues have been provided by multinational comparisons using aggregate data in the contemporary world. Using information from Banks and Textor's *Cross Polity Survey* (1968), Philip Coulter discovered a moderately strong inverse relationship between an active police role in politics and economic development. That is, police were more active in countries with low per capita gross national products.[6] The only other strong association was with the political character of regimes. Other variables—such as linguistic homogeneity, population, urbanization, industrial employment, and racial homogeneity—showed at best very weak relationships. The finding that police activity in politics and the character of regimes are linked is not tautological, because regime character was operationalized without reference to police activities.[7] Another study based on the same cross-national data found that police activity in politics was related to a measure of administrative centralization (Holmes 1972, chap. 6). While the character of the regime and economic development would both seem plausibly to underlie police activity in politics, rather than the other way around, the direction of causation cannot be inferred between police activity in politics and administrative centralization. Further research on this point is required. Together, the findings from contemporary cross-national research can be summarized as follows: an active police role in politics is less common in countries that are relatively well developed economically, have democratic regimes, and are administratively decentralized.[8]

That regimes based on limited political participation need police to maintain those processes, thus giving police a larger role in political life, is obvious. What isn't obvious is why there are significant differences in the police role in politics among countries that have similar kinds of governments. Though regime character clearly influences the police role, variations in tradition are possible as a result of other factors. What are they? One of them appears to be the manner in which state power was consolidated territorially. For example, police development in Austria, Russia, and France was intimately tied to achievements of dynastic hegemony by the Hapsburgs, Romanovs, and Bourbons, respectively (Payne 1966, pp. 3–26; Radzinowicz 1957, pp. 570–574; Squire 1968, pp. 228–229; Rosenberg 1958). On the other hand, police were created in Great Britain, Canada, and the United States to enforce the king's peace under the common law rather than sustain a particular political regime. In these countries police traditions were not marked by the need for political espionage or repression. The point is that police are more likely to be active in politics if they have been created initially to defend the interests of regimes. If the impetus to their creation were law-and-order needs of the populace generally, they are likely not to be active in politics.

The point about the consolidation of dynastic power can be subsumed in terms of a larger, more powerful principle. The specific factor that catalyzes police entrance into political life is group violence that is perceived to be threatening to establishments of state power. By implication, criminal insecurity does not impel police into politics; only political insecurity does. And the earlier that politically relevant criminality, particularly violence, occurs in statebuilding, the more likely a tradition of police intrusion is to be developed. Russia offers a dramatic illustration. Russia has confronted bloody rebellions, coups, and assassinations since Ivan I subdued the Boyars in the seventeenth century. Fear on the part of tsars for the crown and of landowners for their estates combined to produce a political alliance that resulted in systematic repression against dissident political elements and land-bound serfs (B. Moore 1967, part 3). The legacy of police control was confirmed rather than expunged by the Bolshevik Revolution and the civil war that followed. The French, too, forged police institutions amidst violence against a consolidating state. Special police institutions were created in the latter half of the seventeenth century after Bourbon kings were confronted with regional rebellion in the Fronde in 1648 and 1649 (Gruder 1968). On the other hand, police intrusion into politics in Prussia developed much more slowly than in either Russia or France, reflecting the more consensual pattern of consolidation. Not until the nineteenth century did violence internally threaten the regime, notably in 1815 and 1848, with the most severe restrictions on political freedom being applied in 1878 after two unsuccessful assassination attempts against the emperor. The laws passed then allowed the police to crush the Social Democratic Party and to hound its members into exile.[9]

The rule that group violence threatening political order impels police into politics is again confirmed by the experience of Britain, Canada, and the United States. The Special Branch of Scotland Yard was formed in 1884 expressly to deal with violence associated with agitation for Irish home rule.[10] The Chartist agitation of the 1830s and 1840s, though involving vast numbers of people, did not pose a violent threat to the political system, which is not to say that there were not many people who thought otherwise. The demonstrations were con-

tained without violence, and covert penetration was not undertaken by
the police. Intelligence gathering *was* done by the Home Office, but it
was haphazard and informal, done by private persons, largely gentry.
The authorities were very concerned not to jeopardize the growing reputation of the New Police for aboveboard behavior (Mather 1959, chap.
6). In Canada, intelligence gathering of a political sort by the Royal
Canadian Mounted Police was not extensive until the early 1920s,
when it expanded sharply in response to increased labor agitation immediately following the First World War, the Winnipeg general strike of
1919, and the "red scare" of the same years (L. Brown and C. Brown,
chap. 3). In the United States, secret repressive activity by police began
in the 1880s and was justified by anarchist violence attributed to European immigrants and the growing labor movement. This was a turbulent
time, with bombings in Chicago, repeated outbreaks of violence in the
Pennsylvania coalfields, the assassination of President McKinley, and
attempted murders of industrialists J. Pierpont Morgan and Henry C.
Frick (International Association of Chiefs of Police 1976, p. 3). A second surge of unrest and reaction took place after World War I. America's "red scare" produced arrests and harassment of thousands of immigrants, socialists, Wobblies, and union organizers in a campaign led
by the federal attorney general. Law enforcement officials were actively assisted by numerous citizens' associations, such as the notorious American Protective League, in what amounted to a national witch-
hunt (International Association of Chiefs of Police 1976, chap. 2).
During the 1920s and 1930s, police penetration of unions and "leftist"
political groups became routine, conducted primarily by local rather
than federal agencies. The connection between group violence directed
at the political order and police reaction can be seen a third time during
the 1960s, when riots, demonstrations, and bombings, stemming from
racial unrest and dissatisfaction with the Vietnam War, led to an enormous intensification of covert police action, both passively and actively.

It is worth noting that both violent subversion and elite anxiety move
across international borders, rather like communicable diseases. Elites
throughout Europe and North America reacted more or less in concert
to encourage police surveillance and disruption in the face of dramatic
increases in strikes, terrorism, and agitation at the turn of the century,
again after World War I, and finally in the late 1960s. Jacobinism in the

early nineteenth century and communism after 1918 generated the same synergism internationally.

Governments may themselves prompt popular resistance by the mobilization demands they make that in turn leads to increased police penetration. Russia is a classic case. Hardly was power consolidated by the Bolsheviks after the civil war than the government embarked on collectivization and the ruthless dispossession of the *kulaks* from 1928 to 1933. This was followed by wide-ranging purges of the party and bureaucracy from 1934 to 1938, confirming the position of the secret police at the right hand of Stalin (Juviler 1976, pp. 33–39; Conquest 1968, chap. 3). The same thing happens during wartime when resistance to conscription, taxation, or rationing prompts intensified surveillance in the name of national defense.

Thus, a tradition of police activity in politics is more likely where state-penetration and consolidation are coupled with mobilization demands that generate violent resistance.

There is another factor that may be related to variations in one specific form of police intervention in politics: domestic spying and surveillance. Other things being equal, police will be more active in the covert collection of political intelligence in societies that have a tradition of insistence on right thought and right belief.[11] It has always seemed to me significant that the French word for *spy*, which is *mouchard*, is taken from the name of Antoine de Mouchi, theologian of the University of Paris, who was appointed inquisitor by Francis I (1515–1547) (Radzinowicz 1957, p. 544). When a community demands conformity in thought, public penetration of private social life, though not necessarily by the police, knows no effective bounds. Soviet leaders no less than Russian tsars have viewed thought to be as dangerous as action. Their tradition is one of almost paranoid suspicion of nonconforming opinions, especially those emanating from abroad (Florinsky 1953, pp. 283–286). Russian secret police have acted as agents of moral control for generations, believing it necessary to probe behind political action to discern whether family, religion, ideology, party, or regime were being threatened by improper thoughts. One of the major purposes of the Third Section was censorship, just as it is today for the KGB. How different the tradition is in Great Britain, and by inheritance in the United States and Canada, where Elizabeth I is reported to have said, "I shall not build windows into men's souls." Even though England, along with the rest of Europe, was embroiled in religious antagonism between Catholics and Protestants, the English spurned the Inquisition and forged a tradition wherein acts, not thoughts, were the proper focus of government surveillance. Domestic spying was undertaken by Thomas Cromwell, the secretary of state of Henry VIII, as the king struggled to break with the pope. Spies, informers, and agents provacateur were used intermittently by both Protestants and Catholics against one another when they had control of government, but their use sharply declined with the political settlement of the religious issue in the Glorious Revolution, 1688 (Tobias 1972). In the United States, too, insistence on religious conformity was short-lived and confined to the few original colonies. Though persecution of religious believers has occurred from time to time, it has not been at the behest of government. Tolerance is the principle that has become enshrined in the American Constitution (Lipset 1963).

By this argument, theocratic states could be expected to have more extensive police spying, other things being equal, than secular ones— just as countries with serious and persisting religious divisions would be more likely to have traditions of police spying than those that do not.

The relation between spying and right belief is complicated analytically because thought and action are related empirically. Regimes insist on conformity not only because right thought is considered to be morally enjoined, but also because seditious action is linked to thought. Since thoughts expressed are cues to action, successful prevention requires attention to them. This was the justification for intensifying police surveillance of political movements in the United States after both world wars, as well as during the agitation against the Vietnam War. One can expect, therefore, that police spying will be more active where opposition is violent and expressed in ideological terms.[12] Very often, however, the presumption leads not only from thought to action but also from action to thought. Ideological motivations become attributed to people who perpetrate violence or lawbreaking, often in disregard of the palpable grievances underlying the act. The danger of lawlessness is enhanced by associating it with ideological conspiracies. A vicious cycle is generated that allows any disruptive act to excuse political surveillance. Thus, during the 1960s, ghetto violence in American cities was widely attributed to Communist conspiracy rather than rage over discrimination and impoverished living conditions. Ideas can indeed breed violence, but violence is not always ideologically inspired.

The police may also be encouraged to intervene in political life due to factors that relate to their narrow corporate interests rather than those of society at large. It seems logical to expect that the police will be more likely to be fastidious about intrusive political activity if they identify with a regime's challengers. Attachments and sympathy of policemen can be important in moments of political confrontation unless offset by training and discipline; ideological orientations restrain or impel their intervention into politics. In the United States at the turn of the century, police rank and file tended to be antiunion and antiradical, even though they were working class in origin themselves (Richardson 1970, pp. 200–201). This was not the case in Britain, explaining in part why American police appear to have been more willing than British to act covertly against trade-union organizations. British police officials, supported by leading politicans, recognized that in order to ensure the reliability of the police, as well as earn the toleration of the lower strata of the population, tactics against working-class movement had to be scrupulously impartial under law (Miller 1977). Police are probably also more likely to intrude politically when their own interests are threatened. Their mobilization politically to overturn civilian review boards in the United States recently and to raise wages in India are cases in point. Not surprisingly, American police covertly infiltrated groups organized to investigate and expose abuses of police power. It follows that intervention by police in politics for what are perceived as defensive reasons becomes increasingly likely as police develop institutions to express corporate solidarity. Police are more likely, therefore, to intervene in politics when public hostility to them is actively expressed, police self-esteem is low, and organization in their own interest has been undertaken (Janowitz 1960, pp. 426–438).

In summary, then, police will play a more active role in politics if competition for political power is deliberately restricted by government; if public police have been created initially to defend political regimes; if an existing political order is threatened by social violence; and if there is a cultural tradition of insistence on right belief. Intrusion is also facilitated if the police themselves identify with the regimes rather than its attackers and police feel they have been attacked themselves or have been especially disadvantaged.

CONCLUSION

Throughout this book questions have arisen about the relationship between police attributes, such as centralization and their role in politics, and the character of government. In previous chapters regime character was found to be a formative factor in police development. In this chapter, patterns of *mutual* impingement were discovered—the police affecting politics, politics affecting the police. Let us now put both sets of pieces together, clearly setting forth the specific patterns of interaction.

Regime character affects two features of police functioning: centralization of police command and the extent of police intrusion into political life. Regime character does not, however, affect the nature of tasks performed by police, apart from those related to politics. It does not change the amount of nonenforcement tasks that police undertake or the amount of auxiliary administration they do. Regime character does not affect the number of overlapping forces a community has nor the mechanisms by which accountability is achieved.

Conversely, police clearly do affect the kind of governments communities have. One must be careful here to avoid circularity in argument. Police may appear to be affecting the character of government because what they do is itself an indicator of the character of government. Police repression, for example, is assumed to be regime repression. But police behavior does have independent political consequences. Police actions taken on their own critically affect political competition and mold social processes, which in turn shape political life. Even when the police are studiously neutral in terms of direct impingements, they can contribute to the erosion of political legitimacy by being venal, brutal, arrogant, or secretive. At the same time, the organization of the police does not affect politics. Whether police are single or multiple, centralized or decentralized, supervised by politicians or bureaucrats, self-disciplining or not, stratified or egalitarian in rank structure, and specialized or unspecialized makes no difference to the quality of political life. The sole exception may be the creation of interest associations by the police. Yet even here the effects are quite ambiguous.

The words of the British Royal Commission on the Police have caught the essence of the matter:

British liberty does not depend, and never has depended, upon . . . any particular form of police organization. It depends upon the supremacy of Parliament and the rule of law. We do not accept that the criterion of a police state is whether a country's police force is national rather than local—if that were the test, Belgium, Denmark and Sweden should be described as police states. The proper criterion is whether the police are answerable to the law and, ultimately, to a democratically elected Parliament. It is here, in our view, that the distinction is to be found between a free and a totalitarian state. In the countries to which the term police state is applied opprobriously, police power is controlled by the government; but they are so called not because the police are nationally organized, but because the government acknowledges no accountability to a democratically elected parliament, and the citizen cannot rely on the courts to protect him. Thus in such countries the foundations upon which British liberty rest do not exist (Royal Commission 1962, p. 45).

PART V
CONCLUSION

CHAPTER 9

The Future of Policing

Viewed internationally as well as historically, policing displays enormous variety. Cops are not the same everywhere. This statement is meaningful only if the concept of *police* is defined carefully, recognizing that uncertainty will inevitably remain in the characterization of some personnel. If the definition of *police* is left vague, variation in policing may simply be a result of difficulty in recognizing who police are. Accordingly, I have defined *police* as people authorized by a group to regulate interpersonal relations within a community through the application of physical force (Chapter 1). This formulation deliberately decouples the notion of police from authorization by states. Unless this is done, one faces the paradoxical conclusion that policing exists only in states. This limits comparative historical analysis because it renders invisible the evolution of policing from nonstate to state auspices. An alternative solution is to expand the notion of *state* to encompass authoritative regulation by any community, such as tribes, castes, churches, guilds, and industrial corporations. This is awkward because it does violence to common usage.

Since, however, policing in the modern world is dominated by personnel who have been authorized by states—that is, by sovereign, territorially defined, political communities—analysis in this book has focused exclusively on their development and functioning. But even these police vary in a host of fundamental features, such as the number of forces, their coordination, centralization, accountability, impact on politics, work performed, instigation, relations with the public, and strength—all despite essentially similar legal authorization.

What is the future of this variegated institution? Is it possible to predict on the basis of patterns in police activity and development around the world? I think it is. This concluding chapter will recapitulate the important lessons learned in previous chapters and will draw out their implications for the future.

First, although modern policing is dominated by personnel who are paid and directed by the governments of states, it is not clear that this situation will remain unchanged. Public agency in policing is by no means an exclusively modern phenomenon, and there is evidence that even now the trend may be reversing (Chapter 2). The rise in public police can be attributed to two factors: the consolidation of state power in the face of violent resistance and widespread public disenchantment with customary private (nonstate) security arrangements. It follows that as long as states exist, some public police will remain, especially if their monopoly of political power is threatened by violence. At the same time, public disenchantment can turn against any set of security arrangements, whether public or private. It is simply an historical accident that in our recent past private ones were found inadequate. If the public's disaggregate security needs are not met by states, then private police arrangements may be resuscitated. This development is most likely under the following circumstances: where state power is unchallenged politically, where criminality directed at private persons is perceived to be a serious and increasing threat, and where ideology does not preclude private security. These conditions obtain today in the capitalistic West, where private police and security agents sometimes outnumber public ones.

Since the analysis in this book has concentrated on public police under state authorization, the predictions that follow will deal exclusively with that sector of contemporary policing.

Second, there will be an intensification of policing in all countries in the foreseeable future (Chapter 4). The total volume of crime in the world, though not necessarily the crime rate, will undoubtedly increase in the future, because of increases in population as well as the probable breakdown of informal discipline in traditional social groups, especially in rapidly modernizing countries. As a result, the number of police personnel will grow steadily. While the ratio of police to population may not rise, there will be more police in relation to territory. Police will become thicker on the ground and thus more visible than they are today. This may improve their efficacy in crime control; it is arguably easier to impose discipline on a large population in a small space than on a small population in a large space. This remains to be demonstrated, however—a procedure that must overcome significant methodological problems, in particular the difficulty of constructing a reliable measure of variations in the incidence of crime.

Third, the structure of national police systems will remain largely unchanged from country to country, except where there are marked and persistent upsurges in collective, regime-threatening violence (Chapter 3). In the latter places, there will be movement in the direction of increased centralization. These effects will not be the same wherever collective violence occurs, because they can be attenuated by bureaucratic traditions. The structure of police systems is relatively invariant in the face of even major dislocations of a social or political sort. More surprising, perhaps, is the fact that national police structures—described in terms of the number of forces, centralization, and territorial coordination—are independent of the political character of governments. Because of the obduracy of bureaucratic tradition, there is no convergence historically among countries with respect to the nature of police structures, even among countries of similar political stripe. Centralization will be more likely to occur in the future in newer states that are affected by collective violence, in those where bureaucratic traditions are less well established, and in any states undertaking programs of social transformation or resource mobilization that generate violent popular resistance. On the assumption that such circumstances are likely to be common in the future, this hypothesis suggests that there will be an incremental increase in the amount of centralization among world police forces, especially in Africa, the Middle East, and South and Southeast Asia.

Fourth, major changes are unlikely to occur with respect to national modalities for exerting control over the police, except that all countries will feel more compelled than in the past to create at least the appearance of grass-roots consultation (Chapter 7). In some places, this will happen because governments are learning the value of mobilizing populations for public security, both collectively and individually conceived; in others, it will happen because of populist pretenses, often impelled by pressures from minority ethnic groups.

As in the case of national structures of police, mechanisms for ensuring accountability are relatively invariant historically. This statement has meaning with respect to the emphasis placed upon external as opposed to internal supervision and with respect to the exclusiveness of focus by external control agencies. States display remarkable continuity over substantial periods of time in the ways in which they control the police because their choices are governed by two great normative orientations that change very slowly. The first is an orientation toward

government—one polar view being that government is created instrumentally by citizens to achieve individual purposes and the other that
governments embody the distinctive purposes of the collective community (contractual versus statist). The second orientation is toward social
relationships, particularly whether individuals or groups should be regarded as having normative priority (individualist versus communitarian). The degree of social homogeneity may also affect control strategies, with less homogeneous societies emphasizing external modes of
supervision.

The modes of control chosen for achieving accountable police behavior are independent of both the territorial structure of the police
within a country and the character of national government. The easy
assumption that there is an association between devices that ensure accountability, on the one hand, and political character of government
and structure of public administration, on the other, needs to be chal-
lenged. This finding, although it must be subjected to rigorous and extensive testing, has important implications for engineering more accountable police. The essential lesson is that administrative structures
are less important for control than the substantive injunctions that are
passed through them. Accountability does not depend on the structure
of the police or the particular mechanisms chosen to control it. It depends on the activating philosophy of the encapsulating political system. Since controlling devices and the character of government appear
not to be related, it follows that any set of supervisory devices may be
equally effective in conveying the instructions of the political system.
A determined regime can use any set of mechanisms to control the police as it wishes. The medium is not as important as the message.
Therefore, changing formal institutions of control or structures of command, as reformers almost always do, is only important as a means of
underscoring substantive concerns about police operations. This is not
to say that tinkering with formal arrangements should not be done, simply that the effects of such changes wear off rapidly unless the substantive message about reform is reinforced repeatedly.

Fifth, direct and knowing intervention by the police in politics will
become increasingly common in the future. Although all police affect
politics in some ways—directly and indirectly, knowingly and un-
knowingly—explicit attempts by police to shape political life are associated particularly with authoritarian regimes, with political cultures

that insist on ideological conformity, with mobilization regimes faced with popular resistance, and with new states born and nurtured in acute domestic violence (Chapter 8). Since these conditions appear to be waxing in our age, I look for the police worldwide to be even more significant political actors in the years ahead.

Sixth, there is no evidence to suggest that the range of work that police must be capable of handling in the future will change substantially, apart from new forms of crime that are tied to technological development. With respect to the major categories of police work—law enforcement, criminal investigation, human servicing, crowd control, traffic regulation—evolutionary simplification does not appear to be occurring (Chapter 5). Police work is not becoming either more or less specialized. The only powerful exception will occur in states that have high levels of collective violence, where the state will monopolize the direction of police work at the expense of the general public. Where collective violence persists, police forces will concentrate on protecting the interests of the state, although it is not clear that this represents much increased specialization; the requirements of maintaining state security are also varied, especially as the police begin to play a larger role explicitly in politics. Excepting this, countries create police work idiosyncratically in a complicated interaction between police and public that is unaffected, so far as existing evidence shows, by major socioeconomic transformations (Chapter 6). The scope of police work will probably remain as varied as it is in most places today.

Police almost everywhere will continue to perceive an acute tension between law enforcement and servicing. As the volume of crime requests grows in the future, the temptation will be to simplify police work by specializing in law enforcement, even if the proportion of service-related to crime-related demands does not change. This tendency could be offset by increases in police capacity represented in increments of personnel, especially if, as I have suggested, territorial intensification of policing produces unexpected gains in police efficacy. In any case, the disparate demands on the police will most likely continue to produce a dilemma for them. Their primary raison d'être is the protection of life and property; yet as crime problems increase, so too do distractions from the main purpose. The state requires them to contain rising crime. The public agrees but disaggregately requires the police to deal with a large proportion of noncrime matters. The public's aggregate and disaggregate demands are different, a situation intensified in countries that have democratic political systems. The police are caught cruelly in between, with the personnel most intensely affected being the lowest-ranking police officers, who know both the reality of public demand and the pressure of political priorities.

One obvious solution to this problem is to have the police concentrate on crime-fighting and hand over servicing to other government agencies. The police would specialize in emergency intervention when life and property are in danger and in catching criminals after crimes have occurred. In effect, the police would be allowed to do what official policy says and what the public believes they do already. Crime prevention by the police would be accomplished through deterrence, through swiftly and surely bringing criminals to the bar of justice for exemplary punishment, as well as through patrolling while awaiting emergency mobilization. To some extent this has already taken place. Fire and ambulance services have been created in many countries for use in emergency noncriminal situations. Because emergency services are costly, however, further development of specialized rapid-response instruments is unlikely to occur. The police will probably remain the state's primary all-purpose agency for emergency response in the foreseeable future. They will reduce the burden on themselves by developing more effective procedures for establishing priorities on calls and transferring noncriminal matters to other agencies, such as detoxification centers, homes for battered women, drug therapy facilities, juvenile shelters, rehabilitation homes, hostels for unwed mothers, marriage counselors, and mental health hospitals. This, too, has begun to take place in many countries.

Simplifying police work in this way has the effect of highlighting the crime-control responsibilities of the police. That is indeed its rationale, for it takes the police at their word about what they are equipped to do. It also puts them in a political bind. They must now sink or swim in terms of their effectiveness as agents for crime control. They must show that what they do results in enhanced protection, in crimes *not* occurring. It is not enough for the police to publicize arrest statistics, because the public does not want only revenge, it also wants security. But the police know that their deterrent ability is slight unless they turn communities into virtual concentration camps. They admit privately that if the evidence is examined closely, their credibility as crime-fighters might collapse. Curiously, then, while policemen frequently chafe at the noncriminal problems brought to them by the public, they share secret doubts about whether they can spend their time much more profitably as exclusive crime-fighters. Concentrating on crime-fighting may not be as attractive for police as many hard-pressed officers think, because it may force a test of their crime-protection efficacy that they cannot pass.

The political problem that police face is at the root a methodological one. How can they show that their activity has caused something *not* to happen? Most government agencies, such as schools, hospitals, and the postal and fire services, validate themselves by recording and publicizing what they do—teaching people to read, curing the sick, delivering the mail, putting out fires. What they do is closely related to what they accomplish. This is not the case with the police, who pathetically continue to serve up information about their activity—such as arresting people and investigating reported crime—as if it indicated that they were being successful. Records of police activity routinely maintained simply do not prove that patrolling and catching criminals prevents crime. To make that case, the police need to develop ways of measuring variations in the real incidence of crime. This is intellectually tricky and enormously expensive. The irony is that although the police are considered one of the state's most essential services, their utility is uniquely difficult to demonstrate. In the future, therefore, the need for police will be increasingly dramatized but their efficacy increasingly questioned.

Instead of specializing in crime-fighting, the police might resolve the tension between aggregate and disaggregate demands by recognizing the linkage between them. It is already clear that without a sympathetic, cooperative public the efforts of the police to prosecute criminals is undermined. Research evaluating the utility of traditional police practices shows this clearly (Clarke and Heal 1979; Greenwood and Petersilia 1975; Kelling et al. 1974; Skogan and Antunes 1979; J. Wilson and Kelling 1982; Wycoff and Manning 1983). Because police as crime-fighters are dependent on the public, whether they like it or not, they cannot afford to turn their backs on non-law-related requests. Frustrating disaggregate demand creates anger and limits access to the public. Furthermore, the public can be much more effective in crime prevention, if they are willing, than the police. This does not refer only to direct contributions to security through neighborhood watches, patrols, and improvements in physical security. Effective crime prevention comes through attending to the kind of social disintegration that lowers the capacity of communities to discipline themselves informally. The role of the police in lessening the threat of crime, then, comes not exclusively through apprehending criminals and warning them off, but also through actively mobilizing the population to address the causes as well as the symptoms of crime. In order to do this, police cannot distance themselves from disaggregate service demands; they must see these as opportunities to become involved in fundamental processes of social interaction. In short, they must address non-law-related situations in order more successfully to provide effective crime prevention.

Police might even go one step further and assume responsibility within government for diagnosing changes in social structure and interpersonal relations that lead to crime. Fire departments advise urban planners, architects, and builders about conditions that increase the risk of fire. Health experts do the same when industrial plants are located, mining undertaken, and building codes enacted. Yet the police are rarely consulted about whether government policies may have an impact on social processes in ways that increase crime.

Altogether, then, there is no evidence that policing around the world is becoming more specialized, nor is there a persuasive argument that it should do so. On the contrary, specializing in crime-fighting is apt to make the crime problem worse by ignoring not only effective crime prevention but also the enlistment of public cooperation. And, as research has shown, public cooperation, especially in the form of willing testimony, is the key to criminal apprehension and prosecution.

Seventh, as police recognize the outreach requirements for effective crime prevention, major changes will have to be undertaken in training and management. Whether police will be allowed to address these requirements depends in part on whether they are preoccupied with state security. A high incidence of collective violence narrows the ambit of police work. The police agenda becomes that of the state rather than the public. Police attend less to both non-law-related requests and individual security needs. They lose touch with the public. This is true regardless of the character of government: even democratic governments may require police to focus more intensely on collective acts of subversion at the risk of neglecting other duties. India today is an instance. The police in such countries become perceived as political actors, responsive primarily to government. This increases public reluctance to ask for assistance, leading in all probability to reductions in reported crime. Police forces preoccupied with collective violence tend to stress authoritative command rather than delegating responsibility to individual officers. They also usually act in groups and mistrust community input. Professionalization occurs along a military model, if it occurs at all.

On the other hand, the professional requirements for being effective in crime prevention will grow wherever police work is largely determined by disaggregate public demand. In order to accomplish effective crime prevention, whether through deterrence or community mobilization, responsibility for making decisions must shift from senior to junior officers, to persons who are in a position to make instant diagnoses of appropriate actions across an unpredictable range of situations. Managerial style must become more collegial, supplementing and even supplanting reliance on authoritative command. As a result, it will become more difficult to ensure community control of the police through traditional external controls working through the hierarchical command structure. Accountability must be achieved in new ways—in particular, dyadically between sensitive, professional officers and the members of the public whom they encounter time after time. Officers capable of acting in this fashion will have to be more carefully selected than is common in most places—more highly educated, more thoroughly trained, and imbued with the discipline of the autonomous professional. In short, policing in most places needs to become more highly skilled and responsible in order to achieve its primary objective of providing public security. It follows, too, that the costs of effective policing will rise.

Eighth, the approaches that countries take to crime control—their strategies of policing—will vary in the future according to the incidence of collective violence, public perceptions of the seriousness of ordinary crime, and cultural orientations toward the position of individuals in groups. This argument needs to be made at some length, because the determinants of crime-control strategies have not been addressed previously in the book, although bits and pieces of the argument can be found scattered through several chapters. Since crime control is the core function of all police, a view shared by police and public alike, it is fitting to conclude a comparative essay on policing with predictions about the shape this function will take.

Because public police are creations of government, regime needs will always tend to supersede diffuse public ones. This suggests that the nature of police work will be different in countries struggling with collective violence or with police traditions derived from struggling with collective violence early in state-building. Such countries will develop police systems that respond primarily to state needs and emphasize deterrence. I shall call these *regime police systems*. Key elements in the unfolding argument will be found in Table 9.1.

In regime police systems where ordinary crime is relatively unimportant, police will concentrate on state security problems undistracted by disaggregate public demand, whether related to law or to servicing.

Table 9.1
Types of Police Strategies

Determinants	Strategies	Police System Characterizations
I. High levels of collective violence	Regime defense	Regime police
A. Low crime	Public neglect (India)	
B. High crime		
1. Individualistic culture	Deterrence	Formal authoritarian (Russia)
2. Group-oriented culture	Mobilization	Informal authoritarian (Vietnam)
II. Low levels of collective violence	Public defense	Nonregime police
A. Low crime	Regime and public neglect (Norway)	
B. High crime		
1. Individualistic culture	Deterrence	Formal democratic (United States)
2. Group-oriented culture	Mobilization	Informal democratic (Japan)

The police role will be relatively clear, and police and public will be disengaged by what seems mutual agreement. The public may not like the police, but it will not expect much in return except passivity. On the other hand, regime police forces in countries where the level of criminality is high and public concern acute must make a crucial choice in crime-control strategy. They must either rely on deterrence, elaborating laws and penalties in order to ensure swift and certain punishment, or mobilize the community in its own defense, particularly by trying to enhance informal social control. The strategy of community mobilization will always appear risky in regime police systems because it involves creating potentially assertive centers of political power. Instead, regime police systems will find it more congenial to emphasize deterrence through formal controls that emanate from the state. Where regime police work within a context of individualistic culture, this strategic choice is inevitable, because otherwise political authorities would be trying to create cohesive, self-disciplining groups against the cultural grain. This situation may exist today in the Soviet Union, as well as in eastern Europe and parts of Latin America. The formal deterrent orientation adopted by the police will reinforce regime policing to make the system seem unresponsive and draconian. The feelings of the people will be acutely in conflict as they find themselves desperately dependent on a police whose preoccupations and methods reflect expediential decisions by the state. It should be added that minority groups in Western democracies are sometimes caught in the same predicament: they call on the police frequently out of desperate need but regard them as unsympathetic and quixotic agents of a repressive regime.

Countries with regime police systems where there is significant public concern about crime will try the strategy of community mobilization if they place a high value on group life. The needs for crime prevention and state security will work in harness to imbed the police deeply in community life. Both the public and the government will see the value of pervasive penetration by the police, and though each will expect something different out of it, there will be no conflict with respect to the work handled. Such a system need not be draconian and can allow substantial scope for the discretionary use of authority by decentralized administrators as well as lower ranks. Despite having regime police systems, such countries trap their police into paying attention to conditions that cause crime and affect everyone. Their mobilization activities expose them to the demands of the disaggregate community. They are thoroughly totalitarian but more responsive and discriminating concerning ordinary crime matters than regime police systems in individualistic cultures. The public has an active sense of participating in policing, not because they can influence the regime but because they share responsibility with the police for public safety. They are "participant subjects" in policing rather than nonparticipant subjects (Almond and Verba 1965). China, Taiwan, and both Koreas may be cases in point.

Police forces whose work is not shaped primarily by the security needs of the state, largely because collective violence has not played a significant role in political development, I shall call *nonregime police forces*. They, too, face strategic choices in crime control similar to those confronted by regime systems. Of course, if the incidence of crime is low or not a matter of public concern, the police can avoid decision. Unlike regime police forces, they will have little to do, and their establishments will be small by world standards. For countries with a large crime problem, on the other hand, the state's security agenda is identical to that of the disaggregate population. If the cultural tradition is communitarian, government and community will recognize that crime control requires mobilizing the community in its own defense. Crime will be deterred through encouraging informal discipline rather than through formal penalties. The criminal justice system will not be viewed as the first line of defense against crime. Rather, its disciplinary activities will be used when informal discipline has failed. Its more important function will be to encourage vital disciplining by other sectors of society. Matters unrelated to law, but not to informal discipline, thereby become appropriate occasions for police intervention in society. As a result, the police cannot avoid treating noncriminal complaints and problems. Policing will become as extensive and subtle as the disparate public requires. And the police will gain respectability and legitimacy by meeting these demands and associating with grassroots efforts that promote crime prevention. Japan fits this model.

Nonregime police forces in individualistic cultures, on the other hand, face more troubled futures. Community mobilization by the police is suspect in the eyes of the public because it involves injecting coercive organizations created by the state into what has previously been regarded as private life. The boundaries of state authority seem to be expanding under police auspices. The more attractive alternative in such countries, therefore, is to keep the activities of the police tightly focused under law but to make deterrence more effective. New laws are passed, punishments enhanced, and the protections of due process weakened. The Western democracies today, caught between their fear of crime and their cultural predilections, are victims of this dilemma. They cannot happily authorize the police to assist in reinvigorating informal social controls, nor can they easily embrace draconian deterrence. Both strategies conflict with cherished values. They can be neither oriental nor authoritarian. So they vacillate, experimenting with community crime control while at the same time calling for stern criminal penalties. The police become bitter and cynical—unrewarded for what they do most of (servicing), forced daily to recognize the futility of their crime-control efforts, and yet thrust forward as society's best defense against crime. For the Western democracies, the crime problem exposes a weakness in their political foundations traceable to their cultural traditions of individualism: they incline toward the strategy of augmenting the formal disciplinary power of the state. Unlike more group-oriented societies, crime control puts Western democracies between a political rock and a cultural hard place.

This predicament accounts to some extent, I believe, for the astonishing rise in private policing during the last twenty years in the stable, industrialized democracies. Private policing is a way of enhancing security, at least for those with money, without increasing state authority either through formal deterrence or engineering informal discipline. Policing is extended, to be sure, but not state policing. Private policing represents community mobilization under the auspices of the marketplace. It may be the Western democracies' unique way of meeting crime needs while avoiding the authoritarianism of both formal deterrence or pervasive community penetration.

In summary, there are three primary strategies that police forces will choose in meeting their responsibility to create social order, depending on the incidence of regime-threatening collective violence, public concern with ordinary crime, and views about the role of the individual in the community. These strategies are neglect, deterrence, and community mobilization. Each strategy has two variations, depending on whether its purpose is to ensure the regime's or the public's security. (See Table 9.1.)

Thus, *regime police forces*, created in countries that have or have had high levels of politically significant collective violence, will tend to neglect the disaggregate public's security concerns. This may be done with impunity in countries that have low crime rates, as is arguably the case today in India. When crime is high, however, they must merge both goals in a common strategy. Regime police will follow a collectively focused strategy of deterrence enforcement if they work within an individualistic culture; regime police will adopt a collectively focused strategy of community mobilization if they work within a group-oriented culture. These might be called, respectively, *formally authoritarian* and *informally authoritarian* police systems. Russia and Vietnam are possible examples. *Nonregime police forces*, created in countries that have low levels of politically significant collective violence, will adopt strategies that focus on the public's disaggregate security needs. The exception is in the case of countries that have low levels of ordinary crime as well, such as Norway, where they may be quite inattentive in both directions. Nonregime police will follow a strategy of deterrence enforcement focused on individuals if they work within an individualistic culture; nonregime police will adopt a strategy of community mobilization focused also on individuals if they work within a group-oriented culture. These might be called, respectively, *formally democratic* and *informally democratic* police systems. The United States and Japan are examples of each. Obviously, the fit between particular countries and the categories of this schema will always be inexact. Countries employ a mix of strategies, rarely only one. The model explains the inclinations of communities in choosing crime-control strategies.

The strategies that countries adopt for controlling crime have momentous consequences for human freedom. The key issue is how to use public institutions, primarily the police, to deal with crime without creating an authoritarian state and estranging people from it. Countries whose bureaucratic traditions have been forged on the anvil of civil strife will be hard-pressed to create public police capable of enlisting the populace in their own defense. Deterrence will reinforce the authoritarian tendencies of regime police. Such a future is likely in the Soviet Union, eastern Europe, and much of Latin America, but also among some democratic countries of the West, such as Italy and Greece. Countries with traditions of community mobilization under grass-roots auspices, such as China, Korea, and Taiwan, may be more successful in blunting the edge of formal state control despite believing themselves to be faced with threats to state security. Paradoxically, though government penetration in such countries will be more extensive than in authoritarian systems in the West, it is likely to be more subtle, discriminating, and ultimately legitimate. The countries of the democratic West will be tempted to intensify formal deterrence. Crime control and servicing may drift further apart, so that the opportunity for responsive crime prevention through involvement by the police in community life will be lost. Caught within a heritage of individualism, these countries may try to escape from an increasingly authoritarian public police through the wholesale development of private police. Finally, choices are probably least constrained for the host of new states whose traditional ways of life have not yet been wholly shattered. These countries have the precious opportunity to use the state to preserve vital centers of informal social control. Recurrent strife, however, especially if it threatens regimes, may destroy this possibility. Crime-control strategies involving police can undermine primary social relations or enhance them. The choice for this select group of countries is between emulating the West and relying on deterrence or emulating the East and seeking to enmesh the police informally in daily life.

The choices that countries make about crime control, when they are spared the need to defend regimes, are fateful not only for individual security but also for the impetus given political evolution. They constrict or expand the possibilities for the humane as well as the effective achievement of public security at later times.

Description of Research Sites Used in the Analysis of Police Work

All of the facts presented here apply to the years 1976 to 1978, when the fieldwork was done.

I. France

Material on the composition of police work was collected in the Departement l'Essonne, which is adjacent to Paris on the south. The *departement* had a population of 947,052 people, approximately 748,425 covered by the Police Nationale. Though in part agricultural, it was rapidly becoming a built-up suburb of Paris used by commuting businesspeople. The police force numbered approximately thirteen hundred. Data on police work was collected from Lonjumeau Police Station, one of four in the *departement*, as well as Chilly-Mazarin, a substation of Lonjumeau. The data were found in Le Main Courant, the station diary maintained by the duty officer in each station. All events brought to the attention of the police were to be recorded in Le Main Courant.

II. Great Britain

Research in Britain was conducted in Suffolk County, located about thirty-seven kilometers northeast of London. Running from just east of Cambridge to the North Sea, its principal occupations were farming and fishing. The major town and county seat was Ipswich, population 121,500. County police headquarters were located just outside at Martlesham Heath. The rural site selected was Stowmarket subdivision, located about twenty-five kilometers northwest of Ipswich, population 23,580. The Ipswich police division was staffed by just over three hundred officers, Stowmarket subdivision by about thirty-five. All data came from the command-and-control computer system. Not only did it log all calls for police service, but all officers were also required to file contacts with it that have been generated proactively. I have considerable doubt that they did so. The computer printout listed the mode of instigation, location by address and police subdivision, nature of call on reception and again after verification by responding officers, and action taken.

III. India

Indian data came from three states—Uttar Pradesh, Orissa, and Tamil Nadu. In each state two locations were selected, one urban and one rural. Data on police activity came primarily from the Station Diary, sometimes called General Diary, maintained by hand in large bound ledgers. In some places this was supplemented by material from the FIR (First Information Report) Register and Non-FIR Register. In Uttar Pradesh, Kaiserbagh or Quaiserbagh Police Station was located in the center of the old part of Lucknow, covering a population of about 110,000, in an area of thirty-one square kilometers and with a police strength of about one hundred. Mall Police Station was located in a very small farming village thirty-five kilometers northwest of Lucknow on the Hardoi road. It was part of Lucknow District. Mall Police Station's twenty-six officers were responsible for a population of 90,865 in an area of about fifty-six square kilometers.

In Orissa, the urban site was Capital Police Station, located in the heart of the capital city of Bhubaneswar (population 100,000) and covering an area that included the Vidhan Sabha (state legislature), the homes of important government ministers, several bazaars, and a central bus depot. It was the largest police station in Orissa, with 215 officers assigned, covering a population of approximately 68,000. Bologarh Police Station was located about sixty kilometers southwest of Bhubaneswar in a remote corner of Puri District. Bologarh was located in a hilly, partly forested region, known as a haunt of "dacoits," bandits who live in the hills and loot villages at night.

Mylapore was a densely populated area in the southern portion of Madras city, which is the capital of Tamil Nadu state. Staffed by 117 officers, it was responsible for about 108,000 persons in an area of about 2.3 square kilometers. Thiruporur was a small village in Chingelput West District, 50 kilometers southwest of Madras. The police station had 46 officers, covering a population of 129,790 and an area of about 46.7 kilometers.

IV. Norway

The Norwegian information on police tasks came from Oslo and Rjukan. Oslo is the capital, population 465,337. Data on police work came from the log of the computer-assisted dispatch system. Calls for service as well as all contacts generated by officers were supposed to be recorded in the dispatch computer. Rjukan was a small rural community located at the bottom of a steep mountain valley about 120 kilometers southwest of Oslo. Though the town was dominated by a saltpeter factory, the surrounding area was wholly agricultural. Information came from the Duty Diary of the police station.

V. Singapore

Singapore island had a population of 2.28 million in an area of about 602 square kilometers in 1978. It was policed by 7,200 sworn officers. B Division was a densely populated landlocked area of central Singapore city with a population of 250,000. Rural West police division constituted the western tip of the island and, while agricultural in part, was developing rapidly. It contained a population of 282,000 in an area of 30.5 square kilometers. All data came from Station Diaries supplemented by the telephone logs of emergency calls over the 999 number.

VI. Sri Lanka

Both sites in Sri Lanka were located in Columbo District. Pettah Police Station was in the older section of central Columbo, staffed by 197 officers and covering 65,000 persons in an area of 2.1 square kilometers. Kahataduwa Police Station was located 15 miles southeast of Columbo in a thickly vegetated area whose principal crop was rice. The police station had 27 officers, covering a population of 43,849 and an area of 12.5 square kilometers. Information on police work came principally from the Grave Complaints Information Book, Minor Offences Information Book, and the Minor Complaint Information Book. It should be noted that there were also the Traffic Information Book, Detection Information Book, and Telephone Register.

VII. United States

The American data came from five locations in the western state of Colorado. The largest police force was in the capital city of Denver, population approximately 1.5 million in the greater metropolitan area. The police force of 1,383 covered the core city with population of 520,000 in an area of 43.4 square kilometers. Information about police work in all five locations came from the Activity Sheets maintained by each officer during a shift on which he recorded all dispatches and contacts. These sheets were turned in to supervisors at the end of the shift.

The rest of the Colorado data came from two country sheriffs' departments and the encapsulated police departments of the county seats.

Chaffee County, population 11,400, covering 401 square kilometers, was located about 160 kilometers southwest of Denver on the western slope of the Rocky Mountains. The Sheriff's Department had 8 officers. The Salida city police force had 9 officers, covering a population of 4,500. Fort Morgan County was located on the wheat-growing plains 100 kilometers northeast of Denver. Its population was 20,105 in an area of 484 square kilometers. The Sheriff's Department had 9 officers. Fort Morgan City had 16 police officers for a population of approximately eight thousand.

Notes

CHAPTER 1. TOWARD A THEORY OF POLICING

1. Max Weber said that the fundamental characteristic of the modern state is its "monopoly on the legitimate use of physical force within a given territory," and Leon Trotsky that "every state is founded on force" (Gerth and Mills 1958, p. 78).

2. Charles Reith has strikingly described this neglect in his pioneering book, *The Blind Eye of History* (1952).

3. Military personnel may also be neglected and for the very same reasons (Janowitz 1959, p. 15).

4. My definition of *police* and E. Adamson Hoebel's definition of *law* both turn on the relation between community authorization and the application of physical force. "A social norm is legal if its neglect or infraction is regularly met, in threat or in fact, by the application of physical force by an individual or group possessing the socially recognized privilege of doing so" (Kobben 1969, p. 120).

5. As of 1982, Australia, Belgium, Canada, Denmark, Finland, Great Britain, Japan, Norway, the Netherlands, and the United States. Often there is not a fit between the survey samples and police jurisdictions.

CHAPTER 2. THE DEVELOPMENT OF MODERN POLICE

1. Direction of policing and instigation of policing should not be confused. A public system—collectively paid and directed—is not incompatible with private instigation of police action. Officers in modern systems rarely take action on their own recognizance but wait until contacted by someone needing assistance. It is not the nature of instigation—proactive or reactive—that differentiates public from private policing, but rather the nature of the agencies appealed to. For both private and public forces, the amount of individual as opposed to official instigation must be determined empirically.

2. For an argument on the other side, see Strayer 1970, pp. 7–8.

3. Schwartz and Miller would be surprised at this conclusion, but only on terminological grounds. Their criteria for *specialization* are the ones I have used for *publicness*. Though they define police as "specialized armed forces used partially and wholly for norm enforcement," they continually discuss po-

lice as representing a capacity of formal government (1964, p. 161). They confuse *specialization* with *public agency*.

4. Michael G. Mulhall (1903, p. 444) gives the population of Rome in 14 A.D. as about 900,000.

5. William Mildmay (1763, p. 23). Twelve articles establishing the *marechausée* were set forth in 1356. For an excellent account of these lawless gangs, see Barbara W. Tuchman, *A Distant Mirror: The Calamitous Fourteenth Century* (London: Penguin Books, 1979, chap. 10).

6. Sybille van der Sprenkel 1977. For a firsthand description of South China during the period of imperial decline, 1908, see René Onraet, *Singapore: A Police Background* (London: Dorothy Crisp and Co. Ltd., 1945, p. 47).

7. In Japan, for example, in the reign of Saga, ca. 820 A.D., a police department was established at Kyoto for the purpose of arresting criminals and bringing them to trial. In 1186 Minamoto-no Yoritomo took the title *sotsuihosi*, or chief superintendent of police (Ogawa and Tomeoka 1909).

8. As first secretary to Ireland, Peel had already experimented with policing when, in 1814, he created the Peace Preservation Forces. They became the Irish Constabulary and later the Royal Irish Constabulary. The "Peelers" were an armed squad, not stationed among the people but moving from one trouble spot to another (Brady 1974, chap. 1).

9. An earlier formulation appears in Bayley 1975.

10. Tokyo had a full-time training program for lower ranks in 1880, Paris not until 1883, and even then it was only on a part-time basis, interspersed with other duties. London's Police Training School was founded in 1907 (Stead 1957, p. 139; Fosdick 1915 [1975], pp. 211ff.).

11. Professionalization began in London in 1829, when the city had a population of 1.8 million; in Stockholm, 1850, 92,000; in Sydney, 1862, 100,000; and in Calcutta, 1864, 365,000 (Gurr, Grabosky, and Hula 1977, p. 705). At the same time, Eric Monkkonen (1981) argues that American cities developed 100,000 full-time uniformed police after the Civil War as a function of their rank-order in size. I suggest that if there are thresholds of size, as Monkkonen has found, they occur within local climates of opinion about the need to professionalize.

CHAPTER 3. THE STRUCTURE OF POLICING

1. Italy also has municipal police—*vigili urbani*—responsible primarily for directing traffic and enforcing local ordinances.

2. For Belgium as of April 1977 (Vincet 1977).

3. U.S. Department of Justice, Law Enforcement Assistance Agency,

Criminal Justice Agencies in Pennsylvania (1970, foreword). Twenty thousand of these may be local community police (Caiden 1977, p. 29).

4. In 1972, 162 municipalities had done so (Dorey and Swidler 1975, p. 148).

5. Bruce Smith, *Police Systems in the United States* (1949), identified five levels of government that create overlapping police authority: federal, state, county, cities and townships and boroughs, and incorporated towns. Charles E. Merriam found 350 law enforcement agencies in Chicago in the 1930s, including those attached to schools, parks, and sanitation districts. Bruce Smith's survey of the Cincinnati region in 1932 located 147 law enforcement agencies spread over two states and six counties (Walker 1977, p. 145).

6. One hundred thirteen federal agencies have enforcement power in the United States. The FBI is the most important (Shane 1980, p. 157).

7. It was the eighth largest police force in the United States in the late 1960s. The New York Housing Authority's police force was the twenty-fourth largest (Berkeley 1969, p. 27).

8. Private correspondence, Philip C. Stenning, May 1980. Canada reduced the number of forces but not the number of jurisdictions. Whether centralization may be said to have increased depends on how one judges the amount of control exercised by RCMP headquarters in Ottawa over its many forces on contract.

9. The Texas Rangers, created in 1853, were the first state police. After a long pause, Pennsylvania followed in 1908, and then shortly after all the others (Walker 1977, p. 146). Massachusetts established a state police force in 1865, but it was disbanded in 1875 in favor of a state detective squad.

10. There were still 120 forces in 1962.

11. Lilia C. Lopez, "The Philippine Criminal Justice System" (1979, pp. 9ff.). There had been 1467 municipal commands and 61 city police forces previously.

12. According to the International Association of Chiefs of Police (private correspondence), most states had standards of some sort by 1974, but only four had provided mandatory inspection and enforcement penalties.

13. Research by Elinor Ostrom and her colleagues at Indiana University shows that the prevalent notion that very small forces are inefficient may be incorrect. For example, see "Police Agency Size: Some Evidence on its Effects," *Police Studies* (March 1978: 34–46).

14. Max Weber noted the same phenomenon and employed the analogy of loaded dice to describe it (Lipset 1963, p. 7).

15. Information about centralization is from Dorey and Swidler 1975, 1973, and U.S. Department of Defense Area Handbooks. Judgments about authoritarianism are from Raymond D. Gastil (1978), who classified countries as *free, partly free,* and *not free.* I dichotomized the political character variable,

putting *free* and *partly free* as nonauthoritarian, *not free* as authoritarian. The chi-square value for the resulting two-by-two table was 8.47, which is significant at the 1 percent level. The forty-eight countries cannot be considered a representative sample of the world.

16. Hans Rosenberg has said, "Nowhere did the evolution of the absolute system involve a steady growth of governmental centralism and bureaucratization" (1958, p. 168).

CHAPTER 4. POLICE STRENGTH

1. Japan National Police Agency (n.d.), 82.2 percent in fiscal year 1978; Government of Great Britain (1977), 80.9 percent. Bordua and Haurek (1971) reported that 90 percent of the outlays on police in the U.S. went to salaries, compared with 49 percent in secondary schools and 32 percent in the Department of Defense in 1965.

2. New Haven: Yale University Press, 2nd ed., 1973. A third edition was published in 1981 but did not update the data on internal security forces.

3. The CIA's *National Basic Intelligence Fact Book*, which is a public document, does not include any data on police.

4. The figures given by Taylor and Hudson (1973, p. 151) are for "internal security forces," which includes police at all levels and such paramilitary forces as gendarmeries and active militias and national guards. The figures, therefore, overstate the number of police. The ratios for some countries frequently referred to in this study are as follows: Canada, 2,760 persons per police officer; France, 349; Japan, 625; the Netherlands, 702; Sri Lanka 1,145; the United Kingdom, 578; the USSR, 659; the United States, 480; and West Germany, 454. No figures were available for India and Italy.

5. Some countries frequently referred to in this study have police densities as follows: West Germany, 1.9 per square kilometer; the Netherlands, 1.9; Italy, 3.0; United Kingdom, 2.5; France, 3.9; Sri Lanka, 6.67; the United States, 23.2; and the USSR, 62.5.

6. Singh 1977, chaps. 4 and 5. Using Taylor and Hudson's data for seventeen countries for which Singh could supply data on inequality, he found through regression analysis that 86 percent of the variance in police strength per capita could be accounted for in this way.

7. J. Wilson and Boland 1976, pp. 375–376. The relation was with crimes against persons, not crimes against property. They controlled for differences in taxable wealth.

8. This conclusion is not contradicted by the findings of Jackson and Carroll concerning variations in police expeditures per capita in ninety American cities in 1971. Though they argue that their findings show that city governments

increased police expenditures when confronted with the likelihood of civil unrest, only one of their indicators measured dissident mobilization directly. They found that 75 percent of the variance in police expenditures per capita could be explained, in order of importance, by city revenues, percent of population that was black, population density, population size, civil rights mobilization activity, and poverty. Riots, interestingly, were not a significant predictor (Jackson and Carroll 1981).

9. Dates chosen respectively were 1829, 1850, and 1862.

10. Reynolds (1926, pp. 5–16) estimated that there were 7,000 Vigiles plus three urban cohorts of 1,000 each, totalling 10,000.

11. Gurr, Grabosky, and Hula (1977, p. 709). The London data were supported by Hart (1951, p. 34) and Martin and Wilson (1969, pp. 238–248 and Table 92).

12. Bordua and Haurek found that 90 percent of the growth in police strength relative to population in the United States could be accounted for by population, territorial extent, and increases in numbers of motor vehicles. In larger American cities—over 300,000—between 1902 and 1960 there was a constant police-to-population ratio. There were consistently fewer police per population in smaller American cities—25,000 to 50,000—than larger. An analysis of Fosdick's data on the proportion of police per population for European cities in 1913 shows that the plateau is reached when cities achieve populations of about 750,000. However, unlike the United States, smaller cities had more police per population.

13. The data provided by Bordua and Haurek (1971) are the sole exception.

14. Colin Loftin and Alan Lizotte (1974) found in a survey of the United States that willingness to use force is not a lower-class phenomenon. Upper-class persons were more willing to use force to maintain general order. "We derive the proposition that those groups in societies who have the greatest power and privilege in the system of stratification would be subject to the maximum amount of pressure to support the use of force for the maintenance and protection of the social order" (p. 9).

15. According to Lodhi and Tilly (1970), collective violence in France between 1831 and 1931 varied independent of ordinary crime. Collective violence followed its own logic. In "Chaos of the Living City" (1970), Tilly also notes that waves of collective violence were not linked to incremental social changes in France.

16. In earlier work Gurr (1967, p. 28) used twenty as the critical minimum for collective violence. In the reign of England's King Edgar, 959–975, a riot was neatly defined as a breach of the peace committed by at least thirty-five people (Lee 1901 [1971], p. 6).

17. The Anti-Riot Act, 1968, made it illegal to travel between states for the purpose of organizing, inciting, promoting, or participating in a riot or helping people doing the same; the Civil Disobedience Act, 1968, makes it a federal

offense to manufacture, use, or transport fire, incendiary, or expolsive devices in furtherance of civil disorder, also to interfere with firemen or police officers performing official duties during civil disturbances (International Association of Chiefs of Police 1976, p. 92). See Gregory 1976 for the reaction to civil disturbances in several Western countries.

18. Lyman 1964, pp. 150–151; Critchley 1967, pp. 51–53. Consolidation of the metropolitian police force was not completed until 1839, when police powers of magistrates were abolished, ending the famous Bow Street Runners. The Thames Police were merged with the Metropolitan Police at the same time (Reith 1948, p. 92). The police of the City of London, however, have maintained their independence up to the present day.

19. In *The Rebellious Century* (1975), chapter 5, Tilly, Tilly, and Tilly describe the shift in the character of riots from reactive to proactive. See also Radzinowicz 1957, vol. 4, pp. 243–246; Darvall 1934, chap. 13; Critchley 1970, p. 22; Hamburger 1963, pp. 18–19); Woodward 1938; Webb and Webb 1963, pp. 412–413.

20. It is also possible that reform in London was delayed until members of Parliament from outside London had become sensitized to these problems, perhaps by recognizing that London's problems were similar to those in their local constituencies. A study of support for London reform in Parliament would be informative. It may be that urbanization—"Londonization"—had to occur in Manchester, Leeds, Birmingham, Sheffield, etc., before Parliament, dominated by non-London MPs, would support reform.

21. Harring 1983. Pringle (n.d., pp. 205–216) labels this good politics but weak history, at least with respect to England. High Tories and commercial people in the City of London held out against Peel's 1829 reform, while Francis Place's support has already been noted.

CHAPTER 5. POLICE WORK

1. See Bayley 1979, pp. 111–112, for an exhaustive list of the kinds of work performed by the world's police.

2. Bayley 1979 provides a review of the major theories put forward to explain each.

3. Because laws are extensive and subtle, police can usually find some offense that has been committed in most situations. Officers can invent offenses, in the sense of searching for them, if they need arrests in order to appear efficient (Ericson 1982 p. 93).

4. Wycoff, Susmilch, and Eisenbart (1980) review the categories that have been used in role studies to date.

5. Half of de la Mare 1705, comprising four volumes, is devoted to food supply; Williams 1979, chap. 6.

6. Generalizations about auxiliary duties in the United States are difficult to make because each jurisdiction has unique authorizations.

7. B. Smith (1949) showed that assignment specialization and city cize were correlated in the United States.

8. Sperlings (1979, p. 55) has shown that when the modern Stockholm police were created in 1850, almost all constables did the same work. By 1924, 40 percent were in specialized tasks. It would clearly be an error to conclude that the force as a whole was doing utterly new kinds of work.

9. There are a large number of studies in the United States and Britain. For a review as well as an appraisal of what is known, see Sherman 1980. See also Richard Ericson 1982 and Hauge and Stabell 1974.

10. Government of Maharashtra, India (1967, p. 5) found them unusable for determining the nature of police work. This impression has been confirmed through personal inspection.

11. Based on field observations in Canada, Ericson says there are four reasons why officers submit reports of incidents: to refer matters to superiors or other units; to justify their own actions; to respond to requests for information from other units; and to provide required services for private interests such as insurance companies and civil complaints (Ericson 1982, pp. 297ff; McCabe and Sutcliffe 1978, chap. 3). In rural Norway, Hauge and Stabell (1974) found that only 20 percent of thefts and burglaries reported to the police were recorded in the police station charge book, only 38 percent of car thefts and 33 percent of sex crimes.

12. Data was available from several other locations, but the sources overrepresented reactive instigations. For example, data from Dallas, Texas, and Suffolk County, Great Britain, were obtained from computers used in assisting dispatch. The situations reported were almost 100 percent reactive. Although in both locations officers assured me that strenuous efforts had been made to have patrol officers record proactive encounters as well, they do not appear to have done so.

13. Monitoring of police tapes of telephone solicitations may overstate the proportion of law-related requests when the public regularly uses nonemergency numbers that are not covered by the tapes.

14. A thorough review of coding schemes may be found in Wycoff, Susmilch, and Eisenbart 1980.

15. McCabe and Sutcliffe (1978, p. 51) have data on Oxford and Salford in 1973; Home Office Police Scientific Development Branch, "The Policing of Rural Areas" (POL 171 1612/1/5, 1972).

16. Hauge 1979, p. 134. I also recoded and analyzed his data according to my format from his study with Stabell (1974).

17. For a brief examination of the dominant lines, see Bayley 1979, p. 122.

18. The sole exception is the work of Richard D. Sykes in Minneapolis.

CHAPTER 6. A THEORY OF ENCOUNTERS

1. One international study found that police districts high in one kind of situation were high in the other. The conditions that produce a large number of service requests also generate a large volume of crime-related requests (Shane 1980, pp. 172, 196).

2. Ericson (1982, pp. 257–259) observed in Peel County, Ontario, that lower-class people were more likely to bring petty matters not involving violations of the law to the attention of the police. As a result, outcomes were more likely to involve advice and assistance than arrest and constraint.

3. Calls for service increased by as much as 50 percent in New York City when a police emergency number was made available through the telephone system (Wycoff and Kelling 1978, chap. 5).

4. I am indebted to Professor Albert J. Reiss, Jr., for this insight.

5. See Chapter 5 for a discussion of the three operationalizations of crime and noncrime situations.

CHAPTER 7. CONTROL OF THE POLICE

1. The idea for police commissions appears to have originated in the United States in the nineteenth century, when many cities experimented with commissions composed exclusively of elected persons. For an authoritative review of the history of Canadian police commissions, see Stenning 1980. Canada in 1980 had approximately 130 boards. Most municipalities did not have them, but most municipal police officers were supervised by them because they tend to have been established in the larger cities.

2. The City of London is an incorporated city within London. In fact, it comprises the commercial district. Greater London, as it were, is policed by the Metropolitan Police Force, familiarly though inaccurately known as Scotland Yard.

3. American police departments have also acceded to administrative changes mandated by courts as part of consent decrees.

4. American police were emulating the practice of the London Metropolitan Police, which had begun wearing badges in 1829. The addition of individual badges was part of the reforms involved establishing unified municipal police systems.

5. Created first in Sweden, 1809, then in Finland, 1919, in Denmark, 1955, and in Norway, 1962.

6. Sykes and Clark (1974) did a field survey in which they found that less

than 5 percent of the time served by patrol personnel on the street was supervised.

7. The key legislation was "An Act for Policing the Metropolis, 1829"; "The Municipal Corporations Act, 1835"; "Country Police Act, 1839"; "County and Borrough Police Act, 1856"; "Local Government Act, 1888." For a more detailed discussion, see Bayley 1975, pp. 342–343.

8. Stenning argues that the nineteenth-century justice of the peace should really be regarded as a political person because the separation between administration and adjudication was indistinct at that time. JPs were responsible for almost all of local government. Moreover, then as now, the home secretary, a politician, is responsible for policing in London. The classification of JPs as political is certainly arguable. They should be regarded as bureaucratic rather than political, in my view, because they were not chosen by popular election.

9. The roots of these differences may go back to the middle of the nineteenth century (Miller 1977).

10. Some clues are provided by Fosdick (1915 [1975], pp. 258–265) for Europe prior to World War I. For example, in 1915 continental countries did not allow a right of appeal from internal disciplinary decisions. The Royal Canadian Mounted Police still does not.

11. Some readers may recognize the similarity between my analysis and Harry Eckstein's theory of congruence (1966). Although I knew Eckstein's work, I did not consciously have congruence theory in mind when I set to work analyzing mechanisms of accountability. It wasn't until I had compiled the lists of predispositions associated with mechanisms of control that I realized I had discovered congruence theory in a new context.

CHAPTER 8. POLICE IN POLITICAL LIFE

1. Senate Select Committee to Study Government Operations with Respect to Intelligence Activities, known as the Church Committee after its chairman, Senator Frank Church. For complete reference to the Church Committee's work, see Halperin et al. 1976, chap. 3.

2. KGB stands for Komitet Gosudarstvennyi Bezopastnost (Committee for State Security) (Juviler 1976).

3. Deacon 1969, chaps. 1 and 2; Beloff 1938, p. 141. An exception may have been Thomas de Veil, a London magistrate, who was secretly appointed "court justice" in 1729 and made responsible for protecting the court as well as managing the government's spies (Pringle n.d., p. 62).

4. Halperin et al. 1976, chap. 4. According to the Church Committee evidence, Hoover shared such information with Roosevelt, Kennedy, Johnson, and Nixon. Truman and Eisenhower are not mentioned.

5. Police officials may use their careers as a stepping-stone to political office. This is not an example of the police influencing politics, since they have ceased formally to be police. Nonetheless, such transformations ensure that a police point of view is heard in political places.

6. Coulter 1972. The lambda value was 0.54. Police were judged by Professor Banks to be active or inactive—dichotomous variable—on the basis of general reading on each country. Categorization was impressionistic but informed (personal communication).

7. Operationalization of regime character was in terms of such variables as the nature of the electoral system, constitutional status of the regime, status of the legislature, interest articulation, horizontal distribution of power, and character of the bureaucracy.

8. Since economic development and regime character are known to be associated—democratic regimes tending to be advanced economically—I suspect that further analysis would show that regime character and not economic development is the crucial factor.

9. The law was renewed four times before lapsing in 1889 (Eyck 1950, pp. 242–243).

10. The original name was "Special Irish Branch" of the CID.

11. For an earlier formulation of this argument, see Bayley 1975, p. 363.

12. In the words of the Task Force on State Police Non-Criminal Files of the New York State Assembly: "Unfortunately, the extent of information necessary to predict with accuracy any event with the remotest possibility of creating disorder, led the police to develop an intelligence system which basically surveilled political and social ideas. The ideology and membership of groups became extremely important to the police who were attempting to know what people were thinking in order to connect this with a potential for violence, disorder, or subversion" (American Friends Service Committee 1979, p. 230).

Bibliography

Abbott, Robert J. 1972. "Police Reform in Russia." Ph.D. dissertation, Princeton University.

———. 1973. "Police Reform in the Russian Province of Iaroslavl 1856–1876." *Slavic Review* June: 292–302.

Adams, John C., and Barile, Paolo. 1961. *The Government of Republican Italy*. Boston: Houghton Mifflin Co.

Almond, Gabriel A., and Verba, Sidney. 1965. *The Civic Culture*. Boston: Little, Brown & Co.

American Friends Service Committee. 1979. *The Police Threat to Political Liberty*. Philadelphia: American Friends Service Committee.

Andrzejewski, Stanislaw. 1954. *Military Organization and Society*. London: Routledge and Kegan Paul, Ltd.

Armitage, Gilbert. n.d. *The History of the Bow Street Runners, 1729–1829*. London: Wishart and Co.

Arnold, Eric A., Jr. 1969. "Administrative Leadership in a Dictatorship: The Position of Joseph Fouché in the Napoleonic Police, 1800–1810." Ph.D. dissertation, Columbia University.

Bailey, Victor, ed. 1981. *Policing and Punishment in Nineteenth Century Britain*. New Brunswick, N.J.: Rutgers University Press.

Banks, Arthur S., and Textor, Robert B. 1968. *A Cross-Polity Survey*. Cambridge, Mass.: MIT Press.

Banton, Michael. 1964. *The Policeman in the Community*. New York: Basic Books, Inc.

———. 1975. "A New Approach to Police Authorities." *Police* 7: 24–25.

Barker, Ernest. 1927. *National Character and the Factors in Its Foundation*. New York: Harper & Bros.

———. 1944. *The Development of Public Services in Western Europe, 1660–1930*. London: Oxford University Press.

Barzini, Luigi. 1964. *The Italians*. New York: Atheneum.

Basham, A. L. 1954. *The Wonder That Was India*. London: Sidgwick and Jackson.

Bayley, David H. 1969. *The Police and Political Development in India*. Princeton: Princeton University Press.

———. 1975. "The Police and Political Development in Europe." In *The Formation of National States in Europe*, ed. Charles Tilly, pp. 1328–1379. Princeton: Princeton University Press.

————. 1976*a*. "Learning About Crime—The Japanese Experience." *Public Interest* Summer: 55–68.

————. 1976*b*. *Forces of Order: Police Behavior in Japan and the United States*. Berkeley: University of California Press.

————. 1979. "Police Function, Structure, and Control in Western Europe and North America: Comparative and Historical Studies." In *Crime and Justice: An Annual Review of Research*, ed. Norval Morris and Michael Tonry, pp. 109–144. Chicago: University of Chicago Press.

Bayley, David H., and Mendelsohn, Harold. 1969. *Minorities and the Police*. New York: Free Press.

Becker, Harold K. 1973. *Police Systems of Europe*. Springfield, Ill.: Charles C. Thomas.

Becker, Harold K., and Hjellemo, E. O. 1976. *Justice in Modern Sweden*. Springfield, Ill.: Oceana Publications, Inc.

Beloff, Max. 1938. *Public Order and Popular Disturbances, 1660–1714*. London: Oxford University Press.

Berkeley, George E. 1969. *The Democratic Policeman*. Boston: Beacon Press.

Bittner, Egon. 1974. "Florence Nightingale in Pursuit of Willie Sutton: A Theory of the Police." In *The Potential for Reform of Criminal Justice*, ed. Herbert Jacob, pp. 17–44. Beverly Hills: Sage Publications.

Black, Donald J. 1973. "The Mobilization of Law." *Journal of Legal Studies* January: 125–149.

————. 1976. *The Behavior of Law*. New York: Academic Press.

————. 1980. *The Manners and Customs of the Police*. New York: Academic Press.

Bloch, Marc. 1961. *Feudal Society*. Chicago: University of Chicago Press.

Bohannan, Paul. 1957. *Justice and Judgement Among the Tiv*. New York: Oxford University Press.

Bonner, Robert J., and Smith, Gertrude. 1928. *The Administration of Justice from Homer to Aristotle*. 2 vols. Chicago: University of Chicago Press.

Bopp, William J., and Schultz, Donald D. 1972. *A Short History of American Law Enforcement*. Springfield, Ill.: Charles C. Thomas.

Bordua, David J., and Haurek, Edward W. 1971. "The Police Budget's Lot: Components of the Increase in Local Police Expenditures, 1902–1960." In *Police in Urban Society*, ed. Harlan Hahn, pp. 57–70. Beverly Hills: Sage Publications.

Brady, Conor. 1974. *Guardians of the Peace*. Dublin, Ire.: Gill and Macmillan.

Bramshill Police College, Eleventh Senior Command Course. 1974. "A Study of Public Order in Six E.E.C. Countries." June.

Bramstedt, E. K. 1945. *Dictatorship and Political Police*. New York: Oxford University Press.

Brenan, Gerald. 1943. *The Spanish Labyrinth*. Cambridge, Eng.: Cambridge University Press.

Brogden, M. 1977. "A Police Authority—The Denial of Conflict." *Sociological Review* May: 325–350.

Brown, Lorne, and Brown, Caroline. 1973. *An Unauthorized History of the RCMP*. Toronto: James Lewis and Samuel.

Caiden, Gerald E. 1977. *Police Revitalization*. Lexington, Mass.: Lexington Books, D.C. Heath and Co.

Carr, Raymond. 1966. *Spain, 1808–1939*. Oxford: Clarendon Press.

Carsten, F. L. 1954. *The Origins of Prussia*. Oxford: Clarendon Press.

Carte, Gene E., and Carte, Elaine H. 1975. *Police Reform in the United States: The Era of August Vollmer, 1905–1932*. Berkeley: University of California Press.

Chapman, Brian. 1953. "The Prefecture of Police." *Journal of Criminal Law, Criminology, and Police Science* November–December: 505–521.

Chevigny, Paul. 1969. *Police Power: Police Abuses in New York City*. New York: Random House, Vintage Paperback.

Clarke, R. V. G., and Heal, K. H. 1979. "Police Effectiveness in Dealing with Crime: Some Current British Research." *Police Journal* January: 24–41.

Clayton, Tom. 1967. *The Protectors: The Inside Story of Britain's Private Security Forces*. London: Oldbourne Book Co.

Clutterbuck, Richard. 1973. *Riot and Revolution in Singapore and Malaya, 1945–1963*. London: Faber and Faber Ltd.

Coatman, John. 1959. *Police*. London: Oxford University Press.

Conquest, Robert. 1968. *The Soviet Police System*. London: Bodley Head.

Coulter, Philip. 1972. "National Socio-Economic Development and Democracy, A Note on the Political Role of the Police." *International Journal of Comparative Sociology* March: 55–62.

Cox, Sir Edmond C. n.d. *Police and Crime in India*. London: Stanley Paul and Co.

Cramer, James. 1964. *The World's Police*. London: Cassell and Co.

Critchley, T. A. 1967. *A History of Police in England and Wales, 1900–1966*. London: Constable.

———. 1970. *The Conquest of Violence: Order and Liberty in Britain*. London: Constable.

Crozier, Michel. 1963. *The Bureaucratic Phenomenon*. Chicago: University of Chicago Press.

Darvall, Frank Ongley. 1934. *Popular Disturbances and Public Order in Regency England*. London: Oxford University Press.

Day, Robert C., and Hamblin, Robert L. 1964. "Some Effects of Close and Punitive Styles of Supervision." *American Journal of Sociology* March: 499–510.

Deacon, Richard. 1969. *A History of the British Secret Service*. London: Frederick Muller.

de la Mare. 1705. *Traité de la Police*. Paris: n.p.

de Tocqueville, Alexis. 1856. *The Old Regime and the French Revolution.* Repr. ed. 1955. New York: Doubleday Anchor Books.

Dorey, Marcia A., and Swidler, George J. 1975. *World Police Systems.* Boston: Northeastern University Press.

Dupuy, Trevor N.; Hayes, Brace P.; and Andrews, A. C. 1974. *The Almanac of World Military Powers.* 3rd ed. New York: R. R. Bowker.

Earle, Howard H. 1973. *Police Recruit Training: Stress vs. Non-Stress.* Springfield, Ill.: Charles C. Thomas.

Easton, David, and Dennis, Jack. 1969. *Children in the Political System.* New York: McGraw-Hill Book Co.

Eckstein, Harry. 1966. *Division and Cohesion in Democracy: A Study of Norway.* Princeton: Princeton University Press.

Emerson, Donald E. 1968. *Metternich and the Political Police: Security and Subversion in the Hapsburg Monarchy (1815–1830).* The Hague: Martinus Nijhoff.

Ericson, Richard. 1982. *Reproducing Order.* Toronto: University of Toronto Press.

Evans-Pritchard, E. E. 1940. *The Nuer.* London: Oxford University Press.

Eyck, Erich. 1950. *Bismarck and the German Empire.* London: George Allen and Unwin, Ltd.

Farmer, Michael T., and Furstenberg, Mark H. 1979. "Alternative Strategies for Responding to Police Calls for Service: State of the Art: Literature Review and Preliminary Survey Results." Manuscript.

Field, John. 1981. "Police Power and Community in a Provincial English Town: Portsmouth, 1815–1875." In *Policing and Punishment in Nineteenth Century Britain,* ed. Victor Bailey, pp. 42–64. New Brunswick, N.J.: Rutgers University Press.

Florinsky, Michael T. 1953. *Russia.* New York: Macmillan Co.

Fogelson, Robert M. 1977. *Big-City Police.* Cambridge, Mass.: Harvard University Press.

Fosdick, Raymond B. 1915. *European Police Systems.* Repr. ed. 1975. New York: Century Co.

Fossaert, Robert, and Blanc, Edmond, eds. 1972. *La Machine Policière.* Paris: Bertrand des Saussaies, Éditions du Seuil.

Fried, Robert C. 1963. *The Italian Prefects: A Study in Administrative Politics.* New Haven: Yale University Press.

Gash, Norman. 1961. *Mr. Secretary Peel: The Life of Sir Robert Peel to 1830.* Cambridge, Mass.: Harvard University Press.

Gastil, Raymond D. 1978. *Freedom in the World: Political and Civil Liberties, 1978.* New York: Freedom House.

Gerth, H. H., and Mills, C. Wright. 1958. *From Max Weber: Essays in Sociology.* New York: Oxford University Press.

Goedhard, Neil. 1954. "Organization and Administration of the Police in Western Germany, 1945–1950." M.A. thesis, University of Southern California.

Goldstein, Herman. 1977. *Policing a Free Society*. Cambridge, Mass.: Ballinger Publishing Co.

Gorer, Geoffrey. 1955. "Modification of National Character: The Role of the Police in England." *Journal of Social Issues* 11: 25–32.

Government of Canada. 1974. "Report of the Government of Canada—Government of Ontario Study Group on the Role of the Royal Canadian Mounted Police in Ontario." June 27.

Government of Great Britain. 1977. "Report of Her Majesty's Chief Inspector of Constabulary."

Government of Maharashtra, India. 1967. Second Manpower Commission Report, Part 3.

Government of Japan. 1980. *The Police of Japan*.

Great Britain, Police College. 1974. "A Study of Police Recruitment and Training in Europe."

Greenwood, Peter W., and Petersilia, Jean. 1975. *The Criminal Investigation Process*. Santa Monica: Rand Corporation.

Gregory, Frank. 1976. "Protest and Violence: The Police Response." Institute for the Study of Conflict, *Conflict Studies* 75.

Gruder, Vivian W. 1968. *The Royal Provincial Intendants*. Ithaca, N.Y.: Cornell University Press.

Gurr, Ted R. 1967. *Conditions of Civil Strife: First Tests of a Causal Model*. Princeton, N.J.: Center for International Studies.

————. 1979. "On the History of Violent Crime in Europe and America." In *Violence in America: Historical and Comparative Perspectives*, eds. H. D. Graham and T. R. Gurr. Beverly Hills: Sage Publications.

Gurr, Ted R.; Grabosky, Peter N.; and Hula, Richard C. 1977. *The Politics of Crime and Conflict: A Comparative History of Four Cities*. Beverly Hills: Sage Publications.

Hackett, Roger F. 1971. *Yamagata Aritomo in the Rise of Modern Japan, 1838–1922*. Cambridge, Mass.: Harvard University Press.

Hagan, William T. 1966. *Indian Police and Judges: Experiments in Acculturation and Control*. New Haven: Yale University Press.

Hahn, Harlan. 1971. "A Profile of Urban Police." In *The Police Community*, eds. Jack Goldsmith and Sharon S. Goldsmith, pp. 15–38. Pacific Palisades, Cal.: Palisades Publishers.

Halévy, Élie. 1924. *History of the English People*. vol. 2. Trans. E. I. Watkin. Repr. ed. 1948. New York: P. Smith.

Haller, Mark H. 1976. "Historical Roots of Police Behavior: Chicago, 1890–1925." *Law and Society Review* Winter: 303–323.

Halperin, Morton H.; Berman, Jerry J.; Borsage, Robert L.; and Marwick, Christine M. 1976. *The Lawless State: The Crimes of the U.S. Intelligence Agencies*. New York: Penguin Books.

Hamburger, Joseph. 1963. *James Mill and the Art of Revolution*. New Haven: Yale University Press.

Harring, Sidney L. 1983. *Policing a Class Society: The Experience of American Cities, 1865–1915*. New Brunswick, N.J.: Rutgers University Press.

Hart, J. M. 1951. *The British Police*. London: Allen and Unwin.

Hauge, Ragnar. 1979. "Police and the Public: Three Norwegian Investigations." In *Police and the Social Order*, report no. 6, eds. Johannes Knutsson, Eckart Kuhlhorn, and Albert Reiss, Jr., pp. 132–148. Stockholm: National Swedish Council for Crime Prevention.

Hauge, Ragnar, and Stabell, Harald. 1974. *Police Activity: A Study Based on Follo Police Station*. Oslo: Institutt for Kriminologi og Strafferett.

Hazard, John N.; Butler, William E.; and Maggs, Peter B. 1977. *The Soviet Legal System*. 3rd ed. Dobbs Ferry, N.Y.: Oceana Publications, Inc.

Herlihy, David, ed. 1968. *Medieval Culture and Society*. New York: Harper Torchbooks.

Hill, Jim D. 1969. "The National Guard in Civil Disorders." In *Bayonets in the Streets: The Uses of Troops in Civil Disturbances*, ed. Robin Higham, pp. 61–84. Lawrence: University of Kansas Press.

Hjellemo, E. O. 1979. "History of the Nordic Police Systems—The Evolution of Policing in Denmark and Norway." In *Police and the Social Order*, report no. 6, eds. Johannes Knutsson, Eckart Kuhlhorn, and Albert Reiss, Jr., pp. 14–31. Stockholm: National Swedish Council for Crime Prevention.

Holborn, Hajo. 1969. *A History of Modern Germany 1840–1945*. New York: Alfred A. Knopf.

Holmes, Jack E. 1972. "Administrative Decentralization in Developing Areas: A Comparative-Interpretive Study of the Early 1960's." Ph.D. dissertation, University of Denver.

Hopkins, Nicholas S. 1967. "Social Control in a Malian Town." Manuscript.

International Association of Chiefs of Police (IACP). 1976. *History of Police Intelligence Operations, 1880–1975*. Gaithersburg, Md.: International Association of Chiefs of Police.

International Institute for Strategic Studies. Yearly. *Military Balance*. London: International Institute for Strategic Studies.

Jackson, Pamela Irvin, and Carroll, Leo. 1981. "Race and the War on Crime: The Sociopolitical Determinants of Municipal Police Expenditures in Ninety Non-Southern U.S. Cities." *American Sociological Review* June: 290–305.

Jacob, Herbert. 1963. *German Administration Since Bismarck*. New Haven: Yale University Press.

Janowitz, Morris, 1959. *Sociology and the Military Establishment*. New York: Russell Sage Foundation.

————. 1960. *The Professional Soldier*. Glencoe Ill.: Free Press.

Jones, David J. V. 1970. "Law Enforcement and Popular Disturbances in Wales, 1793–1835." *Journal of Modern History* December: 496–523.

Junger-Tas, J. 1978. "The Dutch and Their Police—Experiences, Attitudes and Demands." Manuscript.

Juviler, Peter H. 1976. *Revolutionary Law and Order: Politics and Social Change in the USSR*. New York: Free Press.

Karpets, Igor Ivanovich. 1977. "Principal Directions and Types of Activity of the Militia in the Soviet Union." *International Review of Criminal Policy* 33: 34–38.

Keeton, G. W. 1975. *Keeping the Peace*. London: Barry Rose Publishers.

Kelling, George L., and Lewis, Joseph H. 1979. "Police Research in the United States." In *Police and the Social Order*, report no. 6, eds. Johannes Knutsson, Eckart Kuhlhorn, and Albert Reiss, Jr., pp. 352–366. Stockholm: National Swedish Council for Crime Prevention.

Kelling, George L.; Pate, Tony; Dieckman, Duane; and Brown, Charles E. 1974. *The Kansas City Preventive Patrol Experiment: A Summary Report*. Washington, D.C.: Police Foundation.

Kelly, William, and Kelly, Nora. 1976. *Policing in Canada*. Toronto: Macmillan Co. of Canada, Ltd.

Keppler, Leopold. 1974. "The Gendarmerie in Austria." *Kriminalistic*. Translated in NCJRS 11.

Kobben, Andre J. F. "Law at the Village Level: The Cottica Djuka of Surinam." In *Law in Culture and Society*, ed. Laura Nader, pp. 117–140. Chicago: Aldine Publishing Co.

Kosberg, Erik. 1978. "The Police in Norway." Manuscript.

Kunkel, Wolfgang. 1973. *An Introduction to Roman Legal and Constitutional History*. 2nd ed. Oxford: Clarendon Press.

Lane, Roger. 1967. *Policing the City: Boston 1822–1885*. Cambridge, Mass.: Harvard University Press.

Langer, William L. 1969. *Political and Social Upheaval, 1832–1852*. New York: Harper and Row.

Langrod, Georges. 1961. *Some Current Problems of Administration in France Today*. Puerto Rico: University of Puerto Rico.

Laswell, Harold G. 1941. "The Garrison State and Specialists on Violence." *American Journal of Sociology* January: 455–468.

Lee, W. L. Melville. 1901. *A History of Police in England*. Repr. ed. 1971. Montclair, N.J.: Patterson Smith.

Li, Victor H. 1971. "The Public Security Bureau and Political-Legal Work in Hui-yang, 1952–1964." In *The City in Communist China*, ed. John W. Lewis, pp. 51–74. Stanford: Stanford University Press.

————. 1977. *Law Without Lawyers: A Comparative View of Law in China and the United States*. Stanford: Stanford Alumni Association.

Liang, Hsi-Huey. 1970. *The Berlin Police Force in the Weimar Republic*. Berkeley: University of California Press.

Lintott, A. W. 1968. *Violence in Republican Rome*. Oxford: Clarendon Press.

Lipset, Seymour M. 1963. *The First New Nation*. New York: Basic Books, Inc.

Lodhi, Abdul Q., and Tilly, Charles. 1970. "Urbanization, Criminality and Collective Violence in Nineteenth Century France." Paper presented to annual meeting of the American Society of Criminology. Mimeographed.

Lofland, Lyn H. 1973. *A World of Strangers: Order and Action in Urban Public Space*. New York: Basic Books, Inc.

Loftin, Colin, and Lizotte, Alan. 1974. "Violence and Social Structure: Structural Support for Violence Among Privileged Groups." Paper presented to annual meeting of the American Sociological Association. August.

Lopez, Lilia C. 1979. "The Philippine Criminal Justice System." *Resource Materials*. Tokyo: United Nations and Far East Institute for the Prevention of Crime and Treatment of Offenders.

Lowell, A. Lawrence. 1914. *The Governments of France, Italy, and Germany*. Cambridge, Mass.: Harvard University Press.

Lyman, J. L. 1964. "The Metropolitan Police Act of 1829: An Analysis of Certain Events Influencing the Passage and Character of the Metropolitian Police Act in England." *Journal of Criminal Law, Criminology, and Police Science* March: 141–154.

Manning, Peter K. 1977. "Organizational Problematics: Resolving Uncertainty." Manuscript.

Martin, J. P., and Wilson, Gail. 1969. *The Police: A Study in Manpower: The Evolution of the Service in England and Wales, 1829–1965*. London: Heinemann.

Mather, F. C. 1959. *Public Order in the Age of the Chartists*. Manchester, Eng.: Manchester University Press.

McCabe, Sarah, and Sutcliffe, Frank. 1978. *Defining Crime: A Study of Police Decision*. Occasional Paper no. 9, Oxford University Centre for Criminological Research. Oxford: Blackwells.

Midwinter, E. C. 1968. *Law and Order in Early Victorian Lancashire*. York: St. Anthony's Press.

Mildmay, William. 1763. *The Police of France*. London. (Copy found in Rare Book Collection, Princeton University.)

Miller, Wilbur R. 1977. *Cops and Bobbies: Police Authority in New York and London, 1830–1870*. Chicago: University of Chicago Press.

Monas, Sidney. 1961. *The Third Section: Police and Society in Russia Under Nicholas I*. Cambridge, Mass.: Harvard University Press.

Monkkonen, Eric. 1981. *Police in Urban America, 1860 to 1920*. Cambridge, Eng.: Cambridge University Press.

Moore, Barrington, Jr. 1967. *Social Origins of Dictatorship and Democracy*. Boston: Beacon Press.

Morrison, W. R. 1974. "The North-West Mounted Police and the Klondike Gold Rush." *Journal of Contemporary History* 9: 93–106.

Mulhall, Michael G. 1903. *The Dictionary of Statistics*. London: George Routledge and Sons Ltd.

Nair, Lucy. 1962. *Primitive Government: A Study of Traditional Political Systems in Eastern Africa*. Bloomington: Indiana University Press.

National Police Agency. n.d. *Policy of Japan*. Tokyo: National Police Agency.

Newman, Graeme R. "Social Institutions and the Control of Deviance: A Cross-National Opinion Survey." *European Journal of Social Pyschology* 7: 29–39.

Newspaper Enterprise Association, Inc. 1978. *The World Almanac and Book of Facts*. New York: Newspaper Enterprise Association, Inc.

Niederhoffer, Arthur. 1967. *Behind the Shield: The Police in Urban Society*. Garden City, N.Y.: Doubleday and Co.

Ogawa, Shigejiro, and Tomeoka, Kosuke. 1909. "Prisons and Prisoners." In *Fifty Years of New Japan*, vol. 1, ed. Shigenobu Okuma. London: Smith, Elder and Co.

Oura, Baron Kanetake. 1909. "The Police of Japan." In *Fifty Years of New Japan*, vol. 1, ed. Shiganobu Okuma. London: Smith, Elder and Co.

Payne, Howard C. 1966. *The Police State of Louis Napoleon Bonaparte, 1851–1860*. Seattle: University of Washington Press.

Pfiffner, John M. 1962. "Factors Affecting Police Morale." University of California Yough Studies Center, working paper no. P2.

Philips, David. 1977. *Crime and Authority in Victorian England: The Black Country 1835–1860*. London: Croom Helm Ltd.

Plantin, Lars-Erik. 1979. "The Organization of the Swedish Police." In *Police and the Social Order*, report no. 6, eds. Johannes Knuttson, Eckart Kuhlhorn, and Albert Reiss, Jr., pp. 60–74. Stockholm: National Swedish Council for Crime Prevention.

Police Foundation. 1981. *The Newark Foot Patrol Experiment*. Washington, D.C.: Police Foundation.

Policie Nationale. 1980. Statistical data privately furnished.

Potholm, Christian P. 1969. "The Multiple Roles of the Police as Seen in the African Context." *Journal of Developing Areas* January: 139–158.

President's Commission on Law Enforcement and Administration of Justice. 1967. "Task Force Report: The Police." Washington, D.C.: United States Government Printing Office.

Pringle, Patrick. n.d. *Hue and Cry: The Story of Henry and John Fielding and Their Bow Street Runners*. London: William Morrow and Co.

Punch, Maurice, and Naylor, Trevor. 1973. "The Police: A Social Service." *New Society* May 17: 358–360.

Radzinowicz, Leon. 1957. *A History of English Criminal Law and Its Administration Since 1750*. 4 vols. New York: Macmillan Co.

Radzinowicz, Sir Leon, and King, Joan. 1977. *The Growth of Crime: The International Experience*. New York: Basic Books, Inc.

Raeff, Marc. 1975. "The Well-Ordered Police State and the Development of Modernity in Seventeenth and Eighteenth-Century Europe: A Comparative Approach." *American Historical Review* December: 1221–1243.

Reiner, Robert. 1980. "The Politicization of the Police in Britain." Manuscript.

Reiss, Albert J., Jr. 1971. *The Police and the Public*. New Haven: Yale University Press.

Reith, Charles. 1938. *The Police Idea: Its History and Evolution in England in the Eighteenth Century and After*. London: Oxford University Press.

———. 1948. *A Short History of the British Police*. London: Oxford University Press.

———. 1952. *The Blind Eye of History: A Study of the Origins of the Present Police Era*. London: Faber and Faber Ltd.

———. 1956. *A New Study of Police History*. London: Oliver and Boyd.

Reynolds, P. K. Baillie. 1926. *The Vigiles of Imperial Rome*. London: Oxford University Press.

Richardson, James F. 1970. *The New York Police: Colonial Times to 1901*. New York: Oxford University Press.

———. 1974. *Urban Police in the United States*. Port Washington, N.Y.: Kennikat Press.

Rios, Jose Arthur. 1977. "Police and Development." *International Review of Criminal Policy* 33: 3–10.

Robinson, Cyril D. 1970. "The Mayor and the Police—A Look at the Political Role of the Police in Society." Mimeographed.

Rokkan, Stein. 1970. "The Growth and Structuring of Mass Polities in Western Europe: Reflections on Possible Models of Explanation." *Scandinavian Political Studies* 4. Oslo, Norway: Nordic Political Science Association.

Romig, Clarence H. A. 1977. "The West German Federal Police." *Journal of Police Science and Administration* December: 451–455.

Rosenberg, Hans. 1958. *Bureaucracy, Aristocracy and Autocracy: The Prussian Experience, 1660–1815*. Cambridge, Mass.: Harvard University Press.

Royal Commission on the Police. 1962. *Final Report*. Cmnd. 1728. London. May.

Rubinstein, Jonathan. 1973. *City Police*. New York: Farrar, Straus and Giroux.

Rude, George. 1964. *The Crowd in History: A Study of Popular Disturbances in France and England, 1730–1848*. New York: John Wiley and Sons.

Schwartz, Richard D., and Miller, James C. 1964. "Legal Evolution and Societal Complexity." *American Journal of Sociology* September: 159–169.

Seton-Watson, Hugh. 1967. *The Russian Empire, 1801–1917*. Oxford: Clarendon Press.

Shane, Paul G. 1980. *Police and People: A Comparison of Five Countries*. St. Louis: C. V. Mosby Company.

Shearing, Clifford D., and Leon, Jeffrey S. 1976. "Reconsidering the Police Role: A Challenge to a Popular Misconception." *Canadian Journal of Criminology and Corrections* 19: 348–364.

Sherman, Lawrence W. 1978. *Controlling Police Corruption: The Effects of Reform Politics—Summary Report.* Washington, D.C.: NILECJ, LEAA.

————. 1980. "Causes of Police Behavior: The Current State of Quantitative Research." *Journal of Research in Crime and Delinquency* January: 69–100.

Sherman, Lewis J. 1977. "Policewomen Around the World." *International Review of Criminal Policy* 33: 25–33.

Silver, Allan. 1967. "The Demand for Order in Civil Society: A Review of Some Themes in the History of Urban Crime, Police, and Riot." In *The Police: Six Sociological Essays*, ed. David J. Bordua, pp. 1–24. New York: John Wiley and Sons, Inc.

Singh, Baldave. 1977. "Socio-Economic Inequalities Between Ethnic and Racial Groups: An Exploratory Comparative Study." Ph.D. dissertation, University of Denver.

Skogan, Wesley G., and Antunes, George E. 1979. "Information, Apprehension, and Deterrence: Exploring the Limits of Police Productivity." *Journal of Criminal Justice* Fall: 217–241.

Skolnick, Jerome H. 1966. *Justice Without Trial.* New York: John Wiley and Sons, Inc.

Smith, Bruce. 1925. *The State Police.* New York: Macmillan Co.

————. 1949. *Police Systems in the United States.* New York: Harper and Row.

Sperlings, Sven. 1979. "The Evolution of the Police During the Period of Industrialization—The Stockholm Example." In *Police and the Social Order*, report no. 6, eds. Johannes Knutsson, Eckart Kuhlhorn, and Albert Reiss, Jr., pp. 46–59. Stockholm: National Swedish Council for Crime Prevention.

Spitzer, Steven, and Scull, Andrew T. 1977. "Social Control in Historical Perspective: From Private to Public Responses to Crime." *Correction and Punishment*, ed. David F. Greenberg, pp. 265–286. Beverly Hills: Sage Publications.

Squire, P. S. 1968. *The Third Department: The Establishment and Practices of the Political Police in the Russia of Nicholas I.* Cambridge, Eng.: Cambridge University Press.

Starkarum, Judanath. 1963. *Mughal Administration.* Calcutta: M. C. Sarkar and Sons, Private Ltd.

Starr, Frederick S. 1970. "Decentralization and Self-Government in Russia, 1830–1870." Ph.D. dissertation, Princeton University.

Stead, Philip John. 1957. *The Police of Paris.* London: Staples Press.

Stenning, Philip C. 1980. "The Role of Police Boards and Commissions as Institutions of Municipal Police Governance." Manuscript.

Storch, Robert D. 1975. "The Plague of Blue Locusts: Police Reform and Popular Resistance in Northern England, 1840–1857." *International Review of Social History* 20: 62–90.

Strayer, Joseph. 1970. *On the Medieval Origins of the Modern State*. Princeton, N.J.: Princeton University Press.

Sugai, Shuichi. 1957. "The Japanese Police Systems." In *Five Studies in Japanese Politics*, ed. Robert W. Ward, pp. 1–15. Occasional Papers 7, Center for Japanese Studies. Ann Arbor: University of Michigan Press.

Supreme Commander for the Allied Powers, Historical Monographs. "History of the Nonmilitary Activities of the Occupation of Japan." vol. 5. (1945–1951). Washington, D.C.: United States Government Printing Office.

Sykes, Richard E., and Clark, John P. 1974. "A Socio-Legal Theory of Police Discretion." In *Observations*, Minnesota Systems Research, no. 5.

Taylor, Charles, and Hudson, Michael C. 1973. *World Handbook of Political and Social Indicators II*. 2nd ed. Section I: *Crossnational Aggregate Data*. Ann Arbor: Inter-University Consortium for Political Research.

Tilly, Charles. 1970. "The Chaos of the Living City." Manuscript.

Tilly, Charles; Levett, Allan; Lodhi, A. Q.; and Munger, Frank C. 1974. "How Policing Affected the Visibility of Crime in Nineteenth-Century Europe and America." Ann Arbor: Center for Research on Social Organization, University of Michigan.

Tilly, Charles; Tilly, Louise; and Tilly, Richard. 1975. *The Rebellious Century, 1830–1930*. Cambridge, Mass.: Harvard University Press.

Tilly, Louise A. 1971. "The Food Riot as a Form of Political Conflict in France." *Journal of Interdisciplinary History* 2: 12.

Tobias, J. J. 1972. "Police and Public in the United Kingdom." *Journal of Contemporary History* January–April: 201–219.

Tokyo Metropolitan Police Department. *Keishicho, 1979*. Tokyo: Metropolitan Police Department.

Tönnies, Ferdinand. 1957. *Community and Society: Gemeinschaft und Gesellschaft*. Trans. and ed. Charles P. Loomis. New York: Harper Torchbook.

Tsurumi, Kaguko. 1970. *Social Change and the Individual: Japan Before and After Defeat in World War II*. Princeton, N.J.: Princeton University Press.

Tuchman, Barbara. 1979. *A Distant Mirror: The Calamitous Fourteenth Century*. London: Penguin Books.

United States Government, Bureau of the Census. *U.S. Statistical Abstract, 1979*. Washington, D.C.: United States Government Printing Office.

United States Government, Law Enforcement Assistance Administration, Department of Justice. 1970. "Criminal Justice Agencies in Pennsylvania." Washington, D.C.: United States Government Printing Office.

University Microfilms. 1979. "Criminal Justice and Law Related Titles." Ann Arbor: University Microfilms.

van der Sprenkel, Sybille. 1977. "Urban Social Control." In *The City in Late Imperial China*, ed. G. William Skinner, pp. 609–632. Stanford: Stanford University Press.

Van Maanen, John. 1974. "Working the Street: A Developmental View of Police Behavior." *The Potential for Reform of Criminal Justice*, ed. Herbert Jacob, pp. 83–130. Beverly Hills: Sage Publications.

Viirtanen, Katrina. 1979. "A Comparison of the Historical Development of Police Organization in Finland as Compared to the Other Scandinavian Countries." In *Police and the Social Order*, report no. 6, eds. Johannes Knutsson, Eckart Kuhlhorn, and Albert Reiss, Jr., pp. 32–45. Stockholm: National Swedish Council for Crime Prevention.

Vincet, W. 1977. *Het Post—Unitaire Belgie*. Lier, Belgium: NVJ Van IN.

Walker, Samuel. 1977. *A Critical History of Police Reform*. Lexington, Mass.: D.C. Heath and Co., Lexington Books.

———. 1978. "Research Needs in the Comparative History of the Police." Manuscript.

Wambaugh, Joseph. 1974. *The Onion Field*. New York: Dell Publishing Co.

Webb, Sidney, and Webb, Beatrice. 1963. *The Development of English Local Government, 1685–1835*. London: Oxford University Press.

Weber, Max. 1968. *Economy and Society: An Outline of Interpretative Sociology*. 3 vols. Comps. and eds. Guenther Roght and Claus Wittich. New York: Bedminster Press.

Weinberger, Barbara. 1981. "The Police and the Public in Mid-Nineteenth Century Warwickshire." In *Policing and Punishment in Nineteenth Century Britain*, ed. Victor Bailey, pp. 65–93. New Brunswick, N.J.: Rutgers University Press.

Wildes, Harry Emerson. 1953. "The Postwar Japanese Police." *Journal of Criminal Law, Criminology, and Police Science* January–February: 655–671.

Williams, Alan. 1979. *The Police of Paris, 1718–1789*. Baton Rouge: Louisiana State University Press.

Wilson, James Q. 1968. *Varieties of Police Behavior: The Management of Law and Order in Eight Communities*. Cambridge, Mass.: Harvard University Press.

——— 1980. "The Changing FBI—The Road to ABSCAM." *Public Interest* Spring: 3–14.

Wilson, James Q., and Boland, Barbara. 1976. "Crime." In *The Urban Predicament*, eds. William Gorham and Nathan Glazer. Washington, D.C.: Urban Institute.

Wilson, James Q., and Kelling, George L. 1982. "The Police and Neighborhood Safety." *Atlantic* March: 29–38.

Woodward, Edward W. 1938. *The Age of Reform*. Oxford: Clarendon Press.

Wycoff, Mary Ann. 1982. "Evaluating the Crime-Effectiveness of the Municipal Police." In *Managing Police Work*, ed. Jack R. Greene. Beverly Hills: Sage Publications.

Wycoff, Mary Ann, and Kelling, George L. 1978. *The Dallas Experience: Organizational Reform*. Washington, D.C.: Police Foundation.

Wycoff, Mary Ann, and Manning, Peter K. 1983. "Crime-Focused Policing: Measuring Performance and Effect." *Analyzing Performance in Criminal Justice Agencies*, eds. Gordon P. Whitaker and Charles Phillips. Beverly Hills: Sage Publications.

Wycoff, Mary Ann; Susmilch, Charles E.; and Eisenbart, Patricia. 1980. "Reconceptualizing the Police Role: An Examination of Theoretical Issues, Information Needs, Empirical Realities and the Potential for Revision." Police Foundation, manuscript.

Zane, John M. 1927. *The Story of Law*. Garden City, N.Y.: Garden City Publishing Co.

Zuckerman, Michael. 1970. *Peaceable Kingdoms: New England Towns in the Eighteenth Century*. New York: Alfred A. Knopf.

Index